THE
PEOPLE'S
GAMES

THE PEOPLE'S GAMES

A GAA COMPENDIUM

JOHN SCALLY

BLACK & WHITE PUBLISHING

First published 2020
by Black & White Publishing Ltd
Nautical House, 104 Commercial Street
Edinburgh, EH6 6NF

1 3 5 7 9 10 8 6 4 2   20 21 22 23

ISBN: 978 1 78530 323 4

A CIP catalogue record for this book is available from the British Library.

Typeset by Iolaire Typesetting, Newtonmore
Printed and bound by CPI Group (UK) Ltd, Croydon, CR0 4YY

COVID 0-19
Mayo 1-15
Mayo's curse continues

COVID-19 robbed Leitrim of another All-Ireland.
Seamus O'Rourke

It was the most fun you can have with your long-johns on.
Malachy Clerkin braves the extreme weather as
Wexford beat Kilkenny during Storm Dennis,
rechristened Storm Davy, in February 2020

In my day we had a few farmers, a few fishermen
and a college boy to take the frees.
Paddy Bawn Brosnan

To all working in every corner of the
Irish health care service and frontline services.

Thanks for your heroism during the COVID-19 crisis.

CONTENTS

FOREWORD

I took for granted that I had role models, within my football team we had different people, and I had a good family structure around me. When people do not have those things, don't have the family structure I had or don't have the support from different clubs, it's easy for them to stray off the path and go down a more dangerous route. You see it all along.

I have always been involved with teaching and sports, outside of sports as well. I've been working with special needs students for years and mainstream teaching, as well as my work now in the inner city. So that is where I get my kicks, seeing people develop and grow. I enjoy that side of it.

I do not know how teams can function if they have someone who is maybe too egotistical or looking out for their own interests. Sometimes I wonder how the dressing-rooms look in the Premier League with all the ego that's involved. It is the opposite here with the Dublin dressing-room at the moment, so long may it continue. The group is an impressive collection of human beings in that I think people are aware that there is a higher purpose than themselves or the team.

If individuals came into the team and thought they were bigger for any reason than the team, they'd be quickly weeded out. So I think that's definitely been the crux that we fall on, that we all know that we are doing for something bigger than us. We self-police that at this stage and that creates a humility around the squad that is badly needed in any team.

It was definitely sold to me how socially conscious a lot of the Dublin team of the 1970s were. Even from speaking to them, they were aware of that higher purpose and that there was more to life than football. That kind of stuck with me as well. I think it is very important that those in the GAA are socially conscious.

This book offers a series of significant snapshots into the GAA community. The GAA has a lot of great people with a strong social conscience and I am delighted to see them celebrated in these pages.

Michael Darragh Macauley
September 2020

THE WARM-UP

Let us praise.

Fans of Gaelic Games graciously hear us.

This is a book about the many facets of Gaelic Games but at the outset I wanted to single out one man for special attention because his actions were so counter-cultural.

For Limerick 2019 was a disappointing year when they lost the All-Ireland semi-final to Kilkenny in controversial circumstances. Their manager John Kiely, though, was my man of the year for the grace he showed in defeat and his refusal to enter into any recriminations, even though the match officials gave him an obvious scapegoat.

For those who admire sportsmanship, it showcased the GAA at its very best.

I salute a magic moment.

CLUB TIES

Let us praise again.

Fans of Gaelic Games graciously hear us.

In January 2020 Corofin became the first side to win a third consecutive All-Ireland club football title. The fact that they won those three titles is admirable in itself. But what is so commendable is that they did so playing with style and flair. In 2019, Ciaran Whelan said Gaelic football was coming out of recession. Corofin blazed the trail in that respect.

In the process they proved that Gaelic football can, like hurling, be the beautiful game.

I salute a terrific team.

I salute the beautiful game.

PANDEMIC

Let us praise once more.

Fans of Gaelic Games graciously hear us.

As this book was being written the coronavirus struck the world with the ferocity of a tsunami. Apart from the global trail of illness, economic devastation and death, it sparked a tidal wave of fear. It struck at something deep inside us and shattered many of our cherished certainties. We thought we were in control but nature reminded us of our fragility, vulnerability and mortality not with a gentle whisper but with a primeval scream. It had echoes of a medieval plague but our twenty-first century world struggled to find an adequate response to it.

The COVID-19 crisis caused us to redefine our idea of heroes and the GAA was not found wanting in this respect. A case in point was Mayo hurler Cathal Freeman, who raised over €60,000 by running a marathon in his back garden while soloing a sliotar to raise funds for the Irish Cancer Society and to help the HSE buy personal protective equipment for some of its frontline staff.

The same community spirit was in evidence in the way the GAA community came together to raise over two million euro for little Dan Donoher, son of Laois footballing greats Aisling and Niall, who needs expensive treatment for his rare muscular disease.

Historically, Saint Patrick's Day has been associated with the Railway Cup and latterly the All-Ireland club finals. This year, though, on our national day, Croke Park opened its doors and gates to provide testing for the virus. Other GAA stadia generously followed suit. It was an eloquent statement of what the GAA is all about. Moreover, countless volunteers all around the country brought meals, food parcels and good cheer to many vulnerable people isolated in their communities. It showed how we could come together as a nation while staying apart. In times of bereavement the GAA demonstrated that the grief of one is the wound of all.

These moments illustrated the power of the GAA to be the ties that bind and herald a horizon of hope in one of the darkest chapters of our history. They put humanity front and centre and the Games were pushed to the margins.

I salute their community spirit.

Ernest Hemmingway claimed that the world breaks everyone and afterwards many are stronger in the broken places. The GAA will come through this crisis stronger in the broken places.

BACK TO THE FUTURE

Let us hope.

The centrality of Gaelic Games to Irish life was never more apparent than in 2020 during the COVID-19 crisis. The absence of our games quickly became a real presence. Summer without the championship was like Christmas without turkey.

Fans cannot close their hearts to how they feel. To paraphrase the great Ray Charles: 'Take these pandemic chains from our hearts and set our games free.' The land of hopes and dreams awaited us.

THE THROW-IN

Enter the land of miracles, where the dead are raised and storms at sea are stilled.

When I was a boy there was a traveller who regularly visited Roscommon. He had healing hands and many 'miracles' were attributed to them. As he was a very handsome man, women in particular flocked to avail of his services. Then he stopped coming. There was a great mystery to his absence.

By coincidence his departure coincided with his greatest miracle. A local woman who was considered to be barren gave birth to a fine healthy boy. By another remarkable coincidence the boy grew up in the image and likeness of the traveller rather than showing any similarity to the woman's husband. Now that time's hand rests more heavily on me, I have a better understanding of that mystery.

The individual concept of the nation is now being built on shifting sands, destined to move in parallel with whatever winds might blow. But not so for the GAA. There is no surge of restlessness.

Memories are like a second heart beating inside us. One of my father's enduring legacies to me is a passion for the GAA. I took to this latest infatuation with the intensity of a new lover, drinking in every word and gesture. When it came to Gaelic Games I became as curious as Galileo gazing at the moon through his telescope. My obsession has never worn away.

The GAA is part of all of our autobiographies. No organisation brings that sense of identity like the GAA. It is about how we feel about ourselves, individually and collectively. It inspires what Abraham Lincoln called 'the last full measure of devotion'.

The late Jackie Healy-Rae was once asked to explain the difference between Fiánna Fáil and Fine Gael. He answered, 'Those who know don't need to ask. Those who need to ask will never know.' In a sense the GAA defies classification. It is more than a national movement. It is more than a sporting body. It is more than a cultural entity. It is all of these and more. Yet while the mystery of the GAA eludes easy analysis the one thing that can be said with certainty is that it has been and continues to be driven by remarkable people on and off the field. This book pays homage to the People's Games.

PART I
Threads of a Tapestry

The obvious place to begin this book is with a consideration of the rich history of the GAA. But who wants to be obvious?

The story of my early life is the story of a bygone age when life moved at a gentler pace and there always seemed to be time for chat and laughter. Rural Ireland was totally different than it is today. My summer holidays were spent saving the hay, the country air sweet with the scents of the ripening meadows. The job could go on for days and involved many phases before ending in pikes or cocks of hay. One local farmer was very cautious about ensuring the hay was dry enough to be saved and he was smelling it with great intensity. A neighbour told him: 'It's dry enough. Don't worry about it. You won't be eating it.' A magnificent moment was always when the tea arrived in the hayfield in bottles. Tea never tasted as good as it did in the meadow.

In many ways I had an idyllic childhood. It almost seems like a million years ago.

The whole identity of rural Ireland is changing almost by the year. I loved the old people. It was an education in itself to spend time with them. Many had only travelled a few miles outside their homeland in their entire lives. Yet they had great wisdom. There was a great sense of belonging there and that was why it was so special for me.

It was then that I acquired my love for Gaelic Games. It was also then that I learned that people are at the heart of the GAA. This section takes us into the world of some of the special people that make the GAA great: the fans, the clubs, the volunteers, the families, the administrators and the players.

1

THE DIALECT OF THE TRIBE: JOHN MacKENNA

In these streets and fields where you grew up,
there you will live and there you will die.
Con Houlinhan

The moment called for some form of the poetic, some expression of the heartfelt.

The fans are the lifeblood of the GAA. Their inner worlds. Their passionate loves.

For that reason I felt it was indeed right and fitting that I should begin this book with the story of a fan. But which one should I choose? My own love affair with Gaelic Games began as a fan who worshipped at the altar of Dermot Earley. Like all epic love affairs it had moments of elation and heartbreak.

There was one occasion, however, which was the darkest hour. It was as though I had been cut, the knife having gone so deep that the wound was not yet painful; it produced merely shock. It seemed to me after that conversation that the world was thoroughly altered. It was not something you could explain adequately, why it was that everything was folly. So much of what excited people

11

in normal life seemed wholly and disturbingly petty. An almost Proustian pang of memory came over me as I remembered all his glory days in the Roscommon jersey. I could not remember time looping in on itself in such a manner before, when life had been measured out in minutes rather than in hours and a sadness so deep that no tears could come.

It was the day of Dermot Earley's funeral ten years ago – moments that will live with me forever – looking down on a gathering for an occasion almost unbearably sad: a centre of my life gone. I was near to tears and in my heart there was something stirring, a sense of outrage, a feeling of total despair. I could not bring myself to think of him in the past tense but I had seen the evidence of the previous night as he lay in his coffin. He seemed so calm as he smiled and held his rosary beads in his hand. I hoped fervently his soul had been set free from its anguish and that he would find peace at last in a higher, more perfect world. There was no strain any more, and the features of his face were calm, now that he had been released from the struggle for breath.

After the funeral Mass, as I walked in a daze from the church, I met a Kildare fan, the award-winning writer John MacKenna. I had almost forgotten what it was like to be greeted by the unguarded openness of a friend's smile and in its warmth I felt resurrected from the tomb, called momentarily back into the land of the living by an embrace and a simple expression of kindness. As we walked together to the graveyard after Dermot's funeral, in a scene sculpted in sadness, the emptiness I felt pervaded every-thing and I found I couldn't put my thoughts away. And I began to understand how I would miss my great friend. Like a hidden grieving that rises to grab the heart, my soul was ambushed with old emotions, and my lips began to tremble, and for a brief instant I was swept into the current of all that I had lost. It was John, wearing his Kildare jersey, who sustained me that day on my via dolorosa. Kindness seldom fails. It was John to whom I turned for a fan's perspective. This is his story.

A LILYWHITE LOVE

I have a very early footballing memory set in the county council cottage in which I was born, so I can't have been more than five years of age because we moved house in the summer of 1958 and I was six the following October. So, it must have been the summer of 1958 – my brother would have been 15, my sister 11. The memory is of my father coming in from the garden with a sally rod and my mother cutting a section off an old white sheet and then pinning the sheet to the sally stick with drawing pins to make a Kildare flag for me. The details are still as clear, 60 years later, as they were on that Sunday afternoon. We must have been heading to a match in Athy or Portlaoise – the game is gone from my memory.

But what remains is another Sunday, a bright sunny afternoon. I was ten or 11 and Kildare were playing in Athy.

The ground was crammed with supporters. The huxters were flaunting the *hats, colours and ribbons* – crepe paper hats that ran in the rain; the *Luckie Luckies* – Lucan ice-creams – were on sale outside the gate. Inside, we were urged to get *the last of the choc ices* before the ball had even been thrown in, and the same cry was still going up as the final whistle approached.

There were no fences or security gates back then, children sat on their fathers' shoulders or squatted on the sideline, as close as could be to the action. And that's where I found myself, cross-legged, close to the halfway line, my flag in my hand. At that level, every kick was heard and every tackle was felt and every shoulder made the ground shudder. And, above all others, one player dominated the sky and the ground that afternoon; one man rose to field every high ball and to launch attack after attack from the half-back line. That man was Mick Carolan. To me he was everything I wanted to be. Tall, handsome, athletic, fearless, talented. He was Kildare.

When the heavy, laced football thudded out of play beside me and he came to take a sideline kick, I was as close to him as I'd ever been, so close that I must have been in his line of fire but, instead of asking me to move, he reached down and ruffled my hair before steadying himself and putting the ball over the bar. Had the hand of God reached from the clouds and anointed me, I wouldn't have felt any more deeply or wonderfully blessed. I had been anointed by the touch of greatness.

Days like that, moments like that, were the ones that sowed the seed of passion in my younger self. There would be bad days to follow – many, many bad days – but the fire of that memory has kept me warm for well over 50 years.

The darknesses, when they came – and they came regularly – were often in Newbridge, St Conleth's Park, that drab, dull, decaying stadium that has something of the Soviet era about it. There were last minute goals that ended the dream; sodden league Sundays when nothing could go right; Glenn Ryan like a Trojan horse trying to drag a team behind him. There were bitter Sundays in Portlaoise and Navan. There was the day Kilkenny beat us in an O'Byrne Cup match but that, in its own dark way, became a blessing, a pit from which the only way was up.

And up we went, with the arrival of Mick O'Dwyer. He came in the wake of a man whose work had gone unacknowledged and he built on the foundations laid by Dermot Earley in his short time as manager. O'Dwyer reaped the reward and built on it, lifting us to the heights of 1998.

At his remove it's hard to describe how that summer felt, the energy, the excitement, the passion, the incredulity that winning a Leinster championship after a 42-year gap could bring. And it didn't come easy, but come it did.

The year before we'd beaten Laois and then endured the possibility, the probability and, finally, the inevitability of loss to Meath after three tremendous, nerve-ripping games. July leaked into August as we drew, then drew again after extra time (3-17 to 2-20), then finally lost in the first week of August by two points. To have gone so high, to fall so far was as bleak as sporting bleak can be. We had been in sight of the holy grail ...

But out of that loss came 1998. Another draw, in early June, with Dublin didn't augur well but the replay, two weeks later, saw us through by a point. A month later we decimated Laois and on 2 August we laid the Meath ghost with a goal I'll never forget. Hill 16 burst like a white-hot volcano when Brian Murphy's shot hit the net.

After that match, as we flooded onto the pitch for the presentation, I stood beside Tommy Down – the Meath player – who had stayed to watch. 'Ye deserved it,' he said quietly and I shook his hand. And then Glenn Ryan sang 'The Curragh of Kildare' and I had a sense of what heaven might be.

At the end of August we beat Kerry by a point. Kildare were in an All-Ireland senior football final. The childhood dream was coming true.

All that summer my son Ewan and I had played each championship match on the lawn at the back of the house on the Saturday night before the real thing and the habit had become a superstition. So, on Saturday evening, 26 September 1998, we took our places for the final time and the match began ... but it was never finished. Reaching for a high-ball I came down awkwardly and my ankle was sprained. End of game. The following day I hobbled into Croke Park on crutches. We sat on the Hogan Stand, we sang 'The Curragh of Kildare' at half time, we dared to dream, and we wept at the final whistle, too drained to leave our seats.

As the stadium emptied, a passing, elderly Galway man stopped and shuffled in behind us and, putting a big hand of each on our shoulders, said quietly: 'Always be proud of your team.'

It didn't help then but it does, somewhat, at this remove.

And there were other dark days. Travelling from Tullamore with my Carlow-born brother-in-law Donal, his father and his two Carlow-born daughters after Carlow had beaten Kildare by seven points in 2018 was more a punishment than a pilgrimage. Those are the days that test.

Throughout the late 1980s and the '90s, my son Ewan and his friend Jeffrey were my constant companions at matches. My determination never to be late for a game became a running joke – the punchline coming when we arrived in Cavan for a league match only to find that not only were we early but the pitch gates hadn't even been opened! It was one I was never allowed to forget.

On another Sunday, as the three of us made our way to Croke Park, a two-seater plane crash-landed through a ditch on the road in front of us. 'Not a good omen,' Jeffrey said, drily. He was right: Dublin beat us that day.

But, of course, there's redemption in football. And a day that will live with me forever – as does that day when Mick Carolan ruffled my hair – is 26 June 2010. That morning we had buried Dermot Earley Snr in Newbridge and that afternoon Kildare played Antrim in a Round One qualifier in our ancient holy ground. As the Antrim team stood off to the side of the pitch, the minute of silence became a minute of sustained applause for a dead champion and a living icon. Dermot Jnr had taken his place with the team and would play.

The game ended in a 15-point draw but, for once, the result was irrelevant. I had, for the only time in my life, worn the jersey of another county to the game – my old Roscommon shirt, a small tribute to a man who had been part and parcel of Kildare football and the life of the county for many years.

There is something in the game, in the passion, in the hope, in the loss, but most of all in the commitment of players and supporters that keeps the spirits high and hopeful, even on the down days. And the thing is, despite the imbalances of money and facilities and population, I know there will come a day when, again, Kildare will beat Dublin, and that thought keeps me travelling on. 'Drive on,' we say. 'Drive on, Kildare.'

2

THE VILLAGE PEOPLE:
KAROL MANNION AND JOHN TIERNAN

*There is nothing as special as winning a title with your
own parish, playing with lads you played with all your life.*
John Maughan

If fans are its lifeblood, the heart of the GAA is the club.

The club is the gift that no Gaelic Games' fan can renounce.

Witness one of the all-time greatest hurlers Tommy Walsh's reaction to winning an All-Ireland intermediate club title with Tullaroan in January 2020. This is a man who has no less than nine senior All-Ireland medals: 'The club is so much more. It is the soul of the place. It's like being in Disneyland for the last three months in the place. It's just a magical time. What a time to be a player. We had a parish league and there were 79 people involved in it. There's 600 people in our parish. There were probably about 500 people cheering us on and clapping us at our last training session. That gives you a huge lift.'

As a boy my twin ambition was to become a star player for both St Brigid's and Roscommon. Sadly neither materialised for me.

My underage career with St Brigid's was distinguished. It was distinguished by how undistinguished it was.

The great bard wrote: 'There is nothing so common as the wish to be remarkable.' Sadly I never made any real impact on GAA pitches. The former Dunfermline player Jim Leishman said: 'I was the first professional football player to be forced to retire due to public demand.' I had been the first amateur one in that very same situation. When I played underage for St Brigid's, the only real argument was over the most suitable nickname for my goalkeeping skills: Cinderella because I kept missing the ball, or Dracula because I was terrified of crosses.

FATHER AND SON

As a boy, Karol Mannion shared the same ambitions as mine. The difference is that he made his dreams come true, culminating in a man of the match performance in the 2013 All-Ireland final.

'I remember my father bringing me down when I was about six or seven to play under-10s in St Brigid's. The underage emphasis for the club was only just kicking off around the time, we still only had one pitch and a small dressing-room set up. The complex we have now, with multiple pitches, a gym, hall and clubhouse, was just a dream then, it was pretty basic by today's standards. There was a place we got dressed on a Saturday morning. All the kids in the parish under the age of ten, didn't matter what age you were. There was no nursery or anything organised that there would be today. That pitch was where I fell in love with Gaelic football.

'I remember Frankie Dolan and John Tiernan's age group and a few more that went on to play senior. They were a couple years ahead of me and they had a quality age group. In my underage group we didn't enjoy much success, we weren't competing for county titles. I just loved being part of the club, playing football, hanging out with the lads and that was what kept me going.'

JOHNO

For a generation St Brigid's had been a sleeping giant of Roscommon football, after the retirement of their most iconic player Gerry O'Malley. Then, in 1996, Seán Kilbride persuaded his former Mayo teammate John O'Mahony to coach and manage the side. O'Mahony had just stepped down from managing Leitrim, where he enjoyed great success, notably the never-to-be-forgotten Connacht final triumph in 1994. O'Mahony's Midas touch would work its magic for St Brigid's and he led them to a county title in 1997. Galway then came calling for O'Mahony and while he led the Tribesmen to All-Irelands in 1998 and 2001, St Brigid's did not advance, as Karol Mannion acknowledges:

'As I progressed to the senior team, I was coming into a team that had just won a county title in '97. We had a few barren years where we lost a couple of finals and we didn't really kick on until around 2003 and 2004, with the likes of Ian Kilbride, Mark O'Carroll, Senan Kilbride, Darragh Donnelly and others coming through the ranks. That was what really pushed us from competing for county titles to competing for Connacht titles and beyond.

'We won our first county title together in '05. There was a real sense of having stumbled upon something special. It's hard with a club team to keep everyone together over a number of years, but for whatever reason in those three years when we got to three Connacht finals and an All-Ireland semi-final it just seemed to bond the group, and everyone understood that "we have something special here, we should keep at this".'

Mannion is too modest to speak of his own central role in the club's transformation – notably the big midfielder's stunning last gasp goal against Corofin which salvaged victory from the jaws of defeat to give the club their first Connacht club title in 2006. Off the field his friendships were also having an impact. His closest friend was John Tiernan. Both were now 'county men' with Roscommon but Tiernan was making his mark in foreign fields.

HELP IF YOU CAN

For Roscommon football, 2006 was a great year after a number of years of decline. The high point was Roscommon's minors' victory, over red-hot favourites Kerry, in the All-Ireland minor final replay. It was right and fitting that at the Roscommon People of the Year awards that November players from both teams were honoured.

The St Brigid's star to be singled out was Roscommon's player, John Tiernan. However, despite his considerable achievements on the pitch, Tiernan's fame in Roscommon has as much to do with his off-the-ball activities. It started in February 2006 when he quit his job as a teacher and went to Guatemala, having heard reports of the devastation wreaked by Hurricane Stan in that country.

'I always had a desire to do some work in the Third World. I just always believed we had everything easy over here and we had a huge debt to pay to people less fortunate than us.'

Based in a village called Pacaya, south of Guatemala City, he got immersed in a huge housing project. A landslide had killed hundreds and uprooted thousands in that poverty-infested region. From the moment he entered the area, John was confronted by intense need: 'To see this on television is akin to watching *Game of Thrones* or *The Simpsons*. You say to yourself that this cannot really be happening. But when the stark reality is but feet away from you, it is frightening in the extreme.'

The agonising tyranny of the plight of the majority struck him most forcefully on a visit to the slums, a far cry from the paradisal world of the leafy suburbs which are home to the wealthy elite. There, the diet of mystically nourishing pap and of half-formed truths which he had been fed about the advances in the lot of the poor retreated into the ocean of delusion. Guatemala is a highly stratified, paternalistic society without even a notion of *noblesse oblige*. It seems that the lot of the poor is to live frugally on the crumbs from the wealthy elite's tables. Extreme poverty sucks the vitality out of a community as a bee sucks nectar from a flower. It is a monument to broken hearts and foiled aspirations, to innumerable tales of sadness and dawning shreds of hope. By day, Tiernan built houses. By night he taught English in the local schools. Education was crucial because the whole area was locked into the monstrous barbarism of child labour.

'You could not but be moved by what you saw. I think of getting on a bus to go to work and there would be kids as young as nine and ten there with little machetes going off to cut down trees to make a living. Child labour is horrific to see.'

It sounds like a macabre plot from a novel by Charles Dickens. However, the problem of child exploitation in Guatemala is fact not fiction. There are unknown thousands of child labourers in the country, with poverty being the single most important factor contributing to this human tragedy. Parents with large families hate to send their children to work but the options before them are stark: starve at home or survive at work. On low wages a family cannot survive with just one wage earner. Where child labour is available in the market, employers simply substitute them for their adult labour since they can bully them into accepting low wages.

The biggest offenders are the labour-intensive industries. Employers like children because they learn the lessons of the job quicker than adults. The problem is not the product of inadequate laws but a failure to implement them. Child exploitation is a long way from the top of the political agenda in Guatemala. There are thousands of victims to this modern-day blot on the face of humanity, and everyone tells the same story. Hunger.

The death of hope. A person, it is held, can become accustomed to anything, but child labour for these people is a recurring nightmare. Here, as in most places, money, or more precisely the lack of it, makes all the difference. It is difficult not to succumb to a great sense of the desolation of life which sweeps all round like a tidal wave, drowning all in its blackness. The economic, political and cultural disadvantages suffered by these children are a violation of justice and a serious threat to their lives. For all the talk of children's rights, many children have not significantly improved their lot or achieved legal, economic or cultural parity. Exposure to this environment was to be a watershed for John Tiernan.

'When I came back home, I was a real pain for the first few months. I was questioning everything; why do you need that, why do you need this? But you can't just head off to the mountains and live like a hermit in Ireland. You just have to get back into life here and do what you can for people out there. I only did it for three months, but they have to do it for the rest of their lives.'

John was not content to curse the darkness, he wanted to light a candle. He quickly got involved in a number of fundraising projects such as a dinner dance and sports auction. He knew that charity was not enough. His is a philosophy of a hand-up not a handout. The key was sustainable development. Accordingly, he set up an import-export jewellery business, drawing on the work of a group of widowed women in Guatemala who had formed a co-op. Having returned to teaching in Marist College in Athlone, he recruited the services of its transition year and also the transition year students in the Convent of Mercy in Roscommon to help run the business. One of the signs of his success is that his active campaigning work has made Athlone a recognised Fairtrade Town and he was part of the Athlone Fairtrade Committee on his return from Guatemala. He then spent a lot of his time addressing schools and promoting Fairtrade products to try to guard against child labour and worker exploitation.

'The bottom line is that these people don't need volunteers, they need money. Labour is cheap out there and they can find ten workers out there to do what I did. It's all about awareness because these people have nothing. That's why I've done more work since I came home than I did when I was out there.'

Despite the intensity of his commitment to such a serious cause, the most striking thing about spending time in his company is that he laughs a lot. Laughter is in his genes. He is a first cousin of the uncrowned king of Irish comedy, Tommy Tiernan.

John himself has made his own small mark in the world of showbusiness. After St Brigid's won the Roscommon county title in 2005, John and Karol Mannion became the West of Ireland's answer to Simon and Garfunkel, with a song to the tune of Christy Moore's 'Joxer Goes to Stuttgart'. It became the theme tune to the county final DVD. Karol Mannion nearly chokes with laughter when asked if a career in music or an appearance beckons: 'Let's just say Louis Walsh has not been ringing me to offer me a recording contract!'

The closeness of friendship between the two clubmates is indicated by the fact that John Tiernan was best man at Karol's wedding to Eimir on 30 December 2013. Mannion too caught the social activism bug and with his brother John climbed Mount Kilimanjaro to raise funds to help in the fight against cancer.

GLORY DAYS

Mannion would win a Connacht medal with Roscommon in 2010 but bigger things were in store for him with St Brigid's. There would be a few chapters written on the script of hurt before ultimate glory.

'Lads opted to leave at various times, but that core group stayed together. We got back to win a county in 2010 and went all the way to an All-Ireland final the following March. We had made it to Croke Park, within touching distance of the title, but ultimately lost out to Crossmaglen. Despite the heartbreak of that loss, we had proved a point to ourselves and we realised that it wasn't something that we wanted to throw our hat at now. As a group we knew that we could push on and win the biggest prize of all.

'The following year, we lost the semi-final to Dessie Dolan's Garrycastle. We changed our management team after the Garrycastle loss; the management that had brought us to the previous All-Ireland final against Crossmaglen and the Garrycastle game stepped aside. What we learned in defeat is what made us stronger under Kevin McStay, Liam McHale and Benny O'Brien. It made us into a truly formidable side.

'None of the teams we faced during the 2012–13 campaign got a run on us apart from Ballymun in the first ten minutes of the final. We weren't exposed to a star forward who really went to town on us like Jamie Clarke did in 2011 or Dessie Dolan did the year after. That was a big difference. Kevin and his management team focused on making us tighter at the back, they brought Shane Curran back to go in goal, and that made us probably a five-point better team straight away and we saw the fruits of it.'

THE BOYS FROM ARMAGH

For St Brigid's ever to advance beyond the edge of glory, one great beast needed to be slain.

'When you come out of Roscommon or Connacht you measure up against the best teams in the country and because we lost to Crossmaglen in the semi-final in '07 and then the final in '11, there certainly was a sense that these are the barometer for us if we wanted to win an All-Ireland.

'Without being over-obsessed with them, they were the kind

of team we zoned in on. If we could beat them, if we could get to their level, we could surely win an All-Ireland, and that's just the way it transpired in 2013. They were still at the peak of their powers, they were going for three All-Irelands in a row and we knew that if we could overcome them that day in Mullingar, we would finally get the monkey off our back. Beating Crossmaglen that day showed us how far we'd come. It showed us what we had learned from the disappointments of the past.'

With that psychological barrier breached there was just one more summit to climb. In 2013 they became the first Roscommon side to claim a senior All-Ireland club title at the high altar of Croke Park.

'I don't think we ever worried about our opponents in the All-Ireland final. We were confident enough in ourselves that if we go out and play well, we can beat whoever is put in front of us. We were in this unenviable situation, eight points down in nine minutes. I'd been there a few times with Roscommon and normally you don't get out of those holes. It was tough mentally for sure. But there was no panic. There was no time to panic, such was the intensity of that game.

'We just played the way we always played. Stick to what we're good at. We still needed to do something that would bring us back into the game. Senan Kilbride's goal was the real turning point for us in that game. To recover from the bad start and to bring the game within a manageable deficit, that allowed us to go on and claw back the rest of it. Had we not reduced that margin until after half time it would have been very difficult to pull eight points back in the second half. Without Senan's goal I don't know if we would've won.

'A nice ball fell for me in the second half and the first thing that came into my head was to punch it rather than try to pick it up. Thankfully it went into the bottom corner. I had scored a similar goal in a college game for Trinity years back. It was just pure instinct, it certainly wasn't planned, there's no way I could have reacted that quickly on a premeditated decision. That brought us level. Twenty minutes left and the tension was incredible. I don't think either team went more than a point ahead, it was real tit for tat and it seemed that the first team to blink would lose.

'As it happened both teams probably blinked. It was neck and neck with points scored and easy chances missed on both sides. Ultimately it came down to whoever had possession for the last chance of the game, and I remember it well . . . We had missed an easy chance and John Small got a ball in front of the Cusack Stand. I was thinking with a minute left "Oh my God we're in trouble here." I remember the crowd on the Cusack Stand side lifting into a massive roar as John Small ran down the wing.

'Gearoid Cunniffe just got a hand to John Small's hand pass and Niall Grehan was able to sweep in front of Jason Whelan for the crucial turnover. We worked the ball back up the pitch and Frankie, the man you'd want there to kick a point – other than Senan maybe – got on the ball, as he always wants to do in the crucial moments, and slotted it over. A sweet finish.

'What happened to Frankie in those last few moments with the turnover that led to Jason Whelan's equaliser and then scoring the winner was probably a snapshot of what happened to the whole team that day. We had screwed up so badly in the first ten minutes, but we were able to recover and prove our mental strength. It's the same with Frankie. He had done it for years. Any sports person of his quality takes the rough with the smooth. He would always want to be on the ball irrespective of if he would kick a wide or turn over a ball. He knew the responsibility he carried in our team, as a lot of the senior players did. Frankie was never going to shirk that responsibility and certainly when his brother Garvan was on the ball they have a good understanding. He was always going to get the ball from Garvan and he was always going to try for a score.

'The final whistle blew ... the first few moments are just ecstasy, it's difficult to put into words. You don't get too many moments in your adult life where you're so out-of-control excited. That's the way I felt. I remember Senan Kilbride was the first person in front of me. We had battled for years together with Roscommon and Brigid's, and we would've had a lot of interplay between the two of us. The first thing that came into my head was that we've actually done it, we've won the big one. What we've wanted to do since 2005.'

The rewards of winning were largely spiritual for Mannion.

'I am a father now so I see a lot of things from that perspective. It's like a kid on Christmas morning, uncontrollably excited because he sees a good present under the tree. They don't know how to react, it was the same with me. Time just stands still. You're in the moment with your friends on the pitch. It's an awesome feeling.

'I think representing St Brigid's for all of us is quite important because our families, all of our friends, all of our neighbours, contribute so much to the club. There's a real sense of "it's ours" as opposed to a county setup where it's the management team and the players. There isn't really a tangible contribution or a clubhouse that people in Roscommon can go to and contribute to the county team. In the club you have that, there's great facilities there, not just for playing with the ladies' teams or the men's teams but there's classes run during the week, there's social events with the choir, there is an excellent clubhouse there to run social events. There's a nice bar there for a few pints for people to come together and socialise.

'I believe when everyone has that kind of tangible connection, they feel they contribute to it, and when you go out on the field you are like the public personification of that effort, that collective spirit. I certainly understood that we are representing the club on TV, in Croke Park, the biggest stadium in the country that everyone looks at for big games.

'We are representing the people who are part of our parish and part of our club and I hope that we made them proud.'

They did.

Nothing is more certain.

3

THE HELPING HAND:
PETER McVERRY

It is in giving that we receive.
Saint Francis of Assisi

Mercy has a human heart. Fr Peter McVerry is one of Ireland's best-known humanitarians. But what is less known about him is that he can claim to have helped shape Irish sporting history.

Peter McVerry is a household name because of his campaigning work for the homeless. Before he began this work, though, he taught in Belvedere College and was 'persuaded' to coach the rugby team which included a teenager who was to become one of Ireland's greatest rugby players – Ollie Campbell. Ollie claims, 'We thought he was great and knew everything about rugby.'

Peter's upbringing in Newry shaped his beliefs and values.

'Life is a lottery, none of us chooses where we will be born. I could have been born in Syria with bombs falling all around me, wondering whether I was going to be still alive in the morning. Or in Sub-Saharan Africa, where I might be lucky to get one meal every two days. Or my parents could have had a drug or alcohol addiction which might have sent me into a spiral of addiction, crime and jail.

'But I was lucky with my parents. My father was a doctor in a small town. For many years he did not have a "practice", with assistants or partners to help share the burden at nights or weekends. He was on duty 24 hours a day, seven days a week. Even when we went on holidays in those early years, we went to a seaside town six miles away so that you were still available for your patients. I remember the phone ringing during the night and he would get up and go out to see a patient, and I never heard him ever complain. Sometimes, that phone would ring twice in the same night and he would still get up and out to his patients. He was always there for them. I learnt a sense of service from him, that life is about helping others and making the world a happier, healthier place.

'My mother was a Welsh Protestant, who met my father while working in a hospital in England shortly after he had qualified. In those days, if my father, a Catholic, married a Protestant, the Catholic church would condemn him to hell for all eternity! To spare my father that fate, she became a Catholic, and like many converts, she became more Catholic than the Catholics themselves. So we were brought to Mass every Sunday without fail. Attendance at the family rosary every night was compulsory, no excuses accepted. I got a strong sense of faith from her.

'I think it was a huge sacrifice for her to become a Catholic – I always suspected that she was ostracised by her own family, as I never heard her talk about them or visit them or phone them or write to them. Her family was always a mystery to me, an unknown and unknowable part of my history. In those days, the most sinful thing you could do in that strong Welsh Protestant tradition was to become a Catholic.

'My parents shaped my future life for me. When wondering

what I would do in life, a sense of service, motivated by faith, seemed to me to be the obvious path I should take. I told them I wanted to join the Jesuits, and they questioned me to make sure that this was really what I wanted to do, and then they supported me all the way.

'When I went to work with homeless people in the inner city of Dublin, I think they found that a bit confusing. When people asked what I did, they wanted to be able to say I was a teacher, or a parish priest or something with a recognisable label. But all they could tell them was that they didn't know exactly what I did – I worked with robbers or something! I remember my father coming up to my flat in the inner city one day, and there was a young lad sitting on the floor, drawing on a sheet of paper. Trying to make conversation, my father asked him, "And what does your father do, young fellow?" "Me da was murdered," he answered. That was his first and last visit to the inner city! I never told them that later that young fellow was also murdered.

'I am just so grateful to them both for the life they gave me and the learning I received from living with them.'

THE VOLUNTEER ETHOS

Peter McVerry is an admirer of the GAA because it nurtures an ethos of volunteerism in every parish in Ireland.

'Hundreds of thousands of people give their time and talents, as volunteers, in thousands of projects around Ireland, to improve the lives of others and of their communities. Ireland is unique amongst the nations of the world for the level of volunteerism in our communities. Volunteers represent the best face of Irish society. They are also a threat to the dominant values that are imposed on us by the global economy in which we are, happily and successfully, immersed.

'The economy presents us with its ideal person to which we

should all aspire, namely a self-sufficient individual, a person who can stand on their own two feet, not dependent on anyone but themselves. To be dependent is understood to be appropriate for a child but a failing in someone who is an adult. This self-sufficient person is shielded from the vagaries of life, the unpredictability of others and the insecurity which the future may bring. The more independent the person becomes, the less they have to fear for their future, and their children's future.

'The path to achieving this ideal state is the pursuit of individual gain. It is the person's financial assets that will allow them to achieve this independence. It is the value of their home, their investments, the money in their bank account, which will cushion them from shocks to the economy or possible recession in the future. The most important objective in life is to become financially secure. We owe it to our family and our children.

'This self-sufficient person has little interest in community. Indeed, quite the opposite. The more they have, the more they need to protect what they have. Hence they need to keep others at arm's length, especially those who may pose a threat to what they have accumulated: the stranger, the poor, the homeless, travellers, those who live in social housing, those of a different social class to themselves. They live in fear of losing what they have. NIMBYism ("Not in My Back Yard") is alive and well and thriving: this self-sufficient person cannot tolerate a perceived threat to the value of their house. How many people do not know their neighbours, do not want to know their neighbours and do not see any point in getting to know their neighbours?

'For them, community is for those idealists who feel so inclined and have time on their hands. Building community, trying to improve the lives of others, especially those who are poor or marginalised, providing services and opportunities for the elderly and the young, keeping our towns and neighbourhoods tidy, are all worthwhile activities but peripheral to the main purpose of life, namely pursuing financial independence for themselves and their family.

'The economic crash in 2008 showed how false this ideal of self-sufficiency is. Many who had a lovely home, a good job, several bank accounts, lost everything through no fault of their own. They were made redundant, their home was repossessed and their bank accounts were emptied. Only the super rich (the 1 per cent) can achieve this ideal. They have the resources to ensure that even if their investments collapse they still have more than enough put aside, or hidden away, to make sure that their comfortable lifestyle will not be affected. They are the ones who control the economy and who are the major beneficiaries of the economy. They also control much of the mainstream media and, through it, shape the narrative which promotes this ideal to which we are expected to aspire and the path to achieve it.

'Volunteers offer us a completely different vision of life. They remind us that, actually, we *are* all dependent on each other. The vision and values to which volunteers bear witness to are a challenge to the vision and values which the economy promotes. Solidarity with others, care for those in need, and building community are just as important as building up our finances. Care and compassion for others, reaching out to our neighbours and those in need, stand in stark contrast to the competitive struggle with others to accumulate a share of the limited wealth which the economy creates.

'We owe a debt of gratitude to all those who volunteer in our communities, not only for what they do, but also for reminding us of what makes life worth living, and of what will bring us far more happiness and satisfaction than the self-interested focus on financial gain.

'Volunteers are at the heart of the GAA.

'For that I salute them.'

4

THE PLAYER OF THE FAITHFUL: MICHAEL DUIGNAN

Happiness is a choice that requires effort at times.
Aeschylus

It is life on life's terms.

The most famous quote in the sporting vernacular is perhaps Bill Shankly's claim that 'Some people believe that football is a matter of life and death ... I can assure you it is much more important than that.'

Few people are better equipped to challenge that assertion than Michael Duignan. He was part of the great Offaly team that won All-Irelands in 1994 and 1998, as well as five Leinster titles in 11 seasons from 1988 onwards. He won an All-Star in 1998. Today Duignan is probably best known as a GAA pundit for RTÉ Sport, a job he has been doing for over 20 years, starting when he was still an inter-county player.

However, his toughest battle came off the field through his wife Edel's battle with cancer, which she was eventually to lose at the age of 41. Edel made a routine visit to her GP in 2002. This necessitated an immediate trip to Tallaght Hospital, a diagnosis of breast cancer, an operation, chemotherapy and radiotherapy.

Happy days returned for the family but it was a temporary reprieve only. In 2006, the cancer returned. This time it was a secondary cancer affecting the liver and Edel was given a year to 18 months to live. She bravely told Michael that she would be there for their son Brian's First Communion, three years away. Against the medical prognosis she was.

DOWNTURN

Meanwhile, through Edel's illness, Duignan was grappling with the economic downturn that decimated his auctioneering and property businesses.

'It was a crazy time. In one incident at Punchestown, I recall being in the company of someone who sniffed at the quality of champagne on offer and said: "Take away that sh*t." Instead, he bought a couple of bottles at €250 each.

'It was an incredible transition. Edel and I bought our house in 1994/95 and we, as two permanent pensionable bank employees, struggled to get a mortgage ourselves. That was how they vetted it.

'Banks were just starting to get into the mortgage business then. In a way, the banks decided who could get on in society because they decided who they would back financially. But it went from that to this situation where vast sums of money were given out and everyone became a developer. In 2005, I set up an auction-eering and property company which did extremely well initially. I was in commercial auctioneering and you could see this thing going mental – six and seven times salaries to mortgages. And one part of you knew it couldn't last.

'And another part said you are a fool not to be in on this. I tried to spread myself across the board with shares. I never saw it collapsing so quickly. The one thing that really frustrated me was that the banks took no responsibility. And my attitude would be if you borrow money, then you borrow money. You owe it.

'Still, the banks made the mistake of making it too easily available. The level of personal debt was huge. From my point of view, it was hard to find myself back at square one after working for 25 years. But you deal with it.'

TOUGH TIMES

After Brian's communion the family enjoyed a special summer holiday in the west of Ireland. September 2009 meant that the two Duignan boys, Seán and Brian, returned to school. On the first Sunday of September, Michael did the analysis for the All-Ireland Hurling final. Edel fell ill and was brought to James' Hospital. Deep in her soul she knew that she would not survive and was at peace with this. Then came Duignan's toughest day when he brought Seán and Brian to their mother's bedside to say goodbye.

Nothing equipped Duignan for this battle. 'You hear about cancer but until you get caught up in it you don't really know. When Edel was diagnosed with cancer first, it was terrible but there was some positive news as well in that there are treatments and surgery and so on. Then you have the stage where you're told it's terminal and there's no way out of it. Edel came to grips with it better than me and ultimately came to accept it with no fear of dying.

'Edel was remarkably tough mentally and physically and was always in good form when she went out. She had a code when she needed to be alone – the bedroom curtains would be drawn when she didn't want to see people. But for the most part, people knew that she was sick, but probably never really knew how sick until the end.'

THE GAA FAMILY

Edel had a huge funeral. Grief is a lonely road and should not be walked alone. The GAA community, as always, rallied magnificently for the Duignans. Henry Shefflin and Eoin Kelly pucked a sliotar in the back garden with the two boys. Niall Quinn gave them €50 each. The late Páidí O'Sé rang Michael to sympathise. Michael told him not to travel from Ventry, but the next morning Páidí called to pay his respects, stayed a short time and left quietly.

One parable, though, illustrates the magnificence of the GAA for Duignan. 'Tommy Walsh's greatest ever season was 2009. All-Ireland winner again, and hurler of the year, he was superb. But just a week after beating Tipperary in a thriller, he posted a special package to me. Tommy sent a parcel down to the house with Aidan Fogarty; who used to hurl with Offaly, with jerseys and socks and togs and his red helmet, which my son Seán wore for years after. The helmet, was signed inside. It meant an awful lot. When we won our first minor club title in 2016 I had Tommy up to present the medals. He is a great character. Brian Cody also reached out to me after Edel's death.'

THE BOSS

County boards are not always wise in the ways of the world or its money. Twenty-one years later Duignan's career would take a new twist when he was elected as the new chairman of Offaly GAA. The decision was made at the county convention in Tullamore, with the former county hurler defeating incumbent Tommy Byrne by 76 votes to 62. 'Firsts are always special for me. At my first county convention I was elected chairman of the county board. We put in a huge amount of work and there was huge goodwill for me but even so the result was close enough in the end. I think it was the first time an outgoing chairman had been defeated in such a vote since 1971.'

The Faithful County's hurlers were relegated from the Joe McDonagh Cup in 2019, meaning they would be competing in the third tier championship the following year. Meanwhile, the footballers, who last won the Leinster title in 1997, would be playing in Division 3 of the Allianz League, meaning that unless they reached a first provincial final since 2006, they would be competing in the new second tier All-Ireland championship.

'Meeting every club in Offaly inspired me and motivated me for the future of Offaly GAA. The response we got, the people we met, the ideas people have and the passion there for the future. I was disillusioned with where we were. I think we could be doing better. When I saw Offaly going into the Christy Ring and I saw the draw for the Christy Ring, it really spurred me into life. I thought we were in a position we shouldn't be in. I thought we should be a lot more competitive particularly against our neighbours in bordering counties. We were just finding it difficult to beat anyone of note, hurling or football, at the time. I felt we had to breed ambition and change the culture to get our players back to where they should be. It's about creating a culture from a young age – from 13 or 14 they should be aiming at the top. They should be measured against the top instead of hoping for the best. There was a bit of that going on. We had to set our standards higher.

'The GAA has been a huge part of my life. What I found when I reflect back is that it evolves all the time. When I was playing that was my only focus and I played for a long time, 15 years with Offaly but 27 adult years with clubs, a couple of clubs, from 16 to 43. I finished up with Ballinamere. As a player I was focused on playing and didn't realise the massive work that goes on by hugely respected people in the background doing jobs.

'We were mindful of the fact that there was a lot of people there with experience who have done a lot of work but there is an appetite for change. There is no doubt there was a lot of work going on but to me we are getting the same results. If you keep doing the same thing nothing changes. We had won one Leinster Senior football championship match in ten years, our underage teams had been poor and our hurlers had been relegated to the Christy Ring. It was a slide and no matter what people thought they were doing, the structure wasn't working, the system wasn't working and the games programme wasn't working. Something had to be done as far as we were concerned before it went any further.

'Everyone has to take responsibility but the leadership has to come from the top. To me, the clubs and the schools have to be going much better than they are going. They have to be operating at full capacity in order for the county to be going better. We have to understand every club. Every club in Offaly has different challenges. Some of them might be population, some of them might be big towns like Tullamore and Edenderry not being able to get as many players out as they might like. Some of them might be facilities, some money. We committed to do a full club audit, involve clubs in discussions about what was the issue. We had to understand in every area in Offaly where they needed support. Is it in coaching, national schools, secondary schools? We had to recognise there was very good work going on in certain areas, certain clubs, certain schools. Can we replicate that across the board, that is what we need to do. Get as many of our young people out there playing first of all and then playing at the proper level. That is where we are talking about starting.

'Fixtures and our games programme are so important. The amount of matches our kids are getting is not enough. They are not meaningful. Everyone is saying it to us and we know it ourselves. Training for months and months and for an odd match. You train and you play. I wanted to play a match every day, never mind every week. We need to ignite that interest right across the county. Get our kids out playing games, and we have to look at what we are basing our whole coaching system on. Are the development squads working? Are they the best? Just because they are a nationwide solution, are they the best thing for Offaly? We have to think outside the box. We are a different county and we have to do what is right for Offaly. It is easy for the big county to pick out an odd lad here and there. We have to bring a lot more lads forward. Now some of them have taken over from the clubs where they are training two or three times a week, playing matches and holding up championships. That is not what they are designed for, it is very narrow in terms of the amount of players playing. We have to have a huge look at all those areas.

'I think there is a huge apathy out there. I think a lot of people have given up in ways. That is why when you meet the people in the clubs putting in the work, you have so much admiration for them. They have so much passion. I think there has been a general slide. Whether people feel they are not wanted or had been involved or didn't think they could make a difference. I was looking at people all over Offaly who have so much to offer and they are not involved. I can't answer the question about why they are not involved. Why was I not involved before now? I think we all have to put our hands up here and say why did we leave it so long to have this debate and this challenge?

'This is not personal against any of those people who have put in massive hours and time for Offaly GAA. To me, it was so obvious that there was change needed, to give everyone in Offaly a gee up, whether in clubs and coaching. We have always had a massively passionate Offaly GAA following. All you have to do is look at the crowds at matches. If there is any bit of success they come out in droves.

'There is huge interest out there. A lot of people have gone home, folded the tent and sort of given up on where we are at. They are accepting the position we are in. Now I can't do that, it was never in my make-up. It was never in the teams I played in to accept that. I know we don't have the population of other counties.

I think money wise we do well, we fight well above our weight and I know from O'Connor Park that when you go with a good project, get out to the people and meet them, I don't see money being an object. We need far more people in Offaly involved at club and County Board level and to enjoy what they are doing.

'We are all Offaly GAA people and the people who are there deserve respect in this process. All of our meetings and everything we have said have been hugely respectful of the people who are there. I am an Offaly man and if I believe in a project I will get involved.'

He was surprised at the pace of Offaly's decline after his county retirement, as they reached Leinster senior hurling and football finals in 2004 and 2006. 'A lot of things change in the GAA as it always does. There was also change in the social scene, the Celtic Tiger, teachers and what was expected. The roles of schools and not being paid for after hours stuff changed. Changes were happening and managing that change was a difficulty. It slid on from there and all of a sudden we were getting hammered, 30 points or whatever. We had a couple of terrible days in football and hurling.'

How can Offaly raise their standards?

'It is all about thousands and thousands of hours. The most important thing is you have to develop a love of the game. You develop that if you have it in the house. Then you get down to training and it is structured straight away. You are into a system, there is enjoyment and the basic skills are developed. It is also about keeping up the fitness levels that you should be at. It is about balancing all that.

'We have to manage dual issues. Whatever challenges Offaly has as a county, it is not what the rest of the country has, that is not relevant to us. It doesn't matter. A huge part is getting as many players as possible out playing first of all, giving them a meaningful games programme, instilling that love of the game in them and then we can start worrying about the level we are going to get to. It is not rocket science to me and it never will be. It is about being ambitious and seeing yourself operating at the top level. If you see yourself operating at B and C level, that is where you will always be. You have to see yourself and dream about winning.

'We want to focus everything we are doing in the future on the performance of Offaly teams while also making sure that our operations are properly maintained and run; that the governance of our county is properly run. We will look at every aspect of Offaly GAA but the bottom line is we want to improve our performances on the field.'

THE PUNDIT

Duignan's first experience of *The Sunday Game* was the All-Ireland final in 1996 between Wexford and Limerick. 'I was working with Michael Lyster and Ger Loughnane up on the old Nally Stand. My involvement was unusual because I was still playing, and I continued working on the programme and playing until I retired in 2001. The crowd was making so much noise that we couldn't hear each other and I always remember climbing up a ladder to get a quieter spot. The health and safety people wouldn't allow it today.'

His outstanding memory of his time on the programme is tinged with sadness.

'Galway's win in 2017 stands out. My father was a Galway man, and I went to school in Garbally College in Ballinasloe, so I always had an affinity for Galway. But this was more powerful because it came so soon after the death of Tony Keady, who I had played against at the start of my career and it was so emotional because he was such a legend. I had such time for the man. At half-time, we were looking at the piece on him. It was so heartbreaking for him and his family. Whether it was Waterford or Galway that day, it was going to be special because of what it meant to both those counties. I remember looking over here at John Mullane and he was heartbroken. I was heartbroken for the people of Waterford but I was delighted for the people of Galway. Galway were All-Ireland champions for the first time since 1988, when Keady himself was at the centre of the Tribesmen's defence.

'That's always the way it was going to be that day, what an occasion. What an emotional day. All-Ireland final Sunday is always very emotional for me because it brings back memories of Edel's death in 2009.'

Generally, though, he has relished his time on the programme.

'It has been a great opportunity to get to know well the likes of Ger Loughnane, Tomás Mulcahy, Cyril Farrell and Liam Sheedy, which I really enjoyed.'

There was some initial speculation that his role as Offaly chairman would conflict with his job as a TV pundit.

'I don't see a problem continuing my role as co-commentator on *The Sunday Game*. I think it would have been more difficult I had been a pundit on the programme and I was asked to comment about the GAA's Central Council or their administration in Croke Park because of the importance of relationships in my role as chairman. That said I have always told the truth as I see it and I will always speak out on something that I believe is wrong. I don't know about Offaly hurling now, because obviously it's a *Sunday Game* rule if your county is playing, you're not involved.

'But I'd love to see Offaly back in Croke Park and I'd love to be stepping away from the co-commentary that day, if Offaly were in a Leinster final or an All-Ireland final. I'd have no problem stepping away.'

REST IN PEACE

For Michael Duignan, spring 2020 was a particularly tough time. His 85-year-old father Peadar died after a short illness, unrelated to Covid-19. Peadar Duignan's funeral in the normal circumstances would have been a huge affair but unfortunately because of the social isolation protocols at the time it was just a small family affair.

Despite the sadness and the deep vein of grief, Michael can still see the light through the darkness. 'He did everything for me. When I was in college in Waterford he would drive me down every Monday morning and still be back for work at 8 a.m. He never said it to me; but he was proud of me. I know he was. He had a streak of mischief to him. In 1988 we were playing Galway in an All-Ireland semi-final. I went to first Mass that morning and when I got home he had the Galway flag up waiting for me!'

PERSPECTIVE

On the way into an Offaly management team meeting on a rainy Tuesday evening Duignan delayed to share some outstanding memories for me. Who was his most difficult opponent? 'Although I didn't mark him often Brian Lohan was very tough to mark. They didn't come any better. Willie O'Connor was another one that stands out. He knew a lot of tricks! When I came on to the scene, the celebrated Galway half-back on line were in their pomp: Pete Finnerty, Tony Keady and Gerry McInerney were pretty awesome individually and collectively. In the 1990s Offaly were a big power in hurling so if you were constantly marking Brian Whelahan or Kevin Kinahan in training it really brought you on. Club hurling was also very strong in Offaly back then. I was marking Martin Hanamy or Hubert Rigney so often it also brought me on as a player.'

Who was the greatest character? 'There were so many of that

Offaly team but they were all characters in a different way like Daithí Regan and John Troy. But it is hard to go beyond Johnny Pilkington. My favourite story about him came the morning after we won the 1998 All-Ireland final. Some of us went for a quiet drink in Doheny Nesbitts. Somehow the *Pat Kenny Show* heard about it and rang the pub and asked for one of us to speak on the phone for the programme. To our surprise Johnny volunteered to do so because, contrary to popular perception, he is a very serious lad and doesn't normally put himself forward. He had a great time with Pat and he was taking the p**s out of Pat for being a "great GAA man" which we all found hilarious.

'Pat's last question was about Michael Bond because Johnny was the man who had been fingered for getting rid of Babs: "Well now that he has won the All-Ireland is Michael Bond's job safe for next year?"

'Johnny paused dramatically before he said, "I don't know. I haven't decided yet if I'll keep him on or not."'

Finally, what was the funniest moment of his career?

'My first All-Ireland semi-final in 1988 against Galway. That morning I went to first Mass and when I came home my mother had the breakfast ready. The nutritionists today would have freaked out because she gave me a big fry-up. The problem was that I was so nervous I couldn't eat anything. My father was a very quiet man and he was reading the paper and he asked me "What's wrong, son?" I answered, "I'm too nervous to eat anything."

'He replied, "Eat up. No use making a fool of yourself in Croke Park and being hungry as well."'

5

THEY KNOW THE CALL OF FREEDOM IN THEIR BREASTS: SARAH MacDONALD

Try not to become a man of success,
but rather try to become a man of value.
Albert Einstein

It is a fact universally acknowledged that Larry Gogan was Ireland's greatest ever DJ. What was less well known about Larry was that he was intimately connected with one of the most iconic events in Irish history, the 1916 Rising. His father John, who subsequently owned newsagents and sweetshops in Fairview, fought in the 1916 Rising and was interned in Frongoch. The journey of a relative from the 1916 Rising to Frongoch is a familiar one to journalist Sarah MacDonald. She is the granddaughter of Louth legend Tom Burke. Sarah is a custodian of the past and the keeper of her grandfather's flame.

'You could say that in a GAA context my grandfather did it all. And in a political context he had a remarkable life also. He was a player, referee, administrator and freedom fighter.'

In the world of Gaelic Games, Louth has an honourable pedigree, being at the forefront of the Gaelic Athletic Association since

47

its formation in 1884. In May 1885, a branch of the Association was set up in the county following Michael Cusack's visit to Drogheda. Shortly after, clubs sprung up the length and breadth of the county. Louth were represented by Young Irelands from Dundalk in the first football All Ireland final held at the Benburbs club grounds, Donnybrook on 29 April 1888. In the early 1900s, Louth qualified for three All-Ireland football finals, losing the 1909 final to Kerry but being victorious in 1910 and 1912, wins gained at the expense of Kerry (in a walk-over) and Antrim respectively.

This was a turbulent and complex period in Irish history. While many Irish sportsmen fought and died on the Western Front and at Gallipoli, some chose the path of radical nationalism. Seán Etchingham of the Wexford GAA was such a man, and he proposed in November 1914 that the GAA establish rifle clubs so that members could defend Ireland. A speaker at the meeting expressed concern that the weather might not be suitable for rifle training. Etchingham was infuriated and responded: 'Do you want special weather for war? This opportunity – the like of which you have not had for a century – may pass; an opportunity that may not occur again.'

Sarah explains how her grandfather was caught up in the political turmoil.

'In 1916 he answered the "call to arms" and was interned in Frongoch Prison (North Wales), where he met Michael Collins. In the aftermath of the Insurrection, 3,000 Irish rebels were arrested in all, and were marched to Dublin Port to board boats destined for internment camps in Britain. Over the next six months, the internees included leading lights of the struggle for independence like Michael Collins, Richard Mulcahy, Terence MacSwiney and Sam Maguire, and they formed deep bonds of friendship while sharing their knowledge and skills. The lessons of the Rising had been learnt and republican networks were strengthened within Frongoch's North and South camps.'

The testimony of one of those men arrested, Johnny Flynn, exists today: 'We were lined up at Richmond barracks, marched down along the quays, and along the North Wall. There were two rows of soldiers either side of us, with a lorry behind us with a machine gun mounted upon it.

'We certainly weren't very popular as we were marched down to the boat. But for the soldiers either side of us, we might have fared very badly with the women of Dublin. Many of them were shouting "shoot the bastards".

'The rebels were brought to Britain on cattle ships, many of them thrown into pens alongside the cattle. Of the 3,000 aboard, 1,800 were interned at Frongoch in Wales: an old, disused distillery which had been used as a prisoner of war camp for German soldiers during the First World War. Living conditions were atrocious, with many of the German prisoners at the camp dying of TB.

'In spite of the poor conditions, the proximity of so many Irishmen with similar republican ideals led to a community atmosphere among Michael Collins and the other detainees, and the prison became known as *Ollscoil Na Réabhlóide* or the University of Revolution.'

One of the detainees, Joseph Lawless, recalled the atmosphere in his Bureau of Military History testimony.

'Frongoch has since then been aptly termed the University of the Irish revolution, and so indeed it was. No more certain way of perpetuating the ideals of the executed leaders and ensuring another and bigger effort to throw off the yoke of foreign domination, could have been imagined or desired by them.

'The police in Ireland had done their work well in selecting throughout the country the most likely disaffected persons, most of whom were Volunteers, but not all of them. These, lodged together in a camp with the leaven of those who had had their blood baptism on the streets of Dublin and elsewhere, were bound to be touched by the longing to emulate the heroic deeds of those who fought; and there were those amongst us whose intellects grasped the possibilities of this situation, and strove to make the best use of the opportunity so unexpectedly provided by the enemy.

'One of the aspects key in fostering this collective identity was Gaelic football,' Sarah continues. 'A number of those interned were Gaelic footballers of considerable repute along with my grandfather. Gaelic football matches were frequently organised between inmates to both keep fit and display their national character. As the prison would not allow the detainees to have hurleys, they were forced to play Gaelic football with a soccer ball. The prisoners renamed the field at the camp – a pitch surrounded by barbed wire – as Croke Park.

'At the time, the Wolfe Tone tournament was the secondary competition in the GAA. Louth – captained by my grandfather – and Kerry had qualified for the final, which was postponed owing to the Rising. Such was the volume of players from both teams interned at Frongoch, it was decided that the Wolfe Tone final would be played on the barbed wire-enclosed field the inmates had deemed as Croke Park. It has become known as the "All-Ireland Behind Barbed Wire".

'Attendance at the game was made compulsory, so a crowd of about 1,800 watched a game that has been described as extremely tough and competitive. Perhaps apocryphally, one British officer was recorded as having said: "If that's what they are like at play, they must be bloody awful in a fight!"

'The game was recorded by prisoner Joe Stanley, who was a Louth-based publisher of Republican literature. His report of the game itself is sadly rather vague. All that is known is the game lasted 40 minutes (comprising two 20-minute halves) and that Kerry won the game by a point.'

The Proclamation was read out by piper Cormac Bowell during the interval. After the game each player placed a piece of grass from 'Croke Park' into the box with their medals as a tribute to the men interned there in 1916.

There was an unusual marketing strategy for the game. Posters advertising the Wolfe Tone Tournament final match in Frongoch between old rivals Kerry and Louth informed fans that 'admission was five shillings and wives and sweethearts should be left at home'!

TIME TO SAY GOODBYE

Sarah explains how the saga ended:

'The last Irishman in Frongoch on 23 December 1916 was Dublin priest Fr Laurence Joseph Stafford. In the Dublin Diocesan Archives include one letter dated 23 December, which was written to Archbishop William Walsh of Dublin. In it Fr Stafford writes, "Five months ago when they were releasing the men interned here in hundreds, I said I should be the last Irishman left in Frongoch; and today I am."

'Outlining to the archbishop how he lobbied the British authorities for the prisoners' release he had argued "that Christmas was Christmas".

"Today the gates of the compound are thrown open and tonight there will not be a single Irishman (save myself) left in Frongoch."'

According to Noelle Dowling, archivist at the Dublin Diocesan Archives, when the first World War broke out in August 1914, Fr Stafford asked to become a military chaplain and the following March he signed up.

This proved a difficulty when he was appointed to Frongoch because he wore the military chaplain's uniform. The men looked at him as being a sort of 'Khaki chaplain'. Even though he knew some of them, they did not take to him initially. But through his good work and his perseverance they finally did accept him.

Another letter written by Fr. Stafford from Frongoch is dated 19 July 1916, shortly after he arrived in the camp. He relates how he celebrated Mass for the men in both camps in Frongoch, as well as Confession and the Rosary: 'I need hardly say, the men appreciate the presence of a priest among them and I am up shortly after five every morning to begin my work.'

POSTSCRIPT

Sarah is proud that her grandfather made a significant contribution to the GAA.

'In 1920 at the behest of Michael Collins he was nominated and elected Secretary of the County Board, a position he held until 1925. He later served four years as County Board Chairman from 1928–31. He refereed the 1928 All-Ireland Final and the Tailteann Games and Railway Cup Finals, as well as countless Louth finals. With Drogheda Stars he won two Louth Junior and two Louth Senior medals, before helping to form Wolfe Tones in 1923. He won a third Louth Senior medal with them in 1925. He declined the invitation to represent Leinster in the 1924 Tailteann Games because of his political views. In 1928 he refereed the All-Ireland final, the first occasion Sam Maguire was presented to the winning team, Bill "Squires" Gannon lifting the trophy for Kildare.'

So what became of the camp?

'Today, the barbed wire has been removed from the field and now it is grazed by sheep. Locals in the Welsh village still refer to the field as "Croke Park". There is a small monument to the memory of the game and the men involved, which was erected by a Liverpool branch of the Gaelic League.'

6

THE FIERCE HURLING MAN: ZAK MORADI

Never praise your own spuds.
Páidí Ó'Sé

When you first greet him, it is the accent that strikes you.

Pure Dub.

It is not what you would expect. His father was from Ramadi. So was his mother. Neither were from hurling strongholds. Yet he is a Leitrim hurler.

Semaco 'Zak' Moradi spent the first 11 years of his life in Ramadi, a city in central Iraq located about 110km west of Baghdad. His family are Iranian Kurds – the third largest ethnic group in Iran, who constitute ten million of the country's 80 million inhabitants. Their early days were spent in the mountainous region on the Iranian side of the border with Iraq, where half of his ten siblings were born.

The Iraq-Iran war, which began in 1980, took the lives of over 100,000 civilians on both sides. Consequently, Zak's parents and his older brothers and sisters fled their native country and set up home in Ramadi in central Iraq.

'In 1980 when the war started, things were really tough because my family were right on the border between Iraq and Iran. My grandparents stayed put and I've still uncles all over there now. They're all farmers up in the mountains. Every time a war kicked in, they were in the middle of it. About 20,000 people left their homes and had to move into Iraq. I am the third youngest in the family. I was born in Ramadi in 1991. By then the first Gulf War was well underway.'

THE MOTHER OF ALL BATTLES

Even Saddam Hussein must have foreseen the potential catastrophic consequences, massive loss of life, and the huge destruction of a war. Most people were convinced that he would step back from the brink. When the Gulf War began, they were shocked to the very core. The scary thing was that some of the briefings that were given by the US forces were drawn from CNN reports. It was the first time the world had witnessed a war as a soap opera.

It was an awesome sight to look at images of the battlefield. It was frightening and alarming to see that all of this could happen and to see that it did happen. It was also very sad, almost unreal. One of the first things that struck viewers was the pollution from the massive oil wells. There were 700 burning oil wells and they clouded the skies with their fumes, spewing massive thick clouds of pollution into the air. The wind was carrying it eastward in one huge cloud, covering hundreds of miles. Just before that it had gone southwards and had engulfed the city of Kuwait, turning midday almost into midnight.

Footage showed bodies still lay on the ground. Helmets had obviously fallen from the heads as the faces were buried in the sand. A boot stood standing on its own. Viewers wondered who owned it and where was that person now.

Further up the desert there was a crossroads just north of

Kuwait City, leading into Iraq, where at some stage in the last few days of the war there had been a massive withdrawal of the Iraqi forces. They had been caught by a coalition forces air strike. Few have ever seen such destruction. The vehicles seemed to be piled up on the junction. They lay in a monstrous mess of twisted metal, shattered tanks and burned-out cabs. In all the chaos perhaps there was a tank in the middle which had not been touched at all, that had escaped the destruction. When you saw all this you wondered what the loss of life in this area must have been.

Then as the television cameras moved further north, people saw minefields appearing as the sand of the desert was blown away by the wind. In the distance they could see shepherds coming out with their flocks and carrying on as they had for hundreds of years before the battle took place. People wondered how they were going to survive with all the war debris and all the unexploded mines.

Kuwait had been a magnificent city. Much was now totally burned out. It was just a shell. All the windows were gone. Much of the area was now almost impassable with all the rubble. It was impossible to comprehend.

A LIVING HELL

The Kurdish problem predated the war. The Iraqi defence minister Ali Hassan al Majid spearheaded a campaign of genocide against the Kurds. He was known to the Kurdish people as 'Ali of the Chemicals'. In 1988 he ordered the dropping of chemical bombs on the town of Halabja. More than 5,500 people lost their lives in that one incident. In addition, people were tortured in groups so that when one broke down and confessed, others would follow suit.

At the ceasefire line between Iran and Iraq, villages had been destroyed by the Iraqi forces and the purge against the Kurds.

The villages were absolutely flattened. The houses were lying like scattered stones on the ground. Then people saw how isolated the Kurds were. They were so vulnerable. One picture stands out. It appeared in *Time* magazine shortly after an assault on the Kurds. A father and his child lay dead on the ground having being gassed. It appeared as if he was carrying the baby and, as he breathed in the gassed air, he died and the baby fell from his hands and rolled on the ground. The baby lay beside his head. Both of them looked in perfect condition but both were victims of chemical weapons.

For the refugees, life had become a living hell. They lost their homes. They often had nowhere to lay their weary heads at night. All their worldly possessions could be carried over their shoulders in just one bag, a plastic bag with a few bits and pieces tied with a string. As they went along, they probably lost some of these possessions. They were not sure if they would have food that night or next morning. The babies or very young children might not be able to walk and would have to be carried along distances in difficult situations. Some of those who could walk might not have shoes. Some might have slippers walking through the mud. Others might have sandals, like Irish children might wear on hot summer days, during the torrential rains that were falling in the wintertime.

In the southern part of Iraq, the sand blowing in small tornadoes swirled around. Women tried to protect their children by putting cloaks around their faces to prevent the sand from blowing against them. They had no homes to go to. Perhaps half of their families were missing. The absence of a father or mother's care would be clearly visible in the eyes of the children as they looked with bulging eyes in wonder. They were wondering what all the strangers were doing around them.

The other noteworthy thing was the lines on people's faces. They had been through so much and that was reflected in their appearance. The laughter was gone from their eyes. Instead, there was an emptiness. They had a total loss of belief in society and in all institutions. In a conflict zone nobody smiled at all. There was this sort of pain on people's faces that portrayed the burden they carried with them.

In refugee camps in this troubled country there was often no living just existence. Around the country death stalked the roads and ditches. There were bodies all over the place, laid out side-by-side by the road – bodies and limbs blown away, bloodied and awful. Whether or not the country was previously divisible between political groupings, the effect of the genocide was to confirm a genuine gulf – between those who were the targets of murder and those who did the murdering. It was in the interests of the leaders on both 'sides' to spread their murderous hate. Babies were often the only survivors with the energy to cry.

FROM A DISTANCE

It is often said that the first casualty of war is the truth, but whose truth? In trying to climb the hill of truth such is the complexity of the conflict that it was difficult, if not impossible, to identify the 'good guys and bad guys'. In the thousands of articles which have attempted to analyse the source of the conflict and the search for a political or military solution the human cost of the war sometimes does not get the attention it deserves. Such is the enormity of the horror that it is virtually impossible for any eye-witness to speak dispassionately about the topic.

Asking survivors like the Moradi family about the memories of the atrocities they witnessed in conflict zones during those years is likely suddenly being introduced to a stranger. Their reticence speaks volumes. All they offer is hints of the horrors they witnessed. In those moments there is vulnerability about them, a sadness that clings to them and a sense that their minds often travel in a land uninhabited by the rest of us. It is not difficult to imagine voices which run through their heads like silver bullets, screaming memories into the caverns of their minds, the primitive regions of the unconscious and beyond. When pressed about the worst atrocity they had witnessed, it is not surprising that often it is to shake their head and say softly, 'I don't want to talk about it.'

For Zak Moradi there was not exhaustive detail but significant clues.

'My parents and my brother remember all that violence. They say the Gulf War in 1991 was the toughest because you had the F60s and all these fighter planes going over and bombing us. At the time you had the Americans coming into Iraq. My mam said 1991 was the scariest time.'

Moradi looks back at his time growing up in Iraq under the Saddam regime as if he was living in a time warp.

'The time we were there was under Saddam Hussein's dictatorship. Over there people weren't able to say anything about the government or you couldn't open your mouth about Saddam Hussein. He was kind of the God in Iraq. It would be similar to North Korea now, but Iraq was twice as bad.

'You'd go into school and there would always be pictures of Saddam. You opened your history book and you'd have a big picture of him in the front of it. The second page you opened, there was a little picture of him. The way they had it, he was looking at us the whole time. If there were 30 million people in Iraq, there were 30 million pictures of him.

'You'd be trained not to say anything bad about him. There would have been five TV channels and it was all about Saddam Hussein. The whole day long was all him. If you were listening to music, the Iraqi singers had to sing about Saddam and how great he was. It was a completely different experience altogether.

'People would be brainwashed that way on television. It was

propaganda the whole time. It was the same thing in school, all the teachers had to say how great Saddam Hussein is. Their family ran the country with an iron fist and that was it. There was no real media over there. If you were a journalist, you wouldn't be allowed to write anything bad about Saddam or you'd be gone. You'd be wiped out, you know? You'd pick up a newspaper every day and you wouldn't know if the paper was from last month or if it was today's paper, because it was the same stuff about Saddam.'

The memory of 11 September 2001 still has the power to chill the blood. It will forever remain a template for humankind's experience of evil, a black symbol of humanity. Within minutes our television sets brought the shocking reality into our homes with disturbing immediacy. The television images ensured that the event belonged to everyone. The mourning too, like that for Princess Diana, was a communal experience. We united to grieve but in a safe and private place, even amid millions of other viewers, to grapple with the sadness that enveloped us. For Zak Moradi, though, these events had a special significance.

'I remember 9/11. Over there, everyday it was about war: "Iraq is going to war, how great Iraq is. We took over Kuwait. We won the war against Iran."'

In the wake of 9/11, conflict started simmering once again between Iraq and the US. It was as plain as the nose on his face to Zak that another war was coming on the horizon, and the family opted to get out. There was, though, a serious fly in the ointment.

'The Iranian government wouldn't take back the Kurdish people. They wouldn't allow the people that had left in the 1980s to go back to the country. And the Iraqi government didn't want you staying there either because you weren't from there. So you were kind of stuck between the two of them.'

Zak remembers how his older brother, who worked for the United Nations, helped engineer a move out of the troubled region. In 2002, the family made the move to Ireland. A year later the Americans invaded Iraq, starting a war that lasted almost nine years. A study in 2011 estimated that half a million Iraqis died as a result of the conflict from the invasion. Zak's family were the lucky ones.

'My older brother used to work for the United Nations over there. He spoke perfect English, as well as fluent Kurdish, Persian and Arabic. He spoke four languages, he was always a very intelligent man. His job with the UN was to take a lot of people out of the country.

'When he got his job with the UN, a lot of countries around Europe started taking all these people in, because they were going through terrible times. I have aunties that are living in Sweden since the 1990s. I have uncles in England. I've got family everywhere around the world. That's one of the hardest things, because you don't have your family around you. They're all over the place. It's not the same.'

Zak's family came to Leitrim to start a new phase of their lives and it was a long way from where they started. Uprooting and moving halfway across the world was tough but the problems for Zak were exacerbated because he had to learn a whole new language at 11 years old.

'Even though it was terrible in Iraq, we didn't want to leave because we were used to the system over there. The lads you went to school with were all over there. I was close to 12 by the time we left so you'd miss the people you grew up with.

'Coming to a different country was weird – a real green one! The weather, everything was different about it. When I started school I couldn't speak a word of English. That was a nightmare. But I have to say fair play to the school, we had an English teacher in primary school who gave us extra lessons so that helped. It took maybe 15 months to pick it up fluently and get to know everything.

'The people were actually very friendly. I'd say because we went over to Leitrim and we were the first foreigners a lot of lads had seen over there. It was something different for them to look at and you've a different skin colour. You didn't speak English and they all wanted to help you.'

Zak fell under the spell of a new game.

'Running would have been the only sport we played in Iraq. When we were kids we'd always be racing each other. In Iraq back then it was very hard to play any sports, because there was an embargo on them. You weren't even able to buy a football. If you were going to buy a football you had to be from a wealthy family.

'I remember Clement Cunniffe, who would have been the main hurler in Leitrim, he came into our school shortly after we arrived in Ireland. He was doing some sort of coaching at the time. He used to come in and teach us how to play hurling and Gaelic. I didn't know what type of sport this was. Some lads were well able to strike the ball and I was going, "How am I going to do this?"

'It took a while to get into it, but I made friends quicker when I started to play GAA. When you're a kid you'll play any sport. If you're given a ball, you'll hit a ball. If you're given a cricket ball you'll play cricket. I was interested in sport, but Gaelic was obviously easier to pick up.

'I always liked hurling. When you drive the ball 40 or 50 yards you get a bit of craic out of it. I got more enjoyment out of the hurling, but I loved Gaelic football as well. I was playing both, but I got more into the hurling as I got older. I remember playing midfield at under-14 in Leitrim and I couldn't strike the ball! But I always had my speed and could always hook and make sure my man didn't win the ball.

'I remember when Clement came into the school he gave me a hurl and a sliotar and said, "You take that home with you. You can play any sport you want." Clement gave me the hurl to keep. I took it home and started practising. I just practised and practised. A few years after I started, I was able to hit the ball off left and right. I went to the hurling wall every day, trying to strike the ball off left and right. That's how I learned. Clement got his hurling because his family were from Galway. I would have looked up to him because everyone talked about how good at hurling he was. Six or seven years later, I ended up playing with him.'

When Zak was 15, the family upped sticks and moved to Dublin where work was more plentiful. Despite living in Leitrim for less than four years, Zak retained his love affair for the county. He developed greatly as a hurler at his new Dublin club Thomas Davis, where he also picked up the nickname 'Zak'. When he arrived in Tallaght he was still going by his first name Semaco, but Con Deasy, who trained the Thomas Davis under-16s, had trouble pronouncing it.

Deasy said, 'I can't pronounce your name at all. I don't know what to call you. I keep forgetting your name. It's too long. I'll call you Zak, is that fair enough?'

Zak explains, 'So he called me Zak. Then everybody started calling me Zak. Even my family at home call me Zak now.'

Leitrim stayed in his heart and when the opportunity presented itself to hurl with the Connacht side, he jumped at it.

'I still had loads of friends in Leitrim and I used to go down every second or third weekend when I didn't have a match. It kept me in contact with all the lads I played with.'

The Leitrim management offered 18-year-old Moradi the opportunity to play in a few trial games.

'I played a few challenge matches. I was only 18 or 19 and scored a few goals and points and they kept me in there. Once I came out of minor, I got mad into the hurling. We won the intermediate hurling championship in Dublin in 2011 and I was good that year.'

In 2016 Moradi was one of just two Leitrim players to be named on the Lory Meagher Cup Champions 15 selection – their version of the All-Stars – after scoring in every one of the county's championship games that year.

It's a long way from Ramadi to Carrick-on-Shannon.

7

WHEN A MAN LOVES A WOMAN: CHARLIE REDMOND

Parce mihi, Dominie, nihil enim sunt dies mei.
Spare me, O Lord, for my days are nothing.

There is nothing colder than loneliness.

Charlie Redmond was and remains an icon on the Hill.

He knows the secrets of pain and heartbreak.

The Erins Isle star played with Dublin for more than a decade. As a forward he did his scoring with chilling efficiency. He is perhaps most famous for scoring what would be the winning goal in the 1995 All-Ireland final. Less happily he also got sent off in the game. It would be 16 years before the Dubs would win the Sam Maguire Cup again.

However, Charlie would face bigger battles off the field. Tragedy would cast a dark shadow on his life when he lost his beloved wife, Grainne, to cancer. Grainne lost her courageous battle to the condition on 2 December 2016, the result of a brain tumour she was diagnosed with back in 2013.

The problem first surfaced when the couple were on holiday when Grainne began having severe headaches and bouts of forgetfulness, so they went to see former Meath footballer and surgeon Gerry McEntee in the Mater Private for a scan. Charlie looked at him with the intensity of an expert inspecting a diamond for a hidden flaw. There was apprehension and agitation in his face.

McEntee's words are forever etched on Redmond's conscious-ness: '"Charlie, it's bad. She has a 5cm tumour." And he said something which is still ingrained in my brain today, he said, "You've got to go to Beaumont and you've got to go now."'

The sound of those words felt like a foreign object in Charlie's mouth, one with sharp edges that pressed painfully against the soft skin of his throat.

Grainne had surgery to remove the tumour on her 51st birthday – but the aggressive cancer was already at stage four and had spread.

'I had difficulty comprehending it,' Charlie recalls with a shudder. The whole nightmarish 30 seconds would stay frozen like a freeze frame in his mind. It would come back to haunt him in subsequent years with monotonous regularity. The rest of the day is blurred like a badly faded photocopy.

'Two weeks previously we were on holiday, and we were having a great time. We got everything we could get, but with this you can't get everything. When we were told Grainne had 18 months to live, I nearly fell off the seat.'

Holding back tears, Charlie poignantly explained how he and Grainne met when he was doing his ambulance training with the Dublin Fire Brigade in a maternity ward. Grainne was a student midwife herself at the time.

'I saw her, and I was smitten immediately,' he recalls. 'I don't think I witnessed the birth to be honest with you! I couldn't take my eyes off Grainne. I asked her out, I said would she like to go for a drink.'

The course of true love faced a perception problem. 'She thought I was the father of the child that had just been born!'

While their first date went well, Charlie had an unfortunate romantic accident after walking Grainne back to her moped.

'I tried to kiss her, give her a little peck.' He smiles at the memory. 'And as I went to kiss her the visor on her helmet fell down and cracked me on the nose, actually cut me on the nose.'

After patching up his nose – and promising never to bust out his favourite white canvas shoes again – Charlie and Grainne fell truly, madly, deeply into love. Marriage followed. They had three lovely daughters – Sarah, Ciara and Ruth. When Grainne became ill, they opted to keep their daughters and their parents in the dark about Grainne's condition for a long time.

'We chose not to tell the children for a long time, until we had to tell them,' Charlie explains. 'Grainne's mother was hale and hearty, and having to tell her was one of the hardest things I had to do. When I told her, we were upstairs in the bedroom in my house. She lay down, and she got up about an hour later, and she had a coat on her.'

She went for a walk alone up to her husband's grave. 'To tell a woman in her 80s that her daughter was going to die – it was so hard,' Charlie recalls. It stirred his sadness like never before. 'It was harder telling her than telling the kids.'

Grainne lived for twice as long as her prognosis: she got three years. 'She was such a strong person, she fought it all the way,' Charlie said – and he remembers her passing with crystal clarity. 'St Francis' have a night up in Blanchardstown, it's a carol ceremony. They have it outside the front door. It was the most beautiful experience I've had in my life. We were on the first floor. I couldn't see anyone, it was a cold, cold winter's night, a clear sky, I could see every star in the sky. All I could hear was "O Holy Night" coming over, the air was really thin, you didn't have to struggle to hear it. It was a surreal experience. I was there on my own, the door was slightly ajar, Grainne was asleep inside, and I know she could hear it. But she never woke up after that.'

The funeral was a very moving occasion. The family's grief though intensely personal was generously shared. The local community as always responded magnificently in times of adversity. Everyone rallied around. Many were weeping. They had good reason to in this court of human suffering.

Charlie is keen to pay tribute to the staff at St Francis Hospice in Blanchardstown who sustained Grainne in her final days. 'Grainne didn't know she was in a hospice, such was the quality of the service. She thought she was in a hotel.'

Through it all, Charlie and the children remained strong, though they still think about Grainne all the time. 'I miss her obviously, hugely. The kids miss her hugely, massively. But we're fine.'

Whoever said time heals all wounds had a very limited experience of heartbreaking grief. Knowing that he will never again hear Grainne's laughter is a blow to his heart.

Her absence lingers in his consciousness. In the hidden folds of the heart Charlie's pain has not dissolved. However, with the passage of time he has begun to not just be sorry for all he has lost but to give thanks for all he had.

He also somehow found the strength to bring some humour into the situation. It feels like a small, silent act of resistance to give him the strength to face whatever lies ahead. He describes how Grainne, who did not really have much understanding of the rules, watched him getting sent off in the 1995 All-Ireland final against Tyrone.

'When is Charlie coming back on?' she asked, her eyes fired with defiance.

'In about three months,' came the immediate reply.

8

THE ONE-OFF: PÁIDÍ Ó'SÉ

*We were walking down the corridor with Mr Haughey, who
was on crutches at the time. He said to him, 'Páidí, did you
break any bones during your career?' And he said, 'Yes,
Taoiseach, but none of my own.'*

Seán Walsh

We were not three minutes into our first conversation when he
launched into a story about a former player with an inappropriate
affection for other men's wives.

To say that he had a love of Kerry is like saying Hitler had a
problem with anger management issues.

On the field Páidí Ó'Sé was one of a kind. He won eight
All-Ireland medals as a player and as a manager led the Kingdom
to two All-Irelands.

Off the field Páidí was unique. In God's garden there was none
rarer. As a shrewd Kerry man, he was often asked for advice,
including by a young woman who sought guidance on how to
'uncouple' herself from a young man she was seeing. Knowing
the young man in question, Páidí said, 'Walk up to him with a big
smile and say, "Congratulations. You are going to be a daddy."
Then watch him run.'

TRUE LOVE WAYS

When a young man of his acquaintance was thinking of getting married, he asked Páidí how he would know if she was 'the one'. Páidí answered, 'She will tell you.'

Páidí did not think the couple were a good match so he felt obliged to discourage his young friend, so he asked him, 'Have you seen her mother?'

'Yes. But I'd rather marry her daughter.'

SO THIS IS CHRISTMAS

Páidí had a generous sensibility. One December he asked a young neighbour: 'Now, Mary, [not her real name] what can I get you for Christmas?'

Mary: 'A unicorn.'

Páidí: 'Ah, Mary, be realistic. What else do you want?'

Mary: 'A boyfriend.'

Páidí: 'What colour unicorn do you want?'

GOOD SAMARITAN

Páidí had a very generous side. One day he went into Tesco and saw a woman who was very distressed. She started to cry uncontrollably. When Páidí asked her what was wrong she explained, between sobs, that she had lost all her holiday money. Páidí immediately put his hand in his pocket and took out a 100 Euro and handed it over to her. The woman was thrilled with his kindness and went home full of gratitude. A Kerry fan came up to Páidí and told him how much he admired his generosity.

Páidí shrugged his shoulders and said, 'Ah sure, God love her. The poor creature was very upset. I had to help her out. Besides I took the money from the thousand euro I had just found in the car park.'

WITH THE RED STUFF ON HER FINGERNAILS

Páidí once told me, 'I once dated a girl who was a twin.'

I said, 'That must have been confusing. How did you tell them apart?'

'Ah sure, 'twas easy. Pauline always wore red nail varnish on her fingers. Patrick wore blue nail varnish on his.'

LOVE AND MARRIAGE

At a party to mark his wedding anniversary, Páidí was asked to give his friends a brief account of the benefits of marriage. He replied, 'Well, I've learned that marriage is the best teacher of all. It teaches you loyalty, forbearance, meekness, self-restraint, forgiveness – and a great many other qualities you wouldn't have needed if you'd stayed single.'

HANGING ON THE TELEPHONE

The classic Páidí story, which I stress is apocryphal, involves the referee who decides that he has to make a quick getaway after an All-Ireland final between Kerry and Dublin in Croke Park in which he sends off three Kerry players and awards two controversial penalties. He drives too quickly, crashes coming round a bend and is thrown through the windscreen on to the road. By coincidence, the car following him is driven by one of the players he sent off, Páidí, and he stops to see if he can help. He finds that the referee is in a bad way and makes a 999 call on his mobile.

'I think the referee's dead,' he shouts down the phone in panic. 'What can I do?'

'Calm down,' says the operator, used to dealing with emergencies. 'First of all, go and make sure the referee is dead.'

The operator hears a choking sound and the cracking of neck bone. Then Páidí returns to the mobile.

'Ok,' he says. 'I've made sure he's dead. Now what should I do?'

I CONFESS

According to legend Páidí went to confession a month after the game and confessed to the priest, 'I lost my temper and said some bad words to one of my opponents.'

'Ahhh, that's a terrible thing for a Kerry player to be doing,' the priest said. He took a piece of chalk and drew a mark across the sleeve of his coat.

'That's not all, Father. I got mad and punched one of my opponents.'

'Saints preserve us!' the priest said, making another chalk mark.

'There's more. As I got out of a shemozzle, I kicked two of the other team's players in the ... in a sensitive area.'

'Oh, Jesus, Mary and Joseph!' the priest wailed, making two more chalk marks on his sleeve. 'Who in the world were we playing when you did these awful things?'

'Cork.'

'Ah, well,' said the priest, wiping his sleeve, 'boys will be boys.'

LOVING CORK

Páidí joked that he had a love-hate relationship with Cork fans. He loved them and they hated him!

He once told me over the phone that at a charity fundraiser he was wearing a Cork jersey for the day.

I asked him: 'How is it going?'

'Not so good.'

'Why?'

'I have been swore at.'

'Gosh, that's not very nice.'

'I've been spat it.'

'That's awful.'

'I've even been punched.'

'That's scary.'

'That's not the scary part.'

'What is the scary part?'

'I still haven't left my own house yet.'

SPEEDY

In his role as a garda Páidí stopped an American in Kerry for driving too fast. Páidí remonstrated with the driver and asked him, in his strong accent, 'What would you do if you were to run into Mr Fog?' The visitor first thought he had stumbled upon a lost tribe in Kerry which personified the weather, speaking of Master Rainfall, Mrs Sunshine, Brother Thunder, etc. Then he thought that Páidí was simply being patronising towards a visiting Yank and answered the question with heavy sarcasm. 'I'd just put Mr Foot on Mr Brake.'

Páidí gave him the sort of look he only reserved for Dublin half-forwards and replied, 'I said *mist or fog*.'

9

WE NEED TO TALK ABOUT KEVIN: KEVIN McSTAY

Finish each day and be done with it. Tomorrow is a new day. You shall begin it serenely and with too high a spirit to be encumbered with your old nonsense.

Ralph Waldo Emerson

It is a grip on the heart. But it comes at a cost.

What is it like to be an intercounty manager today? Three days before the Roscommon team he managed played Leitrim in the 2017 Connacht semi-final, Kevin McStay wrote to me. I reproduce the letter below to give an insight in that respect.

Roscommon Town
Friday June 16th 2017

Dear John,

I am spending the morning catching up with correspondence from the past few weeks – apologies that yours got caught up with the many other 'Good Luck' cards, Notes, 'Best Wishes', 'Resign Now', etc.

Your support is very much appreciated. To follow Roscommon you have to be committed to the 'long haul'. Roscommon as a footballing tradition doesn't hit the podium on an annual basis (the late '70s/early '80s apart) and so we must believe that through perseverance and resilience our day will come.

I cannot deny the past few months have been other than difficult as we attempt to improve the fortunes of Roscommon Senior footballers. The criticism has been unfair in many instances and difficult to understand some of the quarters it emanates from. When the critics are former players and former managements you get a little frustrated – they above all should understand the difficulties and daily pressures.

Whatever about our shortcomings as a management team, I cannot point a finger in the direction of our players: to a man, they have shown massive commitment to, and pride in, the 'Primrose and Blue'.

I fully expect our boys to perform on Sunday – we have trained exceptionally hard, our morale is excellent and, though we have a few injuries we could do without, I believe we are ready for the championship season ahead.

As ever John, sincere thanks for your support to me and the present crop of players. At the end of the day, despite what people might think because of my birthplace, I so desperately want Roscommon to succeed. Indeed, it is my single last ambition in sport – to lead us to a Connacht final win.

It may not happen this year – who knows? It is impossible to guess what life and sport has in store for us. But we will be trying manfully to bring success to the county.

My best regards,

Kevin McStay

Manager, Roscommon Senior footballers

(Proud and Privileged to hold this appointment)

POSTSCRIPT

Roscommon went on to win the Connacht final a few weeks later to ease what McStay calls the 'ferocious pressure' he was under. It is no secret that Kevin's most vocal critic at the time had been Roscommon's legendary goalkeeper and former manager Gay Sheeran. The following year McStay heard that a member of the Sheeran family was facing a serious illness. After a sleepless night he sent Gay a text saying that 'life was too short to bear grudges' and that 'the battles on the field' were 'less important than the battle against illness' and wished him well. Sheeran sent him a text in the same spirit of rapproachment in reply.

10

HYMN TO HER:
ROSANNA McALEESE

There is something special about hurling people.
Michael Duignan

When the celebrity economist David McWilliams said if Ireland leaves the EU it will become 'England with camogie' it was an interesting affirmation of the centrality of the sport in Irish life.

The GAA was late to the party when it came to women. Neil Armstrong took a giant step for humanity on the moon before a woman played in Croke Park. Today, though, a new generation of young women are carrying the flag for camogie. One of them is Rosanna McAleese.

'My home club is Eoghan Rua Coleraine, situated on the north coast in County Derry. I was lucky enough to come into a strong senior panel built on many hard years of struggling by gritty northern women. This set-up of girls went on to win three consecutive Ulster titles, and two consecutive All-Irelands. To play at a senior level in Croke Park at age 15 in my club jersey was something that I only now realise the significance of, and maybe that fearless approach was an asset I did not know I had. I have had All-Ireland success playing at different levels for County Derry, but club camogie has also been my passion and priority.

'I moved up to Dublin at 18, to begin studying law. The Trinity Camogs proved to be an invaluable support network. I became an Ulster GAA sports scholar and went on to captain the college team in my final year. Although sometimes more pints than points focused, I will never forget some of the laughs on cold winter nights in Santry. Shared experiences on and off the pitch with this bunch of bright Irish women, too wise to be afraid that embracing their cultural heritage lessens them as academics.'

The GAA had an important place in Rosanna's upbringing.

'I remember reading that if you draw a straight line from the Loughshore to the Glenshane Pass and another from there to Derry city, you'll find 15 of the county's 16 senior county Derry clubs either on or within a couple of miles of it. Except for my home club Eoghan Rua, sitting on the north coast. Playing the part of my youth's anchor, Eoghan Rua pitch was the backdrop to some of the most important events in my life.

'However, I feel there is often a reluctance to accept that the experience of GAA in the north and the south can be very different. You have my mum's native Sleacht Néill, a true collective of like-minded Gaels, agreeing both on the experience of the north's history and the vision for the north's future. Eoghan Rua is not a Sleacht Néill. My dad, as the chairman, being a prime example of this. A Royal Portrush golfer who's love of the GAA was ignited long after his own sporting days had passed.

'A club in a town shared by nationalists and unionists, the key figures are largely blow-ins from nationalist areas who have been brought to the north coast by jobs, loves or a wish to wake up to the waves. But different does not mean less. My club's recent years of unprecedented success stand on the shoulders of men and women who formed and sustained the club since 1958. The Joe

Passmores, the Schira McGoldricks and the Brendan McLernons having enough grit and passion to turn any abandoned soccer field into a place to raise camogs. A memory of my dad scraping sectarian graffiti off the club's mobile changing rooms as we tried to establish our first pitch. Those who laced up their boots to kick a Gaelic football in 1980s Coleraine. Maybe a tested love of the game is as significant as a habitual one.'

With her degree in Trinity secured in 2019 Rosanna moved to the Big Apple with her great friend Louise Mulrennan in search of new dreams.

'After graduating, I decided to move to New York. A student loan and youthful idealism all crammed into an overweight suitcase. My last night in Portstewart before leaving home was with my club teammates. There was a real pang in my heart that night at leaving behind such a beloved normal, but I always knew I never wanted to be tied to home because of camogie. I am unsure whether this came from a genuine wanderlust, or just a stubborn refusal to feel like I am conforming.

'I joined the Liberty Gaels camogie club in New York. I was on Wall Street bringing a hurl to the office to head training after work. Although the "kind of like field hockey but in the air" explanation of camogie to Americans on the subway lost its initial novelty, I do remember meeting three wee girls in Derry jerseys in 14th Street Station on my way home from a training session out in Hoboken New Jersey. For different reasons, I feel we were both so happy to see each other in that moment. Hundreds of questions and feelings happily remaining unvoiced behind the Irish smile and wave.

'I arrived at my first session at a pitch overlooking the New Jersey skyline, but the thing that was getting me excited was the sound of northern girls pucking and laughing together, a sense of comradery I did not know I was missing. I felt completely at home. Wiping up my hair in a ponytail and having the hurl in my hand gave me that sense of control and sense of self that New York can sometimes beat out of you.'

In 2020 life in New York changed dramatically for Rosanna because of the COVID crisis.

'I was traveling home to spend a week in Ireland in early March and I remember joking with the guys in my office that they might never see me again. Fast forward six days, Trump has issued a ban on European travel and with a flight due to arrive into JFK airport 20 mins after the midnight travel ban deadline, it was time to set up work from home, from actual home.

'Three months later and I am unsure when I will get back to my life in New York, as I watch the City of glittering lights now fighting major fires on all fronts. The $7 dollar lattes have now been replaced by a mug of tea from my daddy. Like many people, the experience has really made me think about what the priorities in my life are, and maybe discovering the list is a little shorter or in a different order than I once thought.

'I was later isolating with my boyfriend. We met in Trinity, and strangely even though both of us played club and county hurling before coming to college, the GAA never played a part in our relationship. Maybe because we met at a time when both of us were actively trying to place it in the backseat to let other ambitions drive. Lockdown is the first time we have pucked with each other, just enjoying the act of hitting the sliotar back and forth without the competitive demands or commitment decisions that sometimes make the hurl feel a bit too heavy. Perhaps this shows us that, as players, our relationship with the game does not have to be an all-in or nothing. We can accept the list of priorities in our lives move with time, without this lessening who you are as a player or a person.'

Gaelic Games are part of Rosanna's DNA.

'The GAA is not perfect, it is flawed just like all of those who engage with it, but it embodies sport's humanising ability to strip life back to unaltered basics. I struggle to imagine another arena in 2020 Ireland that can provide a whistle to signify a new beginning and unforgettable moments that transcend our everyday worries. Bernard Donoghue writes, "Hands still stretched out to reach, not the winning tape but other hands."

'Sport is so important in providing meaning, belonging and togetherness. As a sportswoman, the euphoric wins and antagonising losses will remain with me, but it is not these moments that hold the biggest place in my heart. It is driving the coast road home from the airport and seeing the club's goalpost pepping over the bray of the hill, the flag waving in the wind to welcome me home. Or watching my younger sister, Mia, who has Down's syndrome, run the 100 metres, being cheered on by her team; her arms outstretched not to grab the winning tape, but to grab mine.'

11

THE BOSS: CHARLIE HAUGHEY

*The only difference between the saint and the sinner is
that every saint has a past, and every sinner has a future.*
Oscar Wilde

He grinned but it was the snarl of a cornered animal.

Meeting him was a journey into a different world, like a slumbering country village replaced by the noise and fury of a capital city. His eyes spoke without the necessity of words or gesture, some intuitive seismic register caught the slightest tremor of variance from the norm.

Although best known for his involvement in racing, former Taoiseach Charles J. Haughey played Gaelic football and hurling at club level with some distinction. Born in Donnycarney, he was educated by the Christian Brothers in Fairview, a noted GAA nursery. He won a county medal with Parnells in 1945 – a noteworthy year for him because he also achieved notoriety then for burning the Union Jack outside Trinity College.

On the pitch he was known for his fiery temperament. He was suspended for a year for striking a linesman. His brother Jock won an All-Ireland medal in 1958 when Dublin beat Derry, the county of birth to both his parents.

Charlie regularly engaged in what Donald Trump calls 'plausible hyperbole'. He was fond of talking up his interest in the GAA. Páidí Ó'Se enjoyed the company of the great and the good none more so than that of Charlie Haughey. Páidí recommended one of his tradesmen friends when Charlie needed some work done on his mansion in Kinsealy. His friend travelled to the estate early one Saturday morning and rang the doorbell. Mrs Haughey answered and then called her husband to deal with the situation. When he arrived at the front door Charlie looked at the man and said, 'You should know that in the circumstances you should have gone to the back entrance.'

The man apologised profusely and duly went around to the back door.

Charlie was waiting for him and guided him to the cellar where the work was needed. At the end of the day when the job was done Mr Haughey duly was called to inspect the work. He expressed satisfaction and said, 'I suppose you want to be paid.'

Charlie went away to find his cheque book and returned with a cheque. The man was dismayed at how small the figure was but felt too intimidated to complain.

That night Páidí rang the Taoiseach to express his friend's dissatisfaction. Charlie listened to the complaint, cleared his throat theatrically and said, 'The signature on that cheque is worth much, much more than any money.'

Then he hung up.

CAPTAIN UNDERPANTS

Páidí credited Haughey with one of his biggest achievements. 'In 1985 I was captain of Kerry. I was not that long married, and my wife packed my bag for me the day before the All-Ireland final when we headed to Dublin. That night, though, I discovered to my horror that she hadn't packed my lucky underpants. I had worn them in each of my previous six winning All-Ireland finals and I was absolutely convinced that if I didn't wear them we wouldn't win the final again. So in a panic I rang my mother. She told me to leave it with her. I rang her back an hour later. She said: "I have arranged for them to travel up on the train in the morning. I rang Charlie Haughey. He will send his car to Heuston station to collect them and he will have them in Croke Park for you in plenty of time for the game."'

Pat Spillane had reason to query the depth of Haughey's affinity for Kerry football.

'I missed out on my own meeting with Charlie. I came very close. I was in the Schelig Hotel the morning after the Dingle Regatta and Charlie and his entourage were coiffing champagne. They were loud and boisterous and I heard one of them say: "There's Pat Spillane over there."

'Charlie swanned over to the table beside me and tapped the man on the shoulder and said: "Pat Spillane, I presume."

'The astonished guy replied: "I wish."

'Charlie turned on his heels and walked back to his party as if nothing happened. So much for his great knowledge of Kerry football.'

THE LAMESTREAM MEDIA

In 1998 I interviewed CJH for a book was writing at the time. The interview took place at 9 a.m. on a Saturday morning in his stately home in Kinsealy. When I was shown in, he greeted me stiffly with a hesitant handshake and a smile so tight it would take a crowbar to prize it open. He was clearly weighing me up. Throughout the encounter he was clearly suspicious, especially after I produced a recording machine.

Stories of his lavish hospitality were legendary, so, after he showed me into his study and said 'we will have refreshments',

I was intrigued to see what magnificent hospitality awaited me. How was I literally going to taste the high life for the first time? Would it be croissants specially flown in from Paris that morning or would it be smoked salmon sent from Kinsale? He made a call on the telephone at his desk. Shortly afterwards a 'maid' entered with extraordinary deference – to him, not as much to me. She had a beautiful tray with a stunning silver teapot and cutlery and china to match. At the risk of sounding ungracious I was a little disappointed to see that in this sea of splendour the refreshments amounted to ... a plate with four Digestive biscuits.

As we ate and drank, I expressed great surprise that he had a copy of a biography of Mary Robinson on his desk. The end of his time as Taoiseach had coincided with her time as president of Ireland and relations between them could be described politely as 'tetchy'. He was surprisingly sparing of her in his comments. However, he absolutely lacerated her advisor, Bride Rosney.

When I talked, he looked out the window and did not seem to be paying attention, but then out of the blue he would make the most incisive comment. I was in no doubt that whatever else he might have been this was a man of a formidable intellect, one who got 100 per cent in his Leaving Certificate Latin exam.

At the end of the conversation, when I prepared to leave, Charlie said, 'And of course you will let me see the piece before publication.' It was said in a way that was a command, not a request by a man not used to having his authority questioned. Despite my misgivings I duly sent on him what I had written. Shortly afterwards I received a letter back from him, inviting me to Kinsealy a second time to discuss some minor amendments he wished me to make. Another Saturday morning, I duly made my way there again for 9 a.m. I arrived to meet a different man. All his suspicion had melted away and he was full of the charm that I had seen often during some of his television appearances. Discretion prevents me from revealing too much. But he spoke about the late Irish rugby coach Mick Doyle, who had invited him to launch his autobiography. He had asked Doyler if it was only about rugby. Doyler replied, 'It's 20 per cent rugby and 80 per cent sex.' CHJ said in response, 'You got the balance just right.' We parted after a few more Digestive biscuits.

I thought that would be the end of my dealings with him. Not so. The following Friday evening I received a phone call. The conversation was short and sweet. 'This is Mr Haughey. Could you come out to see me tomorrow morning at 9?' His tone indicated that he clearly did not expect me to decline his invitation, but he gave me no clue as to why he wanted to see me.

The next morning, I had the same anxious feeling in my stomach as I journeyed out to his home as I had the morning of my Leaving Cert Irish exam. In our original interview he had spoken to me about when his horse Flashing Steel won the Irish Grand National in 1995, and that the trophy had been presented to him by the former Taoiseach John Bruton and he had made a complimentary comment about his political adversary. However, that week a series of revelations had appeared in the media about 'irregularities' in his finances. John Bruton was publicly very critical about CJH. Charlie 'instructed' me to take out the kind comments about Bruton. As I left Charlie enquired if I would like a photo of him to use in the book. When I said yes, he invited me back for my fourth visit to Kinsealy.

This was different. Charlie was tied up on the phone so it was his wife who greeted me. She showed me into a room which was clearly where the coats were hung up the sheer size of it gave me an understanding of just how big the parties hosted in that house must be. Sime time later Charlie arrived and gave me a tour of the bottom floor of the house. What struck me was the sheer volume of the number of photos of him with leading figures on the world stage, like President Mitterand and Bob Hawke. Then, as the tour was complete, he brought me back to the cloakroom to collect my coat. I got a revealing insight into what he thought of his cabinets. All his photos with them were hanging there at the very back where virtually nobody would ever see his Ministers. In fact, the photos of his horses were much more prominent than his cabinets.

He was a keen horseman, though he did have a few famous falls in his career. He was once alleged to have said that he chose black and blue as his colours because he was black and blue so often following riding mishaps. He laughed when I quizzed him about the veracity of that remark. 'I think you'd have to take that as apocryphal!'

I asked him what advice he had for me to live a happy life. He answered immediately, 'Life is too short to be drinking bad wine!'

The day before our last meeting Charlie had received a letter from a friend. It included a poem which was written in 1923 by Brian O'Higgins, a Republican prisoner in an internment camp known as Tintown in the Civil War, which had just been discovered in an old photograph album. He felt it particularly pertinent, given the prevailing tide of media comment about him at the time:

> The world will strip your failings
> And hide the good you do
> And with its sharpest thorns
> The ways you walk bestrew:
> You'll toil for men and they'll curse you:
> 'Twas thus, and thus 'tis yet.
> And thus 'twill be forever.
> But God does not forget.

PART II

Standing on the Shoulders of Giants

The late John Moloney was one of the all-time great intercounty referees. John was very active in organising juvenile hurling and football in Tipperary, and was very influential in developing and conditioning them for future life. His club was Galtee Rovers St Pecauns: the latter part of the name came from the fact that within the townland of Toureen there were the ruins of a monastery associated with St Pecaun and every year there was a pattern on 1 August, which was a mix of a religious and social event, and was a huge occasion in the area.

John Moloney would cram 12 or 14 lads into his car for the journey to games. It was an awfully big adventure for them because going on a trip to Golden, Cashel, Tipperary Town, Emely and Lisvernane then was as big a deal as going to New York nowadays. Matt Nugent was a friend of his who was totally committed to the GAA. His life was two-dimensional – farming and the GAA – though I am not sure which came first. He brought kids to many games complete with a flask of tea and sandwiches and a bag of what he called 'beauty bats', which were really sweet apples. A particular thrill was walking down the Ennis Road on the way to big matches in Limerick with all the colour, tension and excitement. He died some years ago watching a Munster under-21 final in Thurles. He could not have died in a more appropriate way. They were just two examples of people with a massive commitment to the GAA.

In an era where time is money everyone seems to be too busy now to take on work of a voluntary nature. One of the healthier legacies of the education system bequeathed by the many religious orders in Ireland was the inclusion of the value of service alongside personal development, emotional satisfaction, monetary reward and occupational status, as the goals of education. With the decline of religious teaching a shift appears to have taken place. There remains an emphasis on personal achievement and personal quality, but notions of communal purpose and social value have abated in Ireland generally.

Yet so many women and men continue to dedicate their lives as volunteers for the GAA. Why? To understand this, it is necessary to explore the history of the GAA in this section. Two central elements of this story are Bloody Sunday and the shadow of the Troubles in the North.

12

THE SUNDAY GAMES: THE PEOPLE'S MOVEMENT

If you don't stand for something, you'll fall for anything.
Gustave Flaubert

The founding of the GAA is part of the story of struggle: the spirit of a nation in chains trying to break free, of wanting something more and finding the courage to run away from the greatest Empire the world had ever known.

The Ireland of the 1840s was a vision of hell – the years of a tragedy beyond belief when over a million people on this tiny island died from famine. Nothing prepared people for it. Nothing could prepare anyone for the sight and smell of death on a massive scale – bundles of corpses where once there had been life.

The mid 1840s saw the plagues of Ireland: hunger, disease and government neglect. Each plague compounded the other like a battleground of contending dooms. Fragile lifelines of aid reached only a minority of the population. In the first year there was barely enough potatoes, in the next only a trickle. Then nothing. Potato stalks withered and died. There was nothing for seed. Many people had nothing to live on and nothing to live for.

The death toll was seemingly unending in many districts. Everything had to be rationed. It would have taken too much land to bury the corpses individually so their relatives normally buried them in a mass grave. There were so many people dying it was impossible to make coffins for them all, or even have a coffin for each family. Timber was very scarce. Sometimes villagers decided to build one proper coffin with a sliding bottom. They solemnly put the corpses into the coffin, carried them up to the grave and slid back the bottom of the coffin and the body tumbled into the grave. The coffin was brought back to the village and passed on to the family of the next casualty.

Fear was the only real sign of life as people died slowly in agony. To the embattled, emotionally bankrupt and hopelessly disorganised, the ordinary joys and sorrows were an irrelevance. The chances of survival were slim. For many, death was a welcome escape from pain and heartache. The afterlife was the only dream they could still cherish. For the strong, life was a victory over death. Where possible the corpses were buried under hawthorn trees – because of their alleged special favour in the eyes of God. These trees were long palls in a parched place. They sang a lament to the angel of death. The memories were too sad ever to be healed.

Ireland was a country of extremes, from the beginning to the end. It seemed simultaneously connected to the Garden of Eden in the landlords' palaces and to some foretaste of doomsday destruction where the peasants lived to die. Nowhere were the gardens more luxuriant or a people more miserable. The tragedy was a moral test which those with power failed.

Deep in their psychic memory the famine was still a painful experience for Irish people right through the nineteenth century and beyond. People used the words 'I'm famished' whenever they were cold or hungry. The frequent usage of these words was just one symptom of the lasting effect of the famine. Often Irish people buried their thoughts of the famine deep in their subconscious. The story of the famine years was so horrific they just wanted to erase it from their memory. There was great shame attached to failing to feed one's family. Parents always blamed themselves for their children's death. Succeeding generations had inherited their shame. Even in the twentieth century some people in rural Ireland would not travel anywhere without bringing a piece of bread in their pocket because the fear of hunger was so strong.

The term 'Great Famine' is itself a misnomer. It is more accurate to say there was a 'Great Starvation'. Famines are caused by natural disasters. There are not famines when there are large quantities of food in a country. There was plenty of food produced in Ireland those years. That food was exported while Irish people starved in the country's greatest human tragedy is an enduring monument to inhumanity, ineffectiveness and indifference.

There were two main options open to these people: emigration, if they could afford it, or the poorhouse/workhouse. In many respects they thought they were safer in their own place. There was so much disease in those coffin ships their chances of surviving that long journey in such a weak state were remote. People by and large did not trust the sea. They all heard the stories of the American sailing ship *Stephen Whitney.* On a foggy December night in 1847 the ship sailing on a voyage from America to Bristol was wrecked off the Irish coast on *Bolig Rinn na mBeann* on the Western Calf Island. Within days, 94 bodies were washed up on the beaches. Some people were desperate enough to try anything, but the majority preferred to meet their maker on their own land rather than on the other side of the Atlantic Ocean.

Nobody knows how many people went on the coffin ships. The one reliable statistic is about a group who went to Canada where they all died of typhoid fever in a place called Grosse Ile just outside Quebec City. Twelve thousand Irish people were buried in mass graves in Canada. They set out to make their mark in the world but the only mark they made was in a grave – a people with no name. It was their final indignity.

The workhouses had a huge stigma attached to them. Like the infamous coffin ships there was so much disease in the workhouse that to sign into the place was often to sign one's death warrant. Generally the poorhouses postponed death for a short while but no more. In the poorhouses and soup kitchens, families were separated from each other. All the men were housed in one section, the women in another. There were separate places for babies, young children, young girls and boys. Once a family went in, they might never see each other again. There were strict rules about communication with other sections. If one person broke the rules the whole family might be thrown out. Through speaking Irish in the workhouses people could sometimes pass on messages without their masters knowing what was being said. In many ways the poorhouse was worse than jail. At least in jail you could get news from your family. It has often been claimed these places could have been called deathhouses.

POWER TO ALL OUR FRIENDS

Ireland had been governed from Westminster since the Act of Union in 1800. In the House of Commons there were about 100 members who represented Irish constituencies. The Viceregal Lodge in the Phoenix Park was home to the Queen's representatives. The Chief Secretary and his staff administered the daily routine of government from Dublin Castle.

One of the main problems faced by administrators in Ireland in the nineteenth century was to reconcile democratic principle with the continuation of ascendancy privilege. County grand juries were non-elective bodies drawn from the largest landholders in the county. Local government was in the hands of the grand juries, non-elective bodies dominated by landowners. The British army had an important and visible presence throughout the country. The Royal Irish Constabulary was an armed body, though the Dublin Metropolitan Police was not.

The close connection between Britain and Ireland made it natural to judge by English standards and, in comparison with England, Ireland was still a poor country. In the conventional portrait the most familiar figures are the greedy and tyrannical landlords squeezing every last penny of rent out of hungry peasants to finance their life of debauchery. While there were a number of such landlords, they were not all like that. The evil was not all on one side. Southern Protestants were slow to forget the stories they had been told of the fanatical fury waged against Protestants during the 1798 Wexford rising and the social intimidation of Protestants which had persisted for years afterwards. Until 1869 the Church of Ireland was the state church. Its disestablishment under an Act of Parliament made a major dent in the exclusiveness of Protestant ascendancy.

The second half of the nineteenth century saw the gradual extension of voting rights in both Britain and Ireland. For the first time the demand for votes for women was being made with conviction. In the Irish context an important milestone was the introduction of the secret ballot after 1872 since it relieved voters from pressure by landlords to vote according to their dictates.

The education system was imperialist rather than Irish, with the prescribed reading books filled with Victorian values and designed to inculcate British loyalties. However, there were a number of counterbalancing forces at work, particularly the press. By 1860 national papers were available cheaply following the repeal of heavy taxes on the newspapers. *The Nation*, founded by Thomas Davis, carried on its national tradition in the 1860s. Songs formed an important agent of political evangelisation

– notably 'God Save Ireland', which became virtually a national anthem in 1867.

The Irish national pulse was strengthening perceptibly. The demand for self-government was being made with more vigour. Political structures were not as secure as they had been. The old establishment was being challenged in various ways. In the countryside the stirrings could be seen among the tenant farmers.

Throughout rural Ireland, agrarian unrest accelerated with increasing demands for tenant right reforms. Landlords were seen as a privileged minority, alienated from the majority of their tenants by differences in both religion and politics. Tenants normally held their holdings from year to year, thus having no security. In times of bad harvests many could not afford to pay the rent. A high number of landlords were absentees, living outside the country and leaving the management of their estates to agents. The great disaster of the famine was followed by mass evictions of tenants. The need for reform of the system was becoming more obvious in the years that followed.

In 1870 a formal demand for Home Rule began when Isaac Butt, a lawyer and member of parliament, founded an association to campaign for a separate Irish parliament. However, the movement really only began in earnest when Butt was replaced as leader by Charles Stewart Parnell, a charismatic figure whose tactics brought increasing success to Nationalist members of the House of Commons and eventually succeeded in making the 'Irish question' the central issues in British politics.

THE BARREL OF A GUN?

For a long time, people who talked about the origins of the Irish state did so in very simple terms. Nationhood was won through a barrel of a gun in a (virginal/pure) David and (dark/demonic) Goliath struggle. The 1919–21 War of Independence was the final episode in a whole series of attempts, including: Grattan's volunteers in 1782; the bold Robert Emmet, 'the darling of Eireann', in 1803; the Young Ireland rising in 1848; the militant revolution of the Fenians in 1867; the 1916 Rising (*A terrible beauty is born*) and the War of Independence. In this perspective there was only one problem in Ireland – the British presence. The way to get rid of this presence was by violence.

As Brian Farrell incisively demonstrated in his groundbreaking work *The Irish Parliamentary Tradition* (1977) the reality is much more complex than the illusion. As the experience of many countries established in the wake of the collapse of the great colonial empires after the Second World War demonstrated, to start a nation state from scratch is very difficult. A number of things need to be in place before nationhood can be sustained, such as literacy, a civil service, civil administration, roads, schools, etc. Farrell identified three essential prerequisites for nationhood: religious freedom, ownership of wealth and participation in the electoral process. Ireland had achieved these conditions in advance of the War of Independence.

Under the Penal Laws, Irish Catholics were denied religious freedom because of the prevalent belief at the time throughout Europe that in Church–State relations you proved your loyalty to the king by being part of the established religion. In 1829, following Daniel O'Connell's election in a by-election in Clare, Catholic Emancipation was won.

The year 1832 brought the Great Reform Bill, which was a very minor bill in itself. It increased the number of people who could vote to two and a half per cent of the adult male population. Its importance was more for what it promised in the future than what it delivered in the present. Although it was to take almost 100 years for women to get the vote, the Act began a process which eventually brought universal adult suffrage. The 1918 British Representation of the People Act was a crucial milestone along the way, as it removed the property qualification on the right to vote.

By a supreme irony, the Act of Union, which so many Irish people considered anathema and fought so long and hard to abolish, was, step-by-step, turning Ireland into a modern state. Each of these important advances were achieved by an Act of Parliament. Thus, in the second half of the nineteenth century, on many different levels, change was driving Irish life like a great engine. All aspects of Irish culture could not but be affected by this dramatic transformation, including the national games. These games are steeped in Irish history.

THE WHIRR OF THE SLITOAR

Apart from the Irish language, nothing is more central and unique to Irish heritage than the game of hurling. In the popular imagination it can be traced back to folklore and stories of Cuchulainn. However, we have tangible historical proof that hurling has been an integral part of Irish life for over a thousand years.

Recently there has been a major debate in the GAA about 'the sin-bin'. However, in previous centuries players who committed a transgression faced a far more onerous punishment, such as two days' fasting or handing over a prize heifer. While top intercounty managers like Seán Boylan fumed about their players having to cool their heels on the sidelines after serious fouls, their seventh-century counterparts were fined cattle or denied food.

These unusual punishments have been discovered by Dr Angela Gleason, a young American academic based for a time at Trinity College Dublin, who has been researching the rules of the ancient stick and ball games which were a precursor to the modern hurling and shinty.

'I have found a number of ancient texts that go into some detail about the penalty system associated with these ancient games. From their inception, Gaelic Games were always seen as "manly activities". However, there have always been sanctions when players stepped over the mark. There were penalties for injuries that resulted from play and as is the norm in Brehon law they were financial and could be expected to be paid in cattle.

'The texts are more vague on the precise nature and rules of the games, but it is believed that they involved teams several dozen strong and were violent affairs.

'These games are seen by many people as the predecessor of hurling, but in some texts they could be referring to hoop and ball games as well as stick and ball. These games should not be considered as in any way resembling the modern sport.

'Law texts dating from as early as the seventh century state that while partaking in games players had a degree of legal immunity from the Brehon laws. But they could be punished with special game-related fines. Penalties were graded according to the age of the player, and the severity of the injury afflicted on an opponent.

'Adults who committed a foul during the play were judged on whether they had set out to injure the other party intentionally. If the offence was deemed intentional, the player was expected to pay full sick maintenance to his victim. In the case of death, not uncommon in these violent sports, the full "honour price" of the victim had to be paid to his family.

'If the injury was unintentional and resulted from "fair play" the penalty was half sick maintenance or one quarter of honour price. The financial levy, usually a payment in cattle, was calculated according to the status of the injured person and whether they were "profitable or idle".

'Children were immune from paying penalties until they reached a culpable age, usually about seven. But if their offence was deemed to be deliberate they could expect to be punished according to the rules applicable to an older age bracket.'

In popular historical texts the first references to hurling seem to have been written in approximately 1272 BC at the battle of

Moytura, near Cong in County Mayo. The Firbolgs were rulers of Ireland and were protecting their position in a battle against the Tuatha de Dannan. While they prepared for battle, the Firbolgs challenged the invaders to a hurling contest in which teams of 27-a-side took part. The Firbolgs won the contest but lost the battle.

There is no historical reference to Gaelic football until 1670 in a poem by Seamus Mac Cuarta. The poem described a game in Fennor – in which wrestling was allowed!

THE HURLING GENESIS

In 1841 a book entitled *Ireland* was written by Samuel Carter and Anne Maria Hall and published shortly after. They begin their section on sport by surprisingly claiming that the great game in Kerry, and throughout the South, is the game of hurley. The authors note:

'It is a fine manly exercise, with sufficient of danger to produce excitement; and is indeed, par excellence, the game of the peasantry of Ireland. To be an expert hurler, a man must possess athletic powers of no ordinary character; he must have a quick eye, a ready hand, and a strong arm; he must be a good runner, a skilful wrestler, and, withal, patient as well as resolute. In some respects it resembles cricket; but the rules, and the form of the bats, are altogether different; the bat of the cricketer being straight, and that of the hurler crooked.

'The forms of the games are these: the players, sometimes to the number of 50 or 60, being chosen for each side, they are arranged (usually barefoot) in two opposing ranks, with their hurleys crossed, to await the tossing up of the ball, the wickets or goals being previously fixed at the extremities of the hurling green, which, from the nature of the play, is required to be a level extensive plain.

'Then there are two picked men chosen to keep the goal on

each side, over whom the opposing party places equally tired men as a counterpoise; the duty of these goalkeepers being to arrest the ball in case of its near approach to that station, and return it back towards that of the opposite party, while those placed over them exert all their energies to drive it through the wicket.

'All preliminaries being adjusted, the leaders take their places in the centre. A person is chosen to throw up the ball, which is done as straight as possible, when the whole party, withdrawing their hurleys, stand with them elevated, to receive and strike it in its descent. Now comes the crash of mimic war, hurleys rattle against hurleys – the ball is struck and re-struck, often for several minutes, without advancing much nearer to either goal; and when someone is lucky enough to get a clear "puck" at it, it is sent flying over the field. It is now followed by the entire party at their utmost speed; the men grapple, wrestle, and toss each other with amazing agility, neither victory nor vanquished waiting to take breath, but following the course of the rolling and flying prize.

'The best runners watch each other, and keep almost shoulder to shoulder through the play, and the best wrestlers keep as close on them as possible, to arrest or impede their progress. The ball must not be taken from the ground by the hand; and the tact and skill shown in taking it to the point of the hurley, and running with it half the length of the field, and (when too closely pressed) striking it towards the goal, is a matter of astonishment to those who are but slightly acquainted with the play.

'At the goal, is the chief brunt of the battle. The goal-keepers receive the prize, and are opposed by those set over them; the struggle is tremendous – every power of full speed to support their men engaged in the conflict; then tossing and straining is at its height; the men often lying in dozens side by side on the grass, while the ball is returned by some strong arm again, flying above their heads, towards the other goal. Thus for hours has the contention been carried on, and frequently the darkness of night arrests the game without giving victory to either side. It is often attended with dangerous, and sometimes with fateful results.

'Matches are made, sometimes, between different town-lands or parishes, sometimes by barony against barony, and not infrequently county against county; with the "crack men" from the most distant parts are selected, and the interest excited is proportionately great.'

The authors then go on to describe the most famous match of them all – the clash between Munster and Leinster in the Phoenix Park in 1790:

'It was got up by then Lord Lieutenant and other sporting noblemen and was attended by all the nobility and gentry belonging to the Vice-Regal Court, and the beauty and fashion of the Irish capital and its vicinity.

'The victory was contended for, a long time, with varied success; and at last it was decided in favour of the Munster men, by one of that party, Matt Healy, running with the ball on the point of his hurley, and striking it through the open windows of the Vice-Regal carriage and by that manoeuvre baffling the vigilance of the Leinster goals-men, and driving it in triumph through the goal.'

However, by the late nineteenth century Gaelic Games were in crisis. Remedial action was needed. One man stood up to the plate.

THE MAGNIFICENT SEVEN

For a considerable time, Michael Cusack had been perturbed about the decline of native Irish games in the face of growing competition from British sports, like the garrison game soccer and rugby. Initially Cusack sought to wrestle control over field games, but also athletics, and introduce a more egalitarian dimension to Irish sport:

'No movement, having for its object the social and political advancement of a nation from the tyranny of imported and enforced customs and manners, can be regarded as perfect, if it has not made adequate provision for the preservation and cultivation of the national pastimes of the people. Voluntary neglect of such times is a sure sign of National decay and of approaching dissolution...

'A so-called revival of athletics was inaugurated in Ireland. The new movement did not originate with those who have ever had any sympathy with Ireland or the Irish people. Accordingly, labourers, tradesmen, artisans, and even policemen and soldiers were excluded from the few competitions which constituted the lame and halting programme of the promoters...

'We tell the Irish people to take the management of their games into their own hands, to encourage and promote in every way, every form of athletics that is peculiarly Irish and to remove with one sweep everything that is foreign and iniquitous in the present system. The vast majority of the best athletes in Ireland are nationalists. These gentlemen should take the matter in hand at once, and draft laws for the guidance of promoters of meetings in Ireland next year...

'It is only by such an arrangement that pure Irish athletics will be revived, and that the incomparable strength and physique of our race will be preserved.'

In the billiards room of Hayes's Hotel in Thurles on 1 November 1884, school teacher Michael Cusack, athlete Maurice Davin (a world record holder in the hammer), stonemason John K. Bracken, District Inspector Thomas St George McCarthy, journalists John

McKay and John Wyse Power, and solicitor P.J. O'Ryan founded the GAA.

Two days later the *Cork Examiner* reported:

'A meeting of athletes and friends of athletics was held on Saturday at three o'clock in Miss Hayes's Commercial Hotel Thurles for the purpose of forming an association for the preservation and cultivation of our national pastimes.

'Mr Michael Cusack of Dublin and Mr Maurice Davin of Carrick-on-Suir had the meeting convened by the following circular: "You are earnestly requested to attend a meeting, which will be held in Thurles on 1st of November, to take steps for the formation of a Gaelic Association for the preservation and cultivation of our national pastimes, and for providing rational amusements for the Irish people during their leisure hours."

'Mr Davin was called to the chair and Mr Cusack read the circular convening the meeting... Mr Cusack then proposed that Mr Maurice Davin – an athlete who had distinguished himself much both in Ireland and in England – should be the president of the association.'

PATRONS

The two most important political figures of nationalist Ireland, the leader of the Irish Party Charles Stewart Parnell and the founder of the Land League Michael Davitt, were quickly persuaded to act as patrons and crucially so, too, was the Archbishop of Cashel, Thomas William Croke, to give an ecclesiastical imprimatur to the fledging body – beginning the patronage of the Archbishop of Cashel at national level which continues to this day.

Stereotypes have done a great disservice to Irish history – none more so than that which depicts Ireland as a priest run society, typified in Austin Clarke's lines:

This land, where every woman's son
Must carry his own coffin and believe,
In dread, all that the clergy teach the young.

The clergy have never had it all their own way in Ireland. Towards the end of the eighteenth century, for example, a bishop in the west of Ireland was afraid to disclose the fact that Rome had suppressed a number of festivals in honour of Our Lady lest the news should provoke a riot. The Irish have always been delighted to follow their clergy – provided they are leading where the Irish want to go!

As Patrick Corish has impressively documented in his study *The Irish Catholic Experience* (1982), the seventeenth century was a profoundly unhappy one for the majority of Irish people because many Catholics lost all their property and were subjected to great cruelty at the hands of the English forces in Ireland. Protestants suffered from many atrocities as their Catholic neighbours sought to extract revenge. The legacy of this century lingers maddeningly to this very day, particularly in Northern Ireland. Another damaging, perhaps the most damaging of all, stereotype emerged: 'Popery' meant treason and the killing of Protestants – 'Protestant' meant loyalty and hatred of Popery. Each took their identity from their opposition to the other.

In the late nineteenth century, thanks in no small part to the work of Cardinal Paul Cullen, the Catholic Church exerted a massive cultural influence in Irish society. To have its blessing and, above all, to be seen to have its blessing was important for the GAA. Archbishop Croke was a shrewd choice. He was one of Parnell's most outspoken supporters among the hierarchy. In fact, he was summoned to Rome by Pope Leo XIII to explain his support for Nationalist politicians. Croke's biases and prejudices were very clear in his letter of acceptance as patron.

'We are daily importing from England not only her manufactured goods... but together with her fashions, her accent, her vicious literature, her music, her dances and her manifold mannerisms, her games and also her pastimes, to the utter discredit of our own grand national sports, and to the sore humiliation, as I believe, of every genuine son and daughter of the old land.

'Ball-playing, hurling, football, kicking, according to Irish rules, "casting", leaping in various ways, wrestling, handy-grips, top-pegging, leap-frog, rounders, tip-in-the-heat, and all such favourite exercises and amusements among men and boys, may be said not only to be dead and buried, but in several localities to be entirely forgotten and unknown. And what have we got in their stead? We have got such foreign and fantastic field sports as lawn-tennis, croquet, cricket and the like – very excellent, I believe, and health-giving exercises in their way, still not racy of the soil, but rather alien, on the contrary, to it, as are indeed, for the most part, the men and women who first imported and still continue to patronize them...

'Indeed if we continue traveling for the next score of years in the same direction that we have been going in for some time past... we had better at once and publicly, adjure our nationality, clap hands for joy at the sight of the Union Jack, and place "England's bloody red" exultingly above "the green".'

We Irish are always happy to blame somebody else. Flann O'Brien claimed that he wrote *At Swim-Two-Birds* in order to become a millionaire – and he liked to complain that Hitler started a war a few weeks after publication just to frustrate this noble enterprise. Croke's fervent anti-English prejudices resonated strongly with Cusack and the other founders, who saw themselves as actors in the age-old battle of good and evil. Accordingly, from its inception, the GAA had a two-fold objective of promoting Irish games and reducing the perceived malign influence of 'foreign games'.

Two further patrons came on board within months, the founder of the Irish Republican Brotherhood John O'Leary and the Nationalist MP William O'Brien.

From the outset, the GAA took on the parish organisation which had been so effectively deployed by Daniel O'Connell in the campaign to win Catholic Emancipation in 1829. The sense of parish identity was further copper fastened by the use of local patron saints or historical figures in the names taken by parish clubs. Davin drew up rules for four sports: football, hurling, athletics and handball. In reality no serious attempt was made to regulate handball until the birth of a new organisation, the Irish Amateur Handball Union, in 1912.

Representations of handball survive from the eighteenth century. Championships tended to be organised on the lines of boxing championships, where the titleholder remained champion until he was successfully challenged and beaten. However, it was not until the Irish Amateur Handball Association was founded that the GAA made a concerted effort to organise handball on a larger scale. In 1973 RTÉ television began its *Top Ace* tournament and televised handball immediately catapulted handballers like Pat Kirby and Joey Maher into national celebrity status. The work of the Irish Amateur Handball Association can be seen in many corners of rural Ireland in the old handball alleys which populate many villages and small towns, many of which have fallen into disuse. In counties like Roscommon, in modern times, handball has attracted many girls and young women to participate to very high standards.

ARE YOU RIGHT THERE, MICHAEL?

Like so many Irish organisations since, almost the first thing the GAA did was to have a split. From the beginning, the GAA has had a history of abrasive personalities, with the gift of rubbing people up the wrong way. Michael Cusack will always be remembered for his role in founding the GAA in 1884. Yet, having given birth to the Association, Cusack almost strangled it in his infancy, because of his abrasive personality. People often miss out on the historical significance of the 'Athletic' in the title of the GAA. In the early years it was envisaged that athletics would play a much greater role in the life of the GAA. One of the people trying to ensure this was John L. Dunbar. He wrote to Cusack in December 1885 suggesting that the GAA and the athletics organisation should meet 'with a view to a possible merger'. Cusack, an enthusiastic hurler, did not mince or waste his words in his response. The letter read as follows:

> GAA
> 4 Gardiners Place
> Dublin
>
> Dear Sir,
> I received your letter this morning and burned it.
> Yours faithfully,
> Michael Cusack.

Cusack suffered from 'Irish bad memory' – which forgets everything but the grudge. He also alienated Archbishop Croke, who stated that he could not continue as patron 'if Mr Michael Cusack is allowed to play the dictator in the GAA's counsels, to run a reckless tilt with impunity and without rebuke'.

Cusack claimed that the new organisation spread like a 'prairie fire'. The GAA was up and running and soon would be firmly established in every parish in Ireland.

Gaelic Games had become the People's Games.

13

I CAN'T BELIEVE THE NEWS TODAY:
BLOODY SUNDAY

Truth is the cry of all, but the game of few.
George Berkeley

It was a time when to quote Henry James in his preface to *The Altar of the Dead* – 'the strange and sinister embroidered on the very type of the normal and easy' – seemed appropriate.

Within a few hours Ireland seemed to be on the edge of sliding into chaos.

It remains the darkest day in the rich history of the GAA.

It colours all the pages of memory.

It should have been a battle of skill.

It became a battle with bullets.

Thirteen people were shot dead by the Black and Tans in Croke Park during a football match between Tipperary and Dublin on 21 November 1920.

BIG MICK

The identity of a people and a nation is determined by a shared recounted story. Bloody Sunday has been central to the 'Irish story'. The enemy of consideration of Bloody Sunday is lack of nuance. Sowing the seed of nuance, though, is tough.

The first challenge is to dispense with the myth. For many younger and, indeed, older people, their abiding image of that day is that from Neil Jordan's film *Michael Collins*: machine-gun equipped armoured cars go into Croke Park and open fire. Jordan would explain his deviation from fact on the understandable grounds that he felt the machine-gunned tank captured the faceless callousness of imperialism more strikingly than soldiers shooting, explaining, 'I wanted the scene to last 30 seconds.' The film was about Michael Collins, not the events in Croke Park, but Bloody Sunday went on for much longer than 30 seconds. The sad reality is that the film did not do justice to the visceral bloodbath that was Bloody Sunday.

There comes a point in every story where different outcomes are possible, roads taken or not taken. There is a case for beginning the story of Bloody Sunday years earlier to take account of the tensions in Ireland that had been fermenting. To take one example in Sackville Street (now O'Connell Street) in the afternoon of Sunday, 31 August 1913, the Dublin Metropolitan Police (DMP) baton-charged crowds attending a banned protest led by Big Jim Larkin. In a five-minute period between 400 and 600 civilians were injured. At a time when politics and religion were so intertwined it is noteworthy that over 80 per cent of the DMP were Catholic.

In 1914 England found itself at war. A new adage came into play: 'England's difficulty is Ireland's opportunity.'

There is a saying in Swahili which has a powerful parallel for Irish nationalists: *Paka akiondoka, panya hutawala*. This partially translates to the traditional Western saying: 'When the cat is away the mouse will play.' However, it has an added twist: 'And be themselves.' There is a very colonial connotation to this which gives it additional resonance in an Irish context.

In the aftermath of the 1916 Rising, the Irish public were initially hostile to those engaged in insurrection. The severe atrocities inflicted by the British subsequently changed the mood of the nation. In political terms the big winners were Sinn Féin, who carried the Nationalist vote in huge numbers in the 1918 General Election. The once dominant Home Rule Party was decimated.

On 21 January 1919 the first shots of the War of Independence were fired in Soloheadbeg, Tipperary, where members of the IRA ambushed Royal Irish Constabulary (RIC) officers who were escorting a consignment of gelignite. The British response was the arrival of the Black and Tans on foot, an idea of Winston Churchill. Only the name Cromwell has attracted such disdain in Irish history as the Black and Tans.

One of the reasons why the Reformation had failed in Ireland in the sixteenth century was that the only ministers who came to spread the new faith in Ireland were those who were so lacking in talent or personality, and sometimes both, that they could not get a job in England. It was a very different story in 1919. Essentially to be a policeman in Ireland was the most lucrative policing job in the world.

Myths abound about the Black and Tans. Inevitably the historical reality was more complex and nuanced. While the popular perception was that English society opened up its prisons to let the 'dregs of humanity' wreak havoc in Ireland, in fact some of the earliest Black and Tans were decorated war veterans. They even included Victoria Cross winners. To these men of honour the atrocities that some of their counterparts inflicted was repugnant, militarily and morally, and they left and went back home. Thankfully, in seeking some element of objectivity about them, we now have a much greater understanding of post-traumatic stress syndrome. Many of them had seen evil and destruction of the most severe degree on the battlefields of the First World War.

GAMES WITHOUT FRONTIERS

Michael Collins took on one of the greatest armies that the world had ever seen with a miniscule force. So he had to change the rules of the military game if he was going to compete on an unequal footing. His solution was to employ 'guerilla warfare' or more colloquially 'hit and run' tactics. The Black and Tans were not going to take this lying down so the pattern emerged of a spiral of reprisals – the IRA committed one atrocity and the Black and Tans responded in kind with another one and vice versa.

It would be, in the main, rural Ireland that would suffer most at the hands of the Black and Tans. A particular target was creameries. The past is a foreign country. To a modern sensibility it is difficult to comprehend just how vital the creameries were in the Ireland of the 1920s.

A big social event for the local farmers was bringing the milk in horse and cart to the local creamery every day. As the farmers waited in the queue outside the creamery, they shared local gossip before presenting the milk for testing. The more cream there was the more money you got. Then they collected the skim milk at the back, which was used to feed the calves. The creamery was the very hub of the rural community.

The best way to unlock the secrets of their identities and personalities was to walk with them, in the softness of the Celtic mist, through the fields, when the constant rain had left the world shimmering with droplets on every leaf. Their lives, just like those of all farmers, were ruled by the state of the rains and the light of the sun.

The creameries' function was twofold: economic and social. Apart from being central to the livelihood of farmers they were also a social outlet where men came to trade gossip. These farmers enjoyed the shrewd talk of men as knowledgeable as themselves. They talked as if talk was what had been denied to them all, as if they were starving for talk. Old controversies emerged from their caves of obscurity and were delicately excavated. Some of the men went home the scenic route – via the pub.

They were, in the main, tough, shrewd farmers who seemed ageless, for sun and hard work and good eating had shaped their bodies into cases of muscle that time can hardly touch. This was their life for years, one of exhausting physical toil, 12 hours a day of sweat and effort in the sun. An ill-chosen phrase could see a farmer emitting the sort of body language that would have made the most severe exponents of the Spanish Inquisitors seem jovial and tolerant. After much drink was taken arguments about old resentments were unloaded. Like all farmers, their senses were intimately synced with the weather and they believed they could read instinctively the signs and were in no need of charts and spreadsheets.

The harsh terrain and small farms made survival difficult. People had very little to celebrate. The only escape, at least for the men, from the problems and anxieties of everyday living lay in Gaelic Games. It allowed people to dream of better days to come. Success at either parish or county level, albeit on a very modest scale, increased people's self-esteem. They talked just a little more boldly, they walked that little bit taller and they waved their flags with pride. It is impossible to explain the intense, almost tribal, loyalty which genuine followers of GAA give to the team. There was close identification between the fans and the players. The players represented the community. The GAA was part of what and who the community was. As Fr Harry Bohan incisively oberved, 'That was all we had. Mass and the match.'

The British would literally pay a high price for the Black and Tans' attacks on the creameries. They had to pay thousands of pounds in compensation. They did not seem to learn from their mistakes. In September 1920 the Black and Tans were responsible for 'the sack of Balbriggan', when many houses and businesses were burned down and two local men were savagely killed. If they were winning small battles, they were losing the bigger propaganda war.

THE DAY OF REST

Sunday was always a leisurely day in Irish households at the time. There was always time for a good long chat after Mass. The church bell tolled, calling the respectable, responsible citizens of the townland to worship. The latecomers frantically scampered up the steps, slipping red-faced into a seat at the back, momentarily disturbing the hushed stillness. Men in dark overcoats shuffled in the porch whispering about the price of cattle over the prayers. Local gossip was traded. Women in their best coats with righteous heads held high thought of the Sunday dinner. Having endured the compulsory fast before communion many tummies were rumbling. Outside the children's screams pierced the fresh air.

Toys, for most kids, were very scarce and the children depended on their imagination for amusement. They played hoops with old cartwheels. Another pastime was making primitive spinning tops. These were simply small coneshaped, brightly coloured pieces of wood. A second piece of wood with a narrow leather strap was used as the top and to get it to spin. The winner was the one whose top would spin the longest. The boys played toss-the-penny on the rare occasions when there were some available. Usually small stones provided an acceptable substitute. Another game was skimming stones on a pond. The dare-devils' greatest mischief was robbing apples in the autumn. The girls learned some of the great Irish dances like 'Shoe the Donkey'.

But this Sunday would be different.

Very different.

HELLO, DARKNESS MY OLD FRIEND

The first flinty hint of winter's breath on the breeze fell on a nice November day. The unseasonal weather was completely at odds with the political temperature. After the countryside the city's waves of noise and movement seem clamorous to the visiting Tipp fans who travelled up on train in the shadow of delight.

That morning, like so many Dubs, Jane Boyle walked to Sunday Mass in the chapel where she was due to be married a mere five days later. There was little drama about her, no apparent depths of intensity or unfulfilled longings that were evident on the surface at least. That afternoon she would travel with her fiancée with indefatigable enthusiasm to watch Tipperary and Dublin play a Gaelic football match at Croke Park. She had no idea that at that very moment nine men lay dead in their beds after a synchronised IRA attack designed to cripple British intelligence services in Ireland. She had no intimations of her own mortality. She had no conception that instead of her wedding her next visit to the Church would be in her coffin.

British intelligence was on a good run and getting closer and closer to nabbing Ireland's answer to the Scarlet Pimpernel, Michael Collins, the mastermind who 'would win the war for Ireland'. Recognising that the tide was turning firmly against him, Collins decided that desperate measures were called for. A storm was approaching. It could not be any darker than his thoughts.

Members of the infamous 'squad', one of Collins' killing machines, were in action. Among there number was 19-year-old Vinny Byrne. He killed two men, Lieutenant Ames and Lieutenant Bennet with an amalgam of mercy and mayhem. Before he shot his victims he whispered into their ears: 'The Lord have mercy on your soul.' However, the autopsies confirm that his victims were riddled with bullets. Standing beside Vinny was Johnny McDonnell. Just a few hours later Johnny would line out in goal for Dublin in the big game and Croke Park. His presence in both venues is a reminder not to accept that the distance between them is unbridgeable.

Today we think automatically of Tipp as a hurling superpower. But in 1920 they were a footballing force. Tipperary had lined out in the All-Ireland final 20 months earlier, only to be beaten by a Wexford side that was winning its fourth title on the trot, a rare feat next emulated in 1981 by Mick O'Dwyer's Kerry. Although Dublin were not the force they were under Kevin Heffernan or Jim Gavin, they were nonetheless a major power too. That's why so many people flocked to Croke Park that day, despite the mutterings there could be trouble after word spread of the killings that Collins' warriors had inflicted.

They all arrived with their Arcadian dreams of escape from the complexities of the world within the limitation of their resources. A natural passion diverted into tributaries. There was to be no slow fade through the amber mutation of autumn for them. The lilting lightness of anticipation in their voices as the game began simmering in its own juices, a sealed cauldron of electrified, motorised and human sweat.

The fans were filled with an extremity of wonder and excitement. As the noise and grit of the city had taken lodgings in his brain a tall, thin man was holding his trousers to stop them falling. His thick and oiled hair suggested that he spent significant time in the grooming.

In between recriminations about the forward who had missed a sitter or the star midfielder who had not bothered to track back and mark there were whispers about the political situation once the match started. Some were in thrall to a misty-eyed version of Romantic Ireland who inevitably claimed some distant lineage to the land.

Then all changed.

Changed utterly.

A terrible lack of beauty was born.

A shadow fell over them, a shadow that would soon lengthen and grow stronger.

CARNAGE

Collins's special units had taken out 14 British intelligence and security servicemen and somebody was going to have to pay a heavy price with their blood. Trucks of police and military sped through the city streets as hundreds of people sought sanctuary in Dublin Castle. Some of the military vehicles were headed for Croke Park. Their mission was supposed to simply be 'a scoping exercise' to gather intelligence but the military leadership was akin to a man wielding someone else's power and as a result being over generous with it. Seeing the military arrive, the crowd panicked and ran. The British forces opened fire on them. Bullets were flying and people caught up in a tempest were running.

The official plan by police was that 15 minutes before the final whistle there would be an announcement by megaphone. Rather than 'stewards to end-of-match positions', the crowd would hear someone telling them to leave by the official exits, where all men would be searched for weapons.

It was a seriously flawed idea, even before it went so badly wrong. Anyone carrying guns would surely have dumped them on the way out. But in the event, no sooner had police arrived at the ground than some of them started shooting. The consequent panic added to the death toll. The folly of all of this was that when the military leadership regained control after a few murderous minutes, the searches yielded nothing.

In this tyranny of terror, to die in your bed became the unspoken dream. For a seeming eternity, like a modern day tower of Babel reigning only confusion and chaos, the attendance were help captive by a cold entanglement of fear in their stomachs – until eventually silence settled and there was only the unsteady beating of hearts. A few sat silently and gave no clue as to whether they had understood what had happened or not.

Some of the wounded sought refuge in nearby homes and were laid out on kitchen tables as inexpert medical care was provided. The corners of the room were folded into shadows and all the light seemed pulled into the centre about the table. Strange thoughts troubled everybody present. Rooted in the inescapable vulnerability of the time it was difficult not to succumb to a maudlin mix of nostalgia and self-pity.

THERE'S A KIND OF A HUSH

That evening the sound of silence was heard all over Dublin. There was a powerful feeling of stillness, as if a heavy fall of snow held the whole world in its grip, but it was still not strong enough to obliterate the pungent scent of fear. Where would the reprisals be? When would they happen?

Shafts of moonlight penetrated the windows across the city. The stars appeared to dance in long silver ribbons. Inside, homes were marked only by a kind of numbness. The 'Fair City' felt like a foreign land to them, as if part of their hearts had been placed in cold storage. For grieving families there were worlds inside their heads that even their closest friends had no path to.

The next morning soft-edged slips of cloud sifted their way through a blue sky like spiralling cigarette smoke. At Masses all over Dublin, priests faced the difficult challenge of finding words of comfort. Some had dark rings under their eyes; those eyes were closing as if succumbing to an overwhelming weakness and they were about to fall asleep on their feet. The clergy described the angels ascending and descending as they read from the Book of Revelation: 'And God shall wipe away each tear. Death shall no more be, neither mourning, neither crying, neither sorrow.'

They intoned the words: *Kyrie eleison, Christie eleison.*

They prayed that the fallen would sleep like the infant Jesus in the arms of Mary and be bathed in some waters purer than the human eye could see. They exhorted the faithful to bear their tribulations with a martyr's grace, assuring them that the dead were not condemned to wander eternity alone. Trials they believed were sent by God to test human mettle. Some said that the bereaved families were waiting like Mary at the foot of the Cross with the promise of comfort and solace to come. Unusually there were no swelling voices spilling out of the churches after Mass. An aura of bewilderment had claimed the worshippers as if they were watching a play being performed in a language they did not understand.

IN THE PAPERS

Elizabeth Hardwick in *Grub Street, New York* observed, 'Making a living is nothing; the great difficulty is making a point, making a difference – with words.' There is a lot of excellent journalism from this period. The newspapers were full of eyewitness accounts. Some of the families of the victims wanted people to hear about the fate of their loved ones and even went to Croke Park and told their stories in the unbroken constancy of love. The tabloid newspapers published pictures of the dead.

Robert Cohen observed in the *International New York Times*, 'There is nothing to understand, they insist, just write the truth! But truths are many and that is the problem.'

Auxiliary Maj EL Mills blamed 'excited and out of hand RIC Constables' for the deaths. He added: 'I did not see any need for any firing at all and the indiscriminate firing absolutely spoilt any chance of getting hold of any people with arms.'

However, subsequent official reaction was less candid. In the

House of Commons, when asked for a statement on what had happened, the Chief Secretary for Ireland Hamar Greenwood at first confined himself to listing Collins's victims, in graphic detail.

When Belfast nationalist Joe Devlin insisted on the rest of the story from Dublin, there were scuffles in the chamber. Then, with calm restored, Greenwood rose again to give a heavily revisionist account of the Croke Park debacle, in which police had been fired on first. Even the more conservative British newspapers struggled to believe him, and the cover story was already thoroughly discredited before the official inquiries.

The fact that there are many truths is evident in the reporting of Bloody Sunday in the two leading Irish newspapers. *The Irish Times* essentially followed the official British line while *The Freeman's Journal* took a much more 'nationalist' position.

Some of the mourners were joined by Luke O'Toole, the general secretary of the GAA, as he meandered through the bloody grass of Croke Park, shadowed by a journalist. They heard a woman sobbing deeply; her attempts to stifle the sound spilled into stuttering gasps. A vigil of sorrow was praying at the spot where the Tipperary player, Michael Hogan, had gone to meet his God – the light had faded from his eyes, like he saw nothing but a trembling darkness.

Having beaten Dublin in the 1920 All-Ireland final (played, confusingly, in 1922), Tipperary would never win the competition again. Perhaps the most direct consequence was that General Frank Crozier, the man in nominal charge of the Croke Park operation, became a committed pacifist later in life.

A plaque in Croke Park carries the name of the Bloody Sunday victims and speaks to the whispering voices of faceless generations, the GAA's unique sacred scripture.

It is a voice for the dead, the names engraved eternally on the hidden chambers of the heart.

They are:

- Jane Boyle (26) Dublin, Assistant to a pork butcher
- James Burke (44) Dublin, Laundry worker
- Daniel Carroll (30) Tipperary, Bar Manager
- Michael Feery (40) Dublin, Unemployed
- Michael 'Mick' Hogan (24) Tipperary, Farmer
- Tom Hogan (19) Limerick, Mechanic
- James Matthews (38) Dublin, Labourer
- Patrick O'Dowd (57) Dublin, Labourer
- Jerome O'Leary (10) Dublin, Schoolboy
- William Robinson (11) Dublin, Schoolboy
- Tom Ryan (27) Wexford, Labourer
- John William Scott (14) Dublin, Schoolboy
- James Teehan (26) Tipperary, Publican
- Joe Traynor (21) Dublin, Labourer

The groundbreaking work of Michael Foley in his powerful book *The Bloodied Field* and the GAA's own Bloody Sunday Graves Project, which seeks to ensure that their final resting place is appropriately acknowledged, has helped us to rewrite their names and their stories back into history.

They are custodians of our troubled past.

They continue to speak to a requiem of voices.

Requiem aeternam dona eis. Domine et lux perpetua luceat eis. Requiescant in pace.

Grant them eternal rest.

LEGACY?

The real political ramifications of Bloody Sunday are difficult to assess. There was a legitimate outrage in Britain about the actions of Collins and his men. Internationally though there was massive condemnation about the actions of the British forces in Croke Park. Not for the first or last time was Collins proven to be prophetic when he said that the ultimate victory would come not to the side that afflicted the most but the side that endured the most. It would take months but the international mood music after Bloody Sunday was such that the British were moved to come to the table. Whisperings grew too loud to be safely ignored.

Was the bloodshed of the War of Independence worth it? That is a political judgement, but what is striking is how quickly disillusionment set in. The sheer energy expended in removing British forces may be one reason. The Civil War is another. Both left people with very little energy with which to reimagine a society. Instead, exhausted revolutionaries lapsed back into the inherited English forms. The Civil War induced a profound caution, making many distrustful of innovation. Fancy theories about a republic had, after all, cost hundreds of Irish lives.

The best way to remember Bloody Sunday is perhaps to pick a few stories to illustrate the bigger story. William Robinson was the first casualty of the Croke Park massacre, a young boy who was sitting in a tree at the corner of Croke Park to watch the game that changed the course of Irish history.

When he heard the rumble of trucks on the bridge behind him, William Robinson turned around from his seat in the crook of the tree. A shot rang out. The bullet whizzed through the air into William's chest and through his right shoulder. He fell from the tree.

Then he lay in hospital waiting to go to his God. There was something smouldering in his eyes but there are no words to describe it. A doctor finally emerged with news. William Robinson had died before noon. The doctor, a gentle man, imbued with diffidence and manners, watching the scene unfold, blessed himself as a mark of respect.

The second victim was ten-year-old Jerome O'Leary, sitting up on a canal wall. An innocent child who came to the greatest harm as he slipped into the great echoing hollow of the night, drifting between worlds, close to home and far away, unsure of how to get there.

So severe was the damage to 14-year-old John William Scott that he was described as being bayoneted to death. That story, in today's parlance, went viral. Later Lady Aston raised the issue of 'the bayonet boy' in Westminster. Her passion blazed like an angry fire.

HEALING HURTS

The War of Independence ended with a Treaty. However, this in turn precipitated a bloody and bitter civil war in Ireland. Gaelic football and hurling were always about more than sport in rural Ireland, and in Kerry in particular. My former teacher, Professor Liam Ryan, told me that the GAA played a greater part in healing the many rifts which have threatened to rupture families and communities throughout Irish history in the last century than the Catholic Church.

'Neighbours, for example, who had shot at one another in the Civil War displayed a greater desire to forgive and forget when gathered around the goalposts than when gathered around the altar. Nowhere was that more apparent than in Kerry.'

The late John B. Keane also spoke to me about the power of the GAA to heal the wounds of the past.

'Football has also been part of our identity here. In Kerry, football was called "CAID", as it referred to the type of ball used. The ball was made from dried farm animal skins with an inflated natural animal bladder inside. We take our football very seriously in Kerry, but we also take politics very seriously. Sometimes our twin passions collide. This was probably most clearly illustrated in 1935 when Kerry refused to take part in the football champion-ship because of the ongoing detention of prisoners in the Curragh.

'The Civil War not alone cost a lot of lives. It split families down the middle and left intense bitterness. The one place in Kerry where the civil war was put aside was on the GAA fields and it did bring old enemies together. Football united what politics divided. It was about our sense of Kerry. If we were playing Dublin in an All-Ireland final politics was put to one side so we would win the match. So in that way football helped clear the bad blood from the Civil War.

'A good example was Con Brosnan. He is one of the great legends of Kerry football and that is saying something. He reached out to his enemies from the Civil War on the football field. One of the things he did was to arrange safe passage for wanted IRA men so they could represent Kerry. Just a year after the Civil War ended, Kerry won the All-Ireland final with a team almost roughly divided between pro- and anti-Treaty players. When Con was nearing the end of his playing days, "one of the other side", Joe Barrett, ensured that he was given the captaincy. It was proof that Con was Kerry's great peacemaker after the Civil War.'

We live in a very different Ireland now, with different national memories, including the 2011 visit to the stadium of the British monarch, and an unforgettable evening in 2007 when GAA headquarters listened in pin-dropping silence to 'God Save the Queen' before roaring an Irish rugby team to a record defeat of England. The English fans were greeted with a polite kindness that appeared not to require any form of return. Almost as if it hid from somewhere in the unknown expanse of darkness, Bloody Sunday was put into a different perspective.

DIFFERENT TIMES

If you praise the sunshine in some parts of Ireland, you'll be told, 'It'll never last.' Yet there are ample reasons for optimism about the ongoing health of the GAA. Chief executive of the Irish Sports Council, John Treacy, who famously won the silver medal in the 1984 Olympics, is ideally equipped to offer a dispassionate appraisal of the role of the GAA in Irish life:

'I think there's a danger that we take them for granted. A number of years ago we hosted a gathering for all the top sports officials in the EU. We showed them a hurling match and they were watching it with their mouths open. They couldn't believe that amateur players could produce a game of such skill and speed. All through the day they kept asking about it.

'For an amateur organisation it is a staggering achievement to have created an incredible stadium like Croke Park, especially in the middle of Dublin. They have shown incredible leadership. The GAA has adapted to the changing times. They are keenly aware of the need to bringing modern marketing methods into Gaelic Games. I think a critical step came in the 1990s with the decision to introduce live coverage of a large number of games on the TV. Young people get their heroes from television. If you go down to Kilkenny, you will see almost every young boy with a hurley because they want to be like their heroes. In recent times you can see some young lads with hurleys walking on the streets of Dublin. You would hardly ever have seen that 30 years ago. That has not happened by accident and shows the forward-thinking approach the GAA has taken.

'They have shown great creativity in the way they have managed to defy the tide and ensure that they continue to get so many people to volunteer. The Economic and Social Research Institute produced a report on the social capital aspect of sport, and it is basically 90 pages of a glowing tribute to the GAA and the way they have harnessed the voluntary capacity. Instead of saying to people, as was done in the past, "give us all your time", they now say give us two evenings and a Saturday morning to train a juvenile team or whatever. We can't put a price on the kind of social value the organisation brings.

'However, their finest hour for me was when they revoked Rule 42 and opened up Croke Park to Ireland's soccer and rugby games while the old Lansdown Road stadium was being demolished and the Aviva was being built. Nobody will ever forget the extraordinarily unique atmosphere the day Ireland played England in that never to be forgotten rugby match in 2007. The emotion that day was unreal – as evident in the sight of big John Hayes bawling his eyes out while the anthems were being played. You could hear a pin drop when they played 'God Save the Queen'. The respect was phenomenal. It was a day when everybody was so proud to be Irish. A special day in the history of a very special sporting body and one I take my hat off to.'

14

TROUBLED TIMES: THE SHADOW OF THE TROUBLES

*Even in its darkest days the GAA
has always come back into the light.*
Eugene McGee

Grief paralyses but anger waits, looking for an opening.

At half-time during the 1981 Ulster final, the Clones playing field was filled with people carrying black flags, supporting prisoners who were on hunger strike for political status in Long Kesh Prison. Ulster football could not escape the dark shadows cast by the Northern Troubles.

In July 1972 Frank Corr, one of the most prominent GAA personalities, was shot dead, becoming one of the first of more than 40 people to die in Northern Ireland because of their involvement with the GAA. In May 1972, during a match between Crossmaglen and Silverbridge, a young British soldier shoved his rifle into the face of Silverbridge player Patrick Tennyson. Indeed, Crossmaglen was to have its ground occupied by the British army for 37 years.

On 21 February 1988, the Troubles also cast a dark shadow when Aidan McAnespie was shot dead by a British soldier as he went to watch his beloved Aghaloo play a football match.

On the playing fields Aidan's main contribution to his club was with the junior team. The closest he normally came to the senior team was watching them from the subs bench and making the occasional appearance in the last few minutes when the result was normally already decided. Yet football and the club dominated his life.

Aidan's sister, Eilish McCabe, subsequently became the best-known opponent of the removal of the GAA's Rule 21, which barred members of the security forces from taking part in Gaelic Games. She shared her memories of that traumatic time with me.

'Aidan was the youngest member of the family, the only one living at home. He had gone through a lot of harassment at the border checkpoint from the British soldiers. He had got a job in Monaghan as a poultry processor in the chicken factory and he travelled up and down every morning and evening, and we were aware that he was getting harassment every day. He had made complaints to the army, his trade union, parish priest, to anybody who would listen and through his own solicitor. In fact, one national newspaper had featured an article on Aidan a year before his death. The headline asked the question, "Is this the most harassed man in Ireland?" Aidan had gone to the media at the time in the hope of embarrassing the security forces for a while and it would have worked to some extent in the short term.'

What form did this harassment take?

'It took different forms. As he drove to work, they might just pull him over to the side of the road and keep him there for five minutes, and other occasions they might come over and search his car, maybe take out his lunch-box and search it with their bare hands and say, "Enjoy your lunch today, Mac." They sometimes called him Mac. On his way back they might keep him back 15 or

20 minutes in the side of the road or ask him where he was coming from or going to or they might pull him into the big shed and take his car apart. But I think the biggest problem was the fear of the unknown – he was never sure of what was coming next. The only thing he was certain of was that they were going to hassle him. He was never going to be in a car that was waved through.'

Was he physically assaulted?

'On some occasions he was. The most recent one prior to his shooting came one evening as he was coming through the checkpoint as he was going home from work. It was raining pretty heavily and the soldiers told him to get out of his car and take off his jacket, which he did. Then they asked him to take off his shoes and socks and he said, "I can't do that. It's pouring rain." They pounced on him and forcibly threw him down on the road and removed his shoes and socks. He came up to me that night and there were marks around his face and neck. I said we were going to have to make a formal complaint. He didn't want to go down to the police station on his own, so my husband went down with him. About six months later he received a letter which said that no disciplinary action would be taken against any member of the security forces.'

When they confronted the army officials, they were smiled at with all the genuineness of a politician.

A DEATH IN THE FAMILY

Dealing with death is always difficult, but the suddenness of a violent death is almost impossible to accept.

'That weekend we had a death in the family,' continued Eilish. 'My mum's sister's husband had died from a long-term illness and we all had been helping my aunt with the wake. He was buried on the Sunday morning and all the family were together. We all went back to my aunt's house for a meal and afterwards Aidan got up from the table and said to me, "I'm away on to see the football match." He had gone back to the family home and lit the solid fuel cooker so the house would be warm when my mum and dad returned home. He walked 269 yards through the checkpoint when a single shot rang out and Aidan died instantly.

'We were still at my aunt's house and I was chatting away with cousins I hadn't seen for a long time. Then my husband came inside and said to me, "Eilish, I need to speak to you immediately." I knew from the tone of his voice that it was quite serious but to be honest I thought it was just that our kids had been misbehaving. When I went out, he said, "There's been an accident at the checkpoint and I think Aidan's been involved and it's serious."

'We got into the car and drove down and just as we were driving through a garda car had arrived and was blocking the road to stop people driving on, but we got through. As we approached the football field, I could also see an ambulance in the background and I thought to myself, "I'm on time and I'm going to make it with Aidan to the hospital." I still wasn't sure what had taken place but I could see a body lying on the ground with a blanket over it but I didn't believe it was Aidan because the body looked small, but I went over towards it. I pulled back the blanket and it was Aidan and he was dead. I immediately held his hand and his hands were very, very warm and I hugged him and embraced him. The crowd all stood in complete silence and I heard my parents coming through. An anger went through my body, but it had gone again as the grief came back. When I saw my parents going to witness Aidan on the roadside that was just unbearable. I couldn't even bear to look at them with Aidan in that situation.'

Aidan had relaxed his hold on life.

'The ambulance came into where the body was and then they said they were going to take him to the morgue. He was put in a body bag and put sitting up in the ambulance, so my dad and I said we were going with him because we couldn't let Aidan go on his own. We sat in the ambulance in total shock down to the morgue in Craigavon and that's probably one of the longest journeys I'll ever have in my life. As we were travelling in the ambulance we went through Armagh. Children were out playing and people were going on with living and it was a sunny day, even though it was February, so people were out walking, others kicking a football, and you just said to yourself, "This can't be happening."

'My husband drove behind in his car and at the morgue my dad formally identified Aidan and then we had to make arrangements for an undertaker and everything else. When we had everything sorted out, we went back to the house, which was packed with relatives and even my poor aunt was there who had just buried her husband, helping my mum, who was in a bad way. Then people were coming to me saying that they had heard it on the news that there was an accidental discharge and an SDLP councillor told me that he had rung up the Northern Ireland office just immediately after the shooting because he was down at the football field and he was absolutely furious that they would claim it was an accident without having the opportunity to question the soldier or to involve forensics.

'It was a long night. We were told around 10 p.m. that Aidan's body was going to be returned that night. The doctor decided that mum, who had stayed up all night the previous two nights with my aunt, should be sedated. I tried desperately to get her to wake up when I realised that Aidan's remains were going to be brought back to the house but to no avail. I looked out just before he was being brought in at around 12.30 a.m. I couldn't believe the crowds that were there at the time. There were footballers, old people, very young people, and people who had come long distances. At that point I had never felt so lonely because everyone else in the family, except my mother knocked out in the bed, were in cars after the coffin. In times like that you clasp on to the smallest things. You wouldn't believe this, but it was a comfort to know that Aidan was going to be home in his bedroom and not in the morgue.

'That night we all sat up and around six o'clock I was making tea for all the people who stayed up with me. Suddenly I heard terrible crying and howling. I looked out in the hall and it was my mum, who had woken up from her sleep in a daze and she was standing in the hall looking in at Aidan's room. Aidan was laid out in his new suit in the coffin, with the candles all lit. My mum had woken up in a nightmare. I suppose she had thought it was a nightmare but the reality of the situation had hit her. It is hard when you are going through a situation like that but when you see your parents going through it – it is unbearable.'

The emotional trauma for the family was compounded by further rumours about the circumstances of Aidan's death and the growing realisation that if they were to extract answers to all their questions drastic measures would be needed.

'On the Monday we heard that the soldier who had shot him had claimed he was cleaning his gun and his finger slipped. That evening we decided we weren't happy with the explanation and nobody from the security forces had come to our door with any comment, so I contacted our solicitor.

'I also contacted our doctor to see if he could carry out an autopsy on Aidan's body. He thought it would be inconclusive if he did that because it was outside his area and that we would be better off getting a pathologist who would be qualified in that field. The Irish government made a statement on the Monday evening that they were going to carry out an investigation. We decided then that we would go ahead with the funeral on the Tuesday morning knowing that there would probably have to be an exhumation of Aidan's body.'

EXTRA STRAIN

A family funeral is always difficult, but how difficult was the burial when there was a strong possibility Aidan would always certainly be exhumed shortly afterwards?

'It was very tough. It was very hard to see Aidan's body leaving the house on a cold February morning. It was hard to believe the amount of people who were there at the funeral from all parts of Ireland, and I mean all parts. When we walked in, we didn't realise that the Cardinal was going to be there saying the Mass or that Mick Loftus, president of the GAA, was going to be there and many representatives from the Ulster Council. All the support helped us in a small bit to carry our cross.

'The sensation of it was almost unbearable, knowing that we were going to exhume him. We didn't know how soon but we hoped it would be sooner rather than later. When Aidan's body was being lowered in the ground, they lowered the supports, that would normally be raised, with his coffin to make it easier to take the coffin out again.

'On the following Saturday we got a phone call from the Irish government saying that we had permission to have the body exhumed the following morning and brought to Monaghan hospital, with the state pathologist, Dr Harbison, in attendance. To me, hearing the news was a relief because I knew an injustice had been done to our family and I had no confidence in British justice so I believed that the autopsy was an opportunity for us to get to the truth.

'For my mother in particular it was unbearable. I remember breaking the news to her that Aidan's body was being exhumed and I could see in her eyes that it was taking a lot out of her, but I knew she too wanted to get to the bottom of it. Indeed on the Wednesday of that week there was a soldier who was charged with the unlawful killing of Aidan, but we had no confidence that he was going to be convicted so we knew the onus was on us to get an investigation.

'On the Sunday night when the police had finished with all their forensics the road was re-opened, but then someone came in and told me that the Monaghan road had been closed again. This made us even more suspicious, and someone came to me later that night and told me that they had a light on and there was a red mark on the road where Aidan's body was. I wasn't quite aware of what was going on and we were told that three shots went off where they were re-marking the road. The media covered the story but the next day the police came back and said no, they had been shot at and returned fire. That was something that had been denied by everyone in the locality that shots were fired at them.'

The family's pain was exacerbated by the portrayal of Aidan by the British media.

'In the British media the phrase they consistently used to describe Aidan was a "Sinn Féin activist". That to our family was very hurtful as well. Aidan was a member of the GAA but had never been involved in any political party or political activity. I myself had stood for Sinn Féin at a local government election in 1985. Aidan had gone out and put up posters for me, as a brother would do for a sister, but neither of us had been involved in any political activity since then. It was like the British media were using this as a stick to beat us. I don't think it's right to treat any person the way Aidan was treated, regardless of their political view, but it hurt more to see him portrayed in this way to justify to people in England what the soldier had done.'

FOREVER YOUNG

Did the fact that Eilish had stood for Sinn Féin contribute to Aidan's problems with the security forces?

'Aidan had been getting the harassment before I stood for

election and he had come in here to me one evening and said, "If you get elected as a councillor, they won't be able to harass me any more."'

The passing of the years has done little to heal the family's pain, as Eilish told me.

'After Aidan's death my husband and I and our two children moved to stay with Mum and Dad for a few weeks. We ended up staying from February until the end of July. Their lives were totally devastated because their lives had revolved around Aidan. When we moved back to our home, I was still expecting Aidan to drop in every evening, the way he always used to. He has been an absent figure from all the happy family events we've had since, like my brother's wedding. You don't ever forget him. You wonder would he be married now and have children. While everybody else gets older Aidan will always be 23 to us.'

GONE TOO SOON

The Troubles would also claim the life of a legend of Mayo football. Of all the matches I have attended the one that stands most in my memory is the Connacht final of 1980. The game is more memorable for the emotion it generated than the actual contest on the pitch. Uniquely the two opposing teams were united in grief for a favourite son on both sides of the county border.

In 1975, Sligo had one of their finest hours when they defeated Mayo in the Connacht final replay. Mayo star of the time Seán Kilbride, who subsequently played with great distinction for Roscommon, attributes Mayo's defeat to one factor – the absence of John Morley, and specifically the failure of the powers that be to lure him out of retirement. Kilbride feels that John's experience was the missing link in what was potentially a very good Mayo team.

It has become a cliché for journalists and broadcasters to refer to a particular player's 'cultured left foot'. Yet every cliché has its truth, and from the days when he first sprang to prominence with St Jarlath's College, Tuam, where he won All-Ireland College senior medals in both 1960 and '61, there was never any doubt that John Morley's left foot merited this soubriquet. This reputation was enhanced once he made his first appearance in the Mayo colours in Charlestown in 1961. His former teammate Willie McGee recalls, 'John was always getting slagged about his right leg but he always defended it by saying that without it he couldn't use his left.'

His versatility was such that he could play in almost any position for Mayo, though he played mostly for the county at centre-back. He played a then record 112 senior games for the county up to 1974, captaining Mayo to their first Connacht senior title in 12 years, and also starred in the 1969 winning side. In the same years he also helped Connacht to Railway Cup successes.

The most famous incident in his illustrious career came in the 1970 league final clash when Mayo defeated Down. John was playing at centre-half back when a Down player grabbed him and tore his shorts. Just as he was about to put his foot into new shorts, the ball came close by, and he abandoned his shorts and in his briefs fielded the ball and cleared it heroically down the field to the adulation of the crowd.

Former Roscommon great Dermot Earley frequently came up against John but his outstanding memory of him was of a match they played together.

'We played together for Connacht and, having won the Railway Cup in 1969, we went out to New York to play in the Cardinal Cushing Games. In our first game against New York in Boston, I was playing very well in midfield. On one occasion the ball was hanging in the air. I went into the clouds, or so I thought, to catch the ball. I touched the ball and then it was wrenched from my hands. As I reached the ground, I turned around quickly to be on the defensive, but I looked around to see that it was my teammate John Morley with the ball tucked in as tight as could be, ready to set up another attack. You would have to consider him as being one of the great players.

'In the west of Ireland there are two things we are known for. One is for saying "mighty". The other thing we are noted for is that we generally refer to people we admire, even though we may never have met them, by their surname. If you go into any GAA setting in the west of Ireland today, indeed all the west of Ireland is a GAA setting, and you say "Morley", everyone will know the name. He remains known by that name with affection and admiration.'

Inevitably any discussion on John Morley's career is overshadowed by the tragic circumstances of his death. The man who gave every ounce of energy on the playing field for Mayo, was prepared to put his life on the line to honour his professional duty and uphold law and order regardless of any risk to his personal safety. The bravery which he had so often exhibited in the green and red of Mayo was to manifest itself even more strikingly in the dark blue uniform of the Garda. A hero in life became a hero in death.

John was murdered on 7 July 1980, just a few days before the Connacht final, with a fellow native of Knock, Henry Byrne. He was just 37 years of age. Another Mayo man and centre-forward for Michael Glaveys, Derek Kelly, was injured in the incident. In June 2020 people in Mayo and Roscommon had a powerful reminder of the tragedy with the killing in the line of duty in Castlerea of Detective Garda Colm Horkan, a Mayo native with long years of distinguished service in Roscommon. He too had been a club player of note with Charlestown and had a deep love of Mayo football.

John Morley had initially been based in Ballaghaderreen on the Mayo–Roscommon border before moving to Roscommon town and finally to Castlerea. In all three places he had fully immersed himself in all manner of community activities.

A robbery had taken place, in a time when the IRA were involved in a campaign to rob banks, and the squad car encountered the getaway car at the crossroads outside Loughlynn on the way to Ballaghaderreen. Shots were fired and Henry Byrne and John Morley were fatally wounded. First on the scene was a retired Garda, the late Garda Kneafsey. Interviewed on the RTÉ news that night he said he had arrived on the scene to discover a guard wounded and badly bleeding on the side of the road and that he had recognised him immediately as 'the footballer'. He spoke to him, but the man was shaking as if registering arrows of pain shooting through his now frail body. John had said to him, 'I'm getting awful cold', which indicated a loss of blood. Then he said an act of contrition. Shortly after, the ambulance arrived, but it was too late to save John.

The human tragedy had a huge effect on Connacht because the Connacht final was just up the road the following Sunday. It was between Mayo and Roscommon, between a county that John had played for, and the county he lived in for many years. Everybody in both counties respected him totally. That Connacht final – played in brilliant weather in an exceptionally bad summer on 13 July – totally reflected that feeling. Fr Leo Morahan, who was on the Connacht Council at the time, gave a poignant and moving oration before the throw-in. In the circumstances, Roscommon's 3-13 to 0-8 win hardly seemed to matter.

15

THE BAN-BREAKER: TOM WOULFE

> . . . . . *there is a dark*
> *Inscrutable workmanship that reconciles*
> *Discordant elements, makes them cling together*
> *In one society.*
>
> William Wordsworth

His story speaks to us like ruins of monasteries surviving from the Middle Ages.

In 1887 Maurice Davin had called for a ban on rugby and soccer. The political leanings of the GAA had been clearly manifested in 1902 when Rule 27, 'The Ban', was introduced. It prohibited members of the GAA from playing, attending or promoting 'foreign games' like soccer, rugby, hockey and cricket. In 1938 the GAA controversially expelled its patron, Ireland's first president, Douglas Hyde, for attending an international soccer match.

The ban was clearly shown to be out of step with the times in 1963 when Waterford hurler Tom Cheasty was banned for attending a dance sponsored by his local soccer club. The ban cost him a National League medal. Mayo great of the 1960s Willie McGee had reason to be worried about being reported on another occasion.

'When I first started playing championship football the ban was still in operation, so you daren't be seen at a soccer or rugby match or play them either. I vividly remember attending a soccer match in Dalymount Park one day when I heard this chant, "Burrishoole, Burrishoole!" coming from behind the goal. I'm from Burrishole and knew it was me who was being identified so I lifted my collar up to hide my face because I was scared stiff of being reported, but it was a Roscommon man and good friend of mine, Noel Carthy. I was glad to know it was him! But the ban did create that kind of climate of fear. It was as if the GAA was saying to the world: "We are not confident enough to trust our own members." Thankfully that situation has changed.'

Thanks, in large measure, to an ongoing campaign of Dublin's Tom Woulfe the GAA ban on GAA players playing or even watching 'foreign' games was revoked by 1971.

PART III
Through the Decades

In the 1950s, Ireland was typified by Eamon De Valera, a veteran of the 1916 Rising, who had survived – only because he was born in New York – to become the dominant figure on the Irish political landscape for the next 50 years. His vision was of an insular Ireland of cosy homesteads, comely maidens and athletic youths.

The sixties, however, were a decade of extraordinary change. The Industrial Revolution had bypassed Ireland, but a new Taoiseach, Seán Lemass, wanted to drag Ireland, kicking and screaming, into the modern age. Through an imaginative series of grants and tax incentives to foreign industrialists he transformed Ireland from an agricultural and rural society with a predominantly old population, because of the haemorrhage of emigration, to a society that was industrial, urban and with a young population. The introduction of free secondary education took Ireland a further step on the road to a meritocracy.

A new era arrived in 1973 when Ireland joined the European Community. The bold decision to become enthusiastic partners in Europe signalled a move away from the economic protectionism which had impeded our development since the 1930s, an abandonment of the notion that we might flourish without involving ourselves in the EEC. The school curriculum reflected the multi-cultural environment. No longer would Irish identity be defined in terms of its separateness and difference from England. Ireland was about to take her place in the fast lane. The possibilities seemed limitless.

The census returns of the previous year had painted an optimistic, even rosy, picture of a nation at last boldly taking its rightful place among the world's elite. New factories and schools were springing up everywhere. The scourge of emigration had not just been halted, it had been reversed, as thousands of people returned from England, America and Australia to the Emerald Isle.

It was a time of extraordinary change. A variety of factors came together like converging lines to produce a social, economic and cultural revolution. Ireland had ceased to be a predominantly agricultural country. Industry and commerce had become more important than farming. As a consequence of this, Ireland had become an urban society, with the majority of people living in towns and cities instead of on the land. Whereas in the 1950s emigration had decimated the Irish population so that most of the country's finest and brightest had left the country, by the early 1970s Ireland had become a country of young people.

For the first time since the Great Famine, the Irish population recorded an increase. For the first time since the Middle Ages, the vulnerable Irish economy was showing promising signs of being able to support itself.

Other changes were less tangible but no less significant. Educational standards were much higher. The introduction of free secondary education in the late 1960s by the Minister of Education, Donogh O'Malley, had far-reaching effects. The most obvious manifestation of this was the myriad of yellow school buses which populated country roads, or early mornings and late afternoons, as they ferried armies of schoolchildren from the country into the towns. However, better education brought new expectations, new ways of thinking and doing, and in many cases a sharp questioning of what went before.

Ireland had now entered the era of the global village. At the flick of a switch the world was at the viewer's finger tips.

The GAA could not but be affected by the profound changes in Irish society. Over the last 100 years the GAA has produced great stars and huge personalities. In this section we look at one representative sample from each of the last ten decades to capture a flavour of them – so that the microcosm represents the macrocosm.

16

1920s

THE MAN BEHIND THE WIRE: DICK FITZGERALD

The dead who shall live forever
and the living who shall never die.
Micheál Ó'Muircheartaigh

Dick Fitzgerald was the quintessential Irish hero. He fought in the Easter Rising, was arrested and was then interned in Wales, where he captained the Kerry team.

He famously wrote *How to Play Gaelic Football*, the first handbook of its kind in the GAA. Fitzgerald won five All-Ireland championships and became the first man to captain a county to consecutive All-Irelands in 1913 and 1914.

Although Limerick won the first All-Ireland in 1887, Gaelic football really came of age in 1903 when Kerry won their first All-Ireland. They beat Kildare in a three-game saga which grabbed the public imagination. Kerry won the first game, but the match was replayed because Kerry had been awarded a controversial goal. So intense was the second game, which finished in a draw, that the referee collapsed at the end. On the third occasion Kerry were comprehensive winners by 0-8 to 0-2.

The following year saw the first taster of what would become one of the great rivalries in the GAA when Kerry beat Dublin to claim their second All-Ireland. By now Fitzgerald had emerged as the first true star of Gaelic football, notably when he appeared to defy the laws of physics in one of the Kildare games when he pointed a late free, only yards from the touchline.

Fitzgerald saw football in very spiritual terms, creating a sense of the immutable bond that victory brings, a feeling of kinship that goes beyond professional loyalty, a camaraderie that overcomes differences of age, sex, even previous fallings out. This was particularly important in Kerry in the 1920s and 1930s where memories of the Civil War lingered very powerfully. His code was not to talk the talk but walk the walk.

Fitzgerald's influence was not just down to his achievements on the playing field. He was pivotal to the decision that Kerry should wear the green and gold, organised street leagues, trained Clare to an All-Ireland in 1917, refereed two All-Irelands and acted as a delegate to Congress.

Tragedy darkened his door in 1929 when his beloved wife Kitty died. Success in Gaelic football is about history and geography – about being in the right place at the right time. Fitzgerald was the right man for his time and was destined to remain one of the chosen few whose name would live on when his stay in this valley of tears had ended. He died prematurely in 1930 two days before the All-Ireland final at the age of 46, when he fell from the roof of Killarney courthouse, a short distance from where he was born. On the Sunday thousands knelt outside the church of his commemorative Mass. Fitzgerald was a selector with the Kerry team that year; after the Artane Boys Band played the national anthem before the All-Ireland final between Kerry and Monaghan, they played Chopin's 'Death March'. Kerry did what the occasion demanded and routed Monaghan by 18 points.

The most obvious reason for Kerry's success has been a phenomenal array of fantastic footballers from Dick Fitzgerald to Paddy Kennedy to Seamus Moynihan.

Dick's name lives on in Fitzgerald Stadium in Killarney, which was opened in 1936. His legacy is to make the green and gold synonymous with Gaelic football.

17

1930s

THE WARRIOR: LORY MEAGHER

Over the bar said Lory Meagher.
Chant in Kilkenny training sessions in the 1930s

It is everything. It is everything and everything again.

Hurling is to Kilkenny what films are to Hollywood: a country-wide obsession that sets a pecking order, discussed endlessly and by everyone, complete with its own arcane laws and rituals. Pubs are the churches of this strange sporting religion. Hurling-talk is no idle form of idle gossip here, but a crucial element in the county's psyche, to which business, love, the land and the weather regularly take second place.

Kilkenny's Lorenzo Ignatius Meagher was perhaps the first true star of hurling. He was to hurling aficionados in the county what Nureyev was to the ballet enthusiast. Tommy Walsh continues to be a flagbearer for Tullaroan club, but it was Lory Meagher who put them on the map.

He won three All-Irelands in the 1930s and entered the club of GAA immortals on foot of his towering performance in dreadful weather in midfield when Kilkenny beat the hot favourites and reigning champions Limerick in the 1935 All-Ireland, having previously won All-Irelands in 1932 and '33. He was chosen at midfield in both the GAA's official Team of the Century and Team of the Millennium, and was known by his contemporaries as 'the prince of hurling'. In 1984, the GAA's centenary year, an official book was published. Only one player was featured on the cover: Lory Meagher.

In Ireland we don't like players or personalities to get too big for their boots. This was best illustrated in the 1970s when someone said to Gay Byrne: 'There are no real stars in Ireland. You are the nearest thing we have to it, but you are not there yet.'

Lory had a funeral fit for a prince when he died in 1973, such was his status within the game. His legacy survives in the museum named after him and in the national hurling trophy that bears his name.

It is said that when a prominent hurler, who shall remain nameless because of the libel laws, dies the presiding clergyman will have to break with liturgical convention. Such is his liking for publicity that instead of saying 'May perpetual light shine upon him' the priest will probably say: 'May perpetual *limelight* shine upon him.' Apart from his genius on the field Meagher is renowned for his modesty off it. This character trait was most vividly illustrated when a journalist met him on the roadside one day and asked where he might track down Lory Meagher. The Kilkenny ace's reply was: 'You've just missed him. He passed up this way a few minutes ago. If you hurry you've a good chance of catching him.'

That was the glory that was Lory.

18

1940s

THE LORD OF THE RINGS: CHRISTY RING

Christy Ring was by far the best hurler I ever saw.
John Doyle

It was a funeral like no other.

He had lived a public life but his death, at the age of 58, was nearly a private affair. He fell down in a quiet street in Cork and a passing teacher, Patricia Horgan, softly whispered an act of contrition into his ear as he took his last breath and prepared to meet his God.

His former teammate and the then Taoiseach, Jack Lynch, delivered a heartfelt eulogy: 'As a hurler he had no peer. As long as young men will match their hurling skills against each other on Ireland's green fields, as long as young boys bring their camáns for the sheer thrill of the tingle on their fingers of the impact of ash with leather, as long as hurling is played, the story of Christy Ring will be told. And that will be forever.'

He was carried to his last resting place on the shoulders of his teammates, one of whom, Paddy Barry, was heard to remark: 'We carried him at last.' One observer said that the crowd was the biggest in Cork since the funeral for 'the martyr Lord Mayor Tomas Mac Curtain'.

In the 1960s Christy Ring was being interviewed by Bob Hyland, a journalist then with *The Irish Press*. The previous week Ring had read a piece that Hyland had written on the Tipperary All-Ireland-winning hurler Seamus Bannon, who had contended that to strike the sliotar cleanly for a sideline cut he needed a soft tuft of grass. Ring took the journalist by surprise when he brought him out on the road. He placed the sliotar on the road and hit it with the sweetest cut of his hurley and drove it into the nearest field. Then he turned to Hyland and instructed him to write to Bannon and to tell him that 'the grass never grew on the Mardyke Road'.

A small fable of Ring's perfectionist streak and of his personality.

The year 2020 marks the centenary of Ring's birth. He has a special place in the annals of the GAA. He first sprang to prominence when, at the age of 16, he played for Cork Minors. In his 24 years playing for the Cork seniors he would amass eight All-Ireland winners' medals, nine Munster championships, three League medals and a staggering 18 Railway Cups – when they were a premier competition. He retired in 1964 when the Cork selectors dropped him, aged 43. His best guess was that he had played over 1,200 games. He left behind a treasure trove of memories but a small archive of interviews because he famously said, 'All my talking was done on the field with a hurley.'

His special status with hurling fans was most tellingly revealed on the day of a Munster final when a Cork fan met him and two of his teammates. She sprinkled holy water on his colleagues but assured the wizard of Cloyne: 'Ringy, you don't need any of this!'

One of the many stories told about Ring begins as he was leading his team out of the tunnel. When they were halfway out, he turned them back to the dressing-room. Then he took off his Cork jersey, held it up and asked his players to look at the colour and what it meant to them. After that the team went out with fire in their bellies and played out of their skins.

He was not a man to call a spade an argicultural implement. Famously after the 1968 Munster final, when Babs Keating gave a magnificent performance, scoring 1-3 for Tipperary, Ring congratulated him by saying: 'Great performance, Babs, but imagine what you would have done if you had concentrated for the whole game.'

In his classic book *Over the Bar* Breandán Ó'hEithir writes about how Ring could match his great skills with toughness. After one game a few young lads shouted to him that he was a dirty player. Ring took great umbrage at this suggestion and swore at them with such viciousness that they ran away terrified.

Legend has it that he had his jaw broken in the first minute of a match but he played on for the full game. Not only that but the two men who marked him both had to be taken off as Ring extracted retibution. While he championed skill greatly, there was one quality Ring valued on the hurling pitch above all others: courage.

In Ring's days as a selector Cork's ace forward Seánie O'Leary got a belt of a hurley across the nose and was withdrawing from the field when Ring shouted at him: 'Get back out there. You don't play hurling with your nose.'

19

1950s

THE MAN WHO PLAYED FOR THREE COUNTIES: JIM FIVES

Rugby is a sport for ruffians played by gentlemen.
Gaelic football is a sport for gentlemen played by ruffians.
but hurling is a sport for gentlemen played by gentlemen.

Raymond Smith

One man who proves the latter part of this adage is Waterford's sole representative on the Team of the Century of players who never won an All-Ireland medal: Jim Fives, right full-back on the hurling team.

It was as a forward, though, that he first made his name with Waterford and his club, Tourin. The club was founded in 1940 and his family played a prominent role in its development. He was the youngest of five brothers who all played senior hurling with their native county. Apart from the club and his family another influence was his school, Lismore CBS, which had a strong team in the 1930s. His heroes were the Waterford hurling team that won the All-Ireland title in 1948, particularly centre half-back John Keane, who had hit the headlines for his fine performances against Limerick in the late 1930s. Although Jim played for

Waterford minors in 1947, he was over age to play for them the following year when they went on to win the All-Ireland. With his substantial physical presence, the six-footer played for the county at minor, junior and senior levels.

In 1949 he entered the Cadets in the Curragh and played a lot of hurling with the army team; and he played with other intercounty hurlers such as Mossy Riordan of Cork, Dublin's Liam Donnelly and Billy O'Neill, who played for Cork and Galway. That same year he made his debut for Waterford against Wexford. It was a baptism of fire, as his immediate opponent was no less a player than Billy Rackard. Waterford's defeat that day was to be an omen of things to come. Fives knew acute disappointment:

'The biggest disappointment of my time with Waterford came when we lost to Tipperary by two points in the Munster championship in 1951. They were the big power then and we were so close. We never put it together after that.'

Why did Waterford have such little success?

'The Waterford team that won the All-Ireland in 1948 was a relatively old team and the team broke up straight after that. We had a poor team while I was there. You have to remember that it's a small county and that the number of clubs playing the game is small. Another problem was that we had not the right management structures. We had far too many selectors and this led to a lot of "political" selection decisions, with selectors sometimes more interested in having players from their club on the team than having the 15 best players. Of course, that was not a problem unique to Waterford, but at the time we couldn't afford to be going out with a weaker side.'

INTO THE WEST

After cadet school, Fives was transferred in Renmore in Galway. For four more years he continued to play for Waterford, though he was playing club football and hurling in Galway. He won a Galway County championship medal with the army playing at midfield and played for two years with the Waterford senior football team, though the closest he got to winning a county hurling medal came in 1955 when they lost the county final. The army team had other intercounty players like Jimmy Brophy from Kilkenny, Billy O'Neill and Dublin's Joe Young.

'It was a very quiet time in Irish history to be a soldier. Ireland had not yet begun its peacekeeping missions overseas, which meant that we had plenty of time for sport. We had ample opportunities to keep fit.'

In 1955 Fives made the difficult decision to forsake his beloved Waterford and declare for Galway.

'It wasn't near as easy then to move around from Galway to Waterford as it is now. I was also often caught between the club and county. The club wanted me for a big match, but Waterford would want me on the same day for a league match or a tournament game. Really for practical reasons the only option for me was to switch to Galway, although I was very sorry not to be playing for Waterford any more.

'The hardest part was the two times I had to play for Galway against Waterford – in the All-Ireland semi-final in 1957 and in 1959 when we played them in the Munster championship because Galway were "in Munster" then. It's a very, very difficult thing to do to play against your native county.'

As was the case with Waterford he was on the Galway team in lean times. The highlight was winning the Oireachtas final by a big score over Wexford in 1958. There were a couple of good performances in the Railway Cup: notably a draw with Munster in 1957 and a victory over Leinster in 1959 in the semi-final. The final was delayed until Easter Sunday due to renovations on the Hogan Stand but Munster won the final.

The move to Galway coincided with Fives' switch from the forwards to the backs.

'I was anxious to play in the backs because I always like to be facing the ball. The thing about forward play is that you always have to turn once you get possession.'

A serious back injury caused him to step down from senior intercounty hurling in 1959. Two years later he was transferred to the barracks in Castlerea and came out of retirement to play junior hurling for Roscommon. Among his teammates was legendary footballer Gerry O'Malley. Although they got to a couple of All-Ireland semi-finals by the time O'Malley finally won his long-awaited All-Ireland medal, a junior hurling All-Ireland medal in 1965, Fives had been transferred to Castlebar the previous year. Having played football for one county and hurling for three counties, Fives came within a whisker of playing for a fourth. He had hardly arrived in Castlebar when he was asked if he would be willing to play for Mayo the following Sunday. The old back injury had returned, and Fives was forced to decline the offer, unable to cross the fitness threshold.

While medals were few and far between, representative honours came his way. In 1953 he played for Ireland against the Universities. The following year the Universities were not considered strong enough to field a testing opposition, so Fives was chosen on the Combined Services team to play Ireland – a blend of players from Universities, the gardai and the army. In 1959 he captained the Rest of Ireland in a prestige fixture against the All-Ireland champions Tipperary.

HURLING IN THE CONGO

Fives twice served on Irish peacekeeping missions abroad, which gave a heightened perception of life.

'I spent six months in the Congo and six months in the Middle

East. It was very interesting but very tense and demanding. Our duties were very heavy. We played hurling in the Congo, which was certainly a strange experience. As you can imagine the conditions were very difficult. The kindest thing I can say about our pitches is that they were very dusty!'

Fives glows affectionately as he recalls some of the more unusual incidents in his career, with the wonder of a baby counting his toes.

'In 1948 I played a senior club match in Waterford. It was a very niggly game and there was a lot of moaning to the referee, the great Limerick player Garrett Howard. At half-time he brought the two teams together and said, "Let's have no more of this whinging. Hurling is a man's game. It's not tennis. Be men and take your challenges and your punishment. Go back out there and play like men not mice." We took his advice to heart and went out and played like men possessed. Nobody held back and there were some fierce challenges and an awful lot of sore limbs the next day!

'I was playing a junior hurling match for Tourin against Ballyduff in Lismore. Our full-forward "manhandled" their goalie and a melee developed around the goal because they tried to lynch him and he ran. Everyone got involved. What made it unusual was that all of us ended up against the railing of the pitch first and then things got so hot and heavy that we all ended up in the next field. It was the most bizarre sight I ever saw on a hurling pitch – actually not on the pitch! Finally, the referee restored order and the match re-started as if nothing had happened.'

20

1960s

IT'S NOT A LONG WAY FROM TIPPERARY: JIMMY DOYLE

When the Gods come out to play they play hurling.
Micheál Ó'Muircheartaigh

In the Tipperary colours, Jimmy Doyle was as eager as a lamb in springtime.

In the closets of his mind, as a boy all his dreams were consumed by thoughts of playing in an All-Ireland final. Like so many of his generation he was converted to Gaelic Games by the GAA's answer to St Paul, Micheál Ó'Hehir. O'Hehir's conversions did not take place on the Road to Damascus but from the 'magic box' on kitchen tables throughout the country. Doyle grew up in an era when Micheál Ó'Hehir was at the height of his extraordinary career, in the days of wet batteries and communal radios. For hundreds of thousands of Irish people, he was the only mediator. A phenomenon never to be emulated, he alone had the power to bring Gaelic Games to the people. And he did. It was he who made Doyle aware for the first time of the unlimited potential that Gaelic Games have for excitement, drama, tension, spectacle, elation and heartbreak, all packaged together in the ebb and flow of the enthralling broadcasts of the man with the golden voice. As one of the greatest forwards in the history of hurling, Doyle would weave his own magic into the lush tapestry of the GAA.

This was a golden era for hurling because there were great teams like Cork, Tipperary and Wexford. Not only that, but these teams had five or six great players competing for each position. In an era of outstanding defenders like John Lyons and Willie John Daly of Cork, Diamond Hayden of Kilkenny, and Billy Rackard and Nick O'Donnell of Wexford it was going to take a formidable talent to shine, but Jimmy Doyle lit up the hurling pitch like a Christmas tree. He could get scores from left or right. However, it comes as a shock that such a classy forward should start and finish his career as a goalkeeper. His Tipperary career was bookended by appearances as goalkeeper on the losing All-Ireland minor final to Dublin in 1954, when he was just 14, and a stand-in appearance in goals against Waterford in 1973.

Even when early childhood memories fade, almost every boy can recall his first football or hurling match. He can remember the score, who got a great goal, who had a bad miss. But mostly he remembers his father. And that is the magic of the GAA. Hurling was part of Jimmy Doyle's family tree. His father Gerry was sub goalie when Tipperary won All-Irelands in 1937 and 1945, and his uncle Tommy was one of the legends of Tipperary hurling, winning five All-Irelands. As a result Jimmy grew up almost from the cradle hearing stories about the Tipperary teams that featured some of the greatest characters in the game, like Mick 'Rattler' Byrne, who was a small man but pound for pound he was the toughest man you could ever meet. He would mark guys from Wexford three or four stone heavier than him, but he would never be beaten. He was a great corner-back for Tipp but also a wonderful storyteller. He did not have much time for all the talk players have today about their injuries, especially about their 'hamstrings'. He always said that the only time in his playing days he heard anybody talking about hamstrings was when they were hanging outside a butcher's shop.

Having won three minor All-Ireland medals, Jimmy Doyle won six senior All-Ireland medals in 1958, '61, '62, '64, '65 and '71, captaining the teams in 1962 and 1965. He also won six National League medals and seven Railway Cups. The ultimate accolade came for the Thurles Sarsfields man when he was chosen on both the GAA official Team of the Century and the Team of the Millennium.

Of course, it helped that his Tipperary team were a well-oiled machine with outstanding players like Babs Keating, Donie Nealon and, of course, Tony Wall, who was one of the great centre-backs of all time. For Babs Keating, Jimmy Doyle was a great role model.

'Long before players were handed out gear for free, we were very conscious of the importance of equipment. Jimmy Doyle was one of the best hurlers I ever saw. He would always arrive in the dressing-room with five spare hurleys. I learned from him the importance of proper preparation.'

An essential element of the appeal of Gaelic games, that extra quality that distinguishes them from all other sports in Ireland, is the tribalism on which the structures are based. No other sports enjoy the intense rivalry that exists in the GAA between clubs. From time to time this creates problems, but in the main it generates a sense of community which has been all but lost in contemporary Irish society. Despite the intensity of the rivalries in hurling, Jimmy Doyle was particularly proud of hurling's tradition of sportsmanship. One parable which illustrates this came in the 1958 All-Ireland semi-final between Tipperary and Kilkenny when he scored eight points off Paddy Buggy. After the match a Kilkenny supporter asked Paddy, 'What happened – why didn't you hit him?'

Buggy replied, 'Why should I? He didn't hit me.'

21

1970s

A STAR IS BORN:
JIMMY BARRY-MURPHY

*He may be 19 but today he's joined the ranks
of the football immortals.*

Micheál Ó'Hehir

Everything that we have, everything that we do, everything that we are is summed up in legends like Jimmy Barry-Murphy.

Gaelic players sometimes suffer from 'Orson Welles syndrome'. Like the famous star of the screen, their crowning moment of glory comes at the very start of their careers. Nothing that follows can match it. Jimmy Barry-Murphy is the exception to the rule. He exploded on to the scene when, at the age of 19, he scored two fine goals in Cork's All-Ireland football final triumph over Galway in 1973.

Galway defender Johnny Hughes still recalls the day vividly:

'We scored 2-13 and lost the All-Ireland by seven points. I have no cribs about losing in 1973 because we were comprehensively beaten. We couldn't match their firepower. Jimmy Barry-Murphy and Jimmy Barrett caused us untold trouble. Jimmy Barry-Murphy even then was a most difficult opponent. He was both very confident and very skilful, and, could take you to the cleaners, and he had two great feet but above all he had a great head. Had he stuck to football he would have gone on to become one of the all-time greats.'

Like other players featured between the covers of this book, though, JBM's collection of football medals is much lower than it should be because his career coincided with the golden era of Kerry football. How difficult was it for him to keep going when Cork were losing the Munster final every year?

'God, there were times when it was hard. It did get demoralising. However, I would have to say that we never went into any of those Munster finals not thinking we were going to win. We never had an inferiority complex even though they beat us well a few times. We always enjoyed those matches, even though Mick O'Dwyer always hyped us up by saying Cork was the most difficult opposition he expected to meet all year. We always got on well with the Kerry lads. I played with most of them on the Munster team and I always felt they gave the Cork lads plenty of respect.

'I suppose what kept us going was the enjoyment we got from playing. We were all passionately in love with the game. We had a lot of craic and fun. Although we had a lot of disappointments in the Munster championship we at least had the consolation of getting to a league final in 1979, which we lost to Roscommon, and of beating Kerry in the league final the following year, which was a big thrill for us to at last win another National title.'

Donegal great Martin Carney saw the more relaxed side of the legend of JBM: 'I played for Ulster in 1975 and remember it as Seán O'Neill's last game for Ulster. Jimmy Barry-Murphy had played the day before in a Senior hurling club final for the 'Barrs against Johnstown and I remember meeting him that night and, let's put it this way, he was enjoying himself, and yet the next day he produced a devastating performance. Jimmy scored 4-1 in that game from five kicks of the ball.'

Having won All-Stars in 1973 and 1974 in football, Barry-Murphy's talents were most often seen on the national stage in hurling because Kerry ruled supreme in Munster. In full flight JBM lit up the stage like a flash of forked lightning, flashing brilliantly, thrilling and, from the opposition's point of view, frighteningly. He is probably the greatest dual star of all time, winning five All-Ireland hurling medals and five hurling All-Stars. With characteristic modesty he downplays his role in Cork's three-in-a-row winning side of 1976–78:

'There are those who will say that we were in the right place at the right time because other teams like Kilkenny were not as strong as they usually were, but look at the players we had at the time such as Martin O'Doherty, John Horgan, Gerald McCarthy, Charlie McCarthy, Ray Cummins and Seánie O'Leary. The fact that we won those All-Irelands had much more to do with their brilliance than anything I ever did.'

He also had the honour of winning an All-Ireland medal in the centenary year on the hallowed sod of Semple Stadium against Offaly. The side's preparation for the game was rather unorthodox, as Barry-Murphy's teammate Tomás Mulcahy recalls:

'Before the 1984 Centenary All-Ireland final our trainer Canon Michael O'Brien wanted the team to be shielded from all the fuss in Thurles. Finding such a sanctuary was difficult, but as a resourceful man Canon O'Brien rang up the local convent and asked if the team could rest up there. They duly did, we were fed by the nuns and had a light puck around in the grounds. To ensure the team's focus was not compromised Canon O'Brien gave strict instructions to the nuns that once the team bus arrived the gates were to be closed and under no circumstances was anybody to be admitted. The problem was that a short while later the chairman of the Cork County Board drove up in his car to the gates of the convent. When he requested entry, he was greeted by two formidable nuns who left no room for ambiguity in the way they told him he had no prayer of being admitted. I think Jimmy Barry-Murphy was the nun's favourite and their prayers for him worked in that final.'

JBM's sublime overheard flick against Galway in the 1983 All-Ireland semi-final was voted as the greatest hurling goal of all time in 2009.

Eileen Dunne sums up JBM's place in the pantheon of the greats: 'Gaelic Games provide an unending theatre of drama, and very often a spectacle that is unique to this country. My late father, Mick Dunne, had a deep love of all things GAA. Growing up, my sisters and I acquired some of his passion for hurling, Gaelic football, handball and camogie. We remember trips to the Grand Hotel in Malahide on All-Ireland Sunday mornings in the 1960s, trips to the Munster final in Thurles to watch the likes of JBM and Ray Cummins in action, or Clones, to meet the McCartans and the O'Neills on Ulster final day. Now we have our own heroes – the whole Dublin team (hurling and football!) – but of course still JBM.'

22

1980s

THE LONGFORD LEADER: EUGENE McGEE

We didn't underestimate Offaly in 1982.
They were just better than we thought.
Pat Spillane

His absence tugs at me like a retreating wave.

One of Longford's most celebrated sons was the late Eugene McGee, who famously managed Offaly to the All-Ireland title in 1982. Although not the most distinguished player of all time, McGee has a unique distinction as a player. He was sent off twice in the one game. He was playing in a club match for UCD and in the first half a player on his side was sent off but gave Eugene's name. In the second half Eugene was sent off himself but was too honest to give anyone else's name – so when the referee checked his report after the match he could not understand how he sent Eugene off twice.

As a manager McGee first came to prominence in club management in the seventies with UCD. Legendary Roscommon footballer Tony McManus had some of his happiest memories in the game during his time in UCD between 1976 and 1980 under McGee's stewardship.

'In 1979 I was captain and Colm O'Rourke was vice-captain. We became good friends. He was tremendously witty and sarcastic. Eugene McGee produced a newsletter about the fortunes of the team, and he named the player who never shut up as the mouth of the team but he added that Colm was a strong contender! O'Rourke is very confident. The only time I ever saw him nervous was when I met him before the All-Ireland semi-final in 2007 when his son Shane was playing. He was never nervous when he played himself but he was that day.

'From our Freshers year Eugene had taken Colm and myself under his wing. He was a complex character but it was very enjoyable working with him. He certainly had a way with him. He commanded respect and had great ideas and was able to communicate them. There were lots of county players around at that time, but he had no qualms about dropping them. Reputations meant nothing to him. You never knew what to expect from him. Days you thought you played well he might lacerate you. Days you thought you didn't play well he would encourage you and compliment you.

'My lasting memory of him came the day we had to play Queens. The night before was the Veterinary Ball and I had gone. The next morning he heard about it and was not happy. He made me travel with him in his car and never said a word to me all the way up to Belfast. In the circumstances I was really keen to do well and I scored 2-3. He said nothing to me after the match. Eventually when all the lads were gone and I was behind waiting for him in the dressing-room to make the journey home he turned to the caretaker and said in his typically gruff accent: "Would you have a jackhammer to widen the door a bit more? This fella's head is so big he won't be able to get out through it."'

McGee continued to be one of the most influential voices in Gaelic football as a pundit. He chaired the GAA's Football Review

Committee, which recommended the introduction of the black card. He was not afraid to take on his critics. When Jim McGuinness challenged the validity of the black card system, McGee replied that McGuinness 'thinks because he won one All-Ireland he is the high priest of football. If he is that good why didn't he win a second or third All-Ireland?'

My abiding memory, though, of Eugene is not of his love of the GAA but of his commitment to those with special needs, giving his support, often hidden from the public eye, to a number of initiatives to secure the care they required.

23

1990s

THE LIFE OF BRIAN: BRIAN LOHAN

What a gift we had from the gods.
Anthony Daly

Brian Lohan should have been called the Postman.

He always delivered for Clare.

He led by his actions and raised the standards of everyone else.

In the 1990s a drinks company sponsored an advertising campaign promoting the game of hurling under the slogan 'Not Men But Giants'. To me the man that embodied this idea more than any other was Clare's full-back at the time, Brian Lohan. It was a time when rumours of the savage intensity of what went on inside the high walls of Clare training sessions had been common currency. Has there ever been a more iconic artefact than Lohan's red helmet as he thundered up the field yet again to turn defence into attack and whip the Banner brigade in the stands into a frenzy? Has there ever been a more inspirational full-back? Was there ever a better full-back?

In 2001 Ger Loughnane predicted that Brian Lohan would go on to manage Clare. In 2019, after a controversial and sometimes turbulent process, he was appointed Clare manager. His first major test as a manager came in the league away to Wexford, managed by his former teammate Davy Fitzgerald. The media went into a frenzy beforehand about whether both men would publicly shake hands afterwards, given the high profile spat between them. There was no grand reconciliation.

Whatever Lohan achieves as an intercounty manager, his place in the annals of Clare hurling is secured because of his achievements as a player: full-back on the All-Ireland-winning teams of 1995 and '97.

TOUGHER THAN THE REST

Ger Loughnane chose to illustrate Lohan's make-up with two snapshots:

'In the All-Ireland semi-final against Galway in 1995 Brian Lohan damaged his hamstring. He was on Joe Cooney and Cooney had got a couple of points off him. I went down to the sideline and looked at him. I did more than look at him, I needn't tell you! He started to hurl out of his skin. Lohan said afterwards, "I saw Loughnane coming down the sideline and decided it was time to start hurling!"

'In the All-Ireland final that year with about 20 minutes to go he pulled a hamstring and he gave a signal. We had built up such an understanding that at any time, whether it was in a dressing-room or out on the field, a look was all it took. There was no need for words most of the time. It was the look, and especially how you sent the look, that sent the message, especially with players like Daly, Seánie [McMahon], Lohan and Doyler [Liam Doyle]. It showed the terrific understanding there was between everybody and that applied with the selectors as well.

'Colm Flynn said to me, "Jesus his hamstring is gone." I replied, "Tell him he's not f**king coming off." I turned my back and walked in the other direction after Lohan called me. Colm went in and broke the news to Brian. No reaction whatsoever. He just got on with it and pretended nothing was wrong with him.

'When you talk about mental toughness, what Lohan did in the All-Ireland, it was out of this world. It would never happen in soccer. If a player pulls his hamstring in soccer, the stretcher is brought in and there's a big exit.

'In the last 20 minutes he used his head, stayed goalside of John Troy and whoever else came on and played away with a torn hamstring. He wasn't able to train for three months afterwards. For those last 20 minutes, he held out by sheer guts. For a Clare player to do that in an All-Ireland final was incredible and said everything about the difference between the team I played on and the team I managed. There's no way I'd have done that when I was playing.

'He got through it by cutting down the angles. It was a measure of his courage and his intelligence. He used his head to survive with a torn hamstring. He was willing to go through the pain barrier because the team needed him to do so.'

Loughnane's other incident also speaks to Lohan's mindset.

'Attention to detail was crucial to our success but I didn't emphasise being spot on time in training. Players get caught in traffic and so on, so laying down strict laws about it was absolutely crazy. The only objection I had to players being late was that they were missing out on the warm-up.

'Attention to detail was most important on the day of champion-ship games. I think no international soccer team planned their day better than we did. The planning depended on where we were. If it was Croke Park most people say ye're 150 miles away, ye have to travel the night before but we never did. We always ensured that the players stayed in their own beds the night before. On Sunday morning we met at 8 a.m. at a hotel in Shannon. I always made a point of almost bouncing out of the car and always gave the message that I was really fresh and had slept very well, even if I hadn't slept at all. Tony Considine would come whistling along and tell a few jokes. Everything was upbeat. You were giving off positive energy straight away. We then got a bus to the airport, where Pat Fitz had everything arranged. There was no checking in. All that was done the night before. The bus took us straight to the plane ramp. Nobody else was allowed to travel on the plane. When the plane landed in Dublin a bus was waiting for us on the runaway and it took us straight away to the hotel. We always had breakfast at 10 a.m.

'Then the players went to bed for two hours. I always had two to a room, with two players who were playing near one another on the pitch like Dalo and Ollie Baker, or an inexperienced player with an experienced one. We usually put an inexperienced forward with Jamesie. It was always a sign of who was going to play if someone was in the room with Jamesie. We'd ask Jamesie when they came down if the other player slept and was all right. This also happened when we went to Cork.

'Lohan and Mike O'Halloran are as close friends as people can be. They always roomed together, but in '98 Hallo didn't make the team. Brian Lohan came to me and said, "Hallo isn't playing. I want to be in the room with somebody who is playing." Lohan will be best man at Hallo's wedding, but this was business. It showed how professional Lohan was.'

LITTLE BROTHER

Loughnane is a contagiously optimistic man. As he talks about some players his face is animated by the genuine joy he derived from his work.

'People say Frank is a totally different person to Brian but he's actually very similar, except his characteristics are not so evident. He's ambitious in the very same way and is even more calculating and ruthless than his big brother. If I was going into battle, Frank would be one of the people I would send for. Frank would do what has to be done. He was blessed with great pace, fantastic vision and an unparalleled instinct for spotting the danger before it comes. He was the perfect corner-back. He was one of the most likable and honourable people you could meet in life. He had a sense of fairness and right, and would never do an injustice to anybody off the field – though he could take out a forward going for goal. If you wanted someone to typify the ideal modern person in Ireland it would be Frank. He was totally ruthless and yet has a great heart.

'The two Lohans are just brilliant men and it was such luck on my part to be there when they were at their prime. They have a typical brothers' relationship. They're seemingly constantly at loggerheads and yet you'd know they'd die for each other. Two of my favourite photos, they're nearly identical, are of the two of them closing in on Johnny Dooley in the All-Ireland final in '95 and on Michael Cleary in the '97 final. When one of them is closing in, you can be sure the other isn't far behind. They had an incredible bond and Hallo was part of that as well.

'Any mistake that would be made in training you'd know it would be Frank that would be blamed for it! Without doubt the most common saying in training was, "For f**k's sake, Frank." Whenever he made a mistake, that's what I'd say to him. Whenever Brian gave away a score, he'd say the same to Frank, only he'd say it with even greater venom than I! Frank would never complain or say anything back.'

As a player Brian Lohan was happy to obey Loughnane. 'We did everything he asked us to do because when we did, we were winning matches and that's what you want from your manager.'

For his part, Loughnane is eager to heap praise on his full-back. 'I know that in the fullness of time Lohan will become a legendary character, even more so than he already is. The characteristics he showed, the nerve for the big occasion, the intelligent play ... I've never seen a full-back like him. In all aspects of his life he's ambitious. He's driven to succeed but he is a totally calm, calculating person. He's good points are too numerous to mention but anyone who's seen him play knows what they are.'

24

2000s

THE COMEBACK KID: KEN McGRATH

The things that used to matter seem so small
When the whole world around you wants to fall.
Michael Duignan

With the intensity of a couple newly in love, Ken McGrath's passion for the Déise set his very soul ablaze.

Ken has known real adversity. The three-times All-Star hurler ran a sports shop in Waterford for four years until, like so many others, the economic crash led to its closure in 2011. But the biggest battle of all was coming down the tracks.

'Every family or every person will have their challenges over their career or their life. I had ten, 15 years playing with Waterford — loved it, loved every minute of it,' recalls the Waterford legend, who played his final championship game for the Déise in 2010.

'The recession hit, and it hit Waterford unbelievably bad. Retail fell off a cliff down in Waterford city and we were probably not in the game long enough to sustain it. The business went. It was a tough couple of years, very tough. We put an awful lot of work into that. Our life and soul went into that for a few years. We knew it was failing in the last year or so, or the last few months, and you're saying, "we'll push on and we'll drive on" the whole time.

'When it didn't succeed, you're nearly embarrassed putting up the closing down signs, or whatever. You know you've failed again in something that you tried to put everything into. It was tough going. It was tough financially as well. But I suppose it all paled into insignificance when the heart problems started arising and started occurring.'

Over so many years for Ken McGrath, the games rushed in against each other until it felt not like a lifetime but a single day shaded in a proliferation of different colours. While he and his wife Dawn were still coming to terms with the financial implications of being forced to close their business, he underwent open heart surgery at the Beacon Hospital in Dublin. In December 2013, Ken — at just 36 years of age — suffered a brain haemorrhage and ended up spending several months at Ardkeen Hospital in Waterford after tests revealed an abnormal valve and infection in his heart. Luckily, he made a full and relatively speedy recovery from the extensive surgery that was required the following April.

'It was hard on me then, but it was much tougher on Dawn, I suppose. She was at home with two kids and trying to work, whereas I was stuck in hospital getting fed every two or three hours, getting antibiotics, no bother. I had an easy enough life just trying to get better. Thankfully I did. The care I got in Waterford and in the Beacon was unbelievable.

'I was in a different place back then than I am now. Thankfully things have turned out for the good. I suppose you don't give up hope. At times when the shop was gone, we were struggling, we were under pressure, but we always felt that things would turn and change for us again.'

Ken is counting his blessings in this sea of strangeness.

'I think if I had let it go any longer, heart failure was my only option. Thanks be to God we got to it in time and the lads dealt with it in Waterford and then up in the Beacon. I'm flying. I'm a new man here. The energy I have is unreal. I was suffering for a few years [and] I didn't really know. I'm probably one of the lucky ones. When you hear stories of young people losing their lives, it would rock you a small bit and it would have you thinking a small bit more about how lucky you are and how much we take life for granted.'

The difficulties for Ken are thankfully in the past. It was like the world had been dim and flat and now suddenly it is in Technicolor 3-D.

'I am working now with my brother Eoin in a coffee business. We were in the right place in the right time. We started the business just as the economic recovery started. People always love coffee! I have two young kids and I am trying to make as much time for them as I can. I am involved in coaching underage teams with the club but that is all I have time for at the moment. Who knows what could happen in the future?'

After Derek McGrath's retirement as Waterford manager the team's fortunes went into decline. Is Ken optimistic? He looks forward to the start of the championship every year filled with possibility and adventure, but not yet sullied by reality. Anything can happen.

'You have to hope. I would like to think we will have our day in the sun again.'

THE FOURTH ESTATE

Since his recovery, Ken has joined the ranks of former stars who have turned to punditry and has climbed the summit as a panelist on *The Sunday Game*. 'After I retired, I drifted from the game a bit. You do lose contact. I love working as a pundit because you have to keep an eye on what it is happening right across the hurling world and it revives the interest. I enjoy the contact it gives me with legends of the games. I keep away from social media most of the time but now and again I use it when I get worked up about some issue in hurling.'

He brings a no-nonsense style to the task. In July 2019, Donal Óg Cusack and Derek McGrath were guests on *The Sunday Game* evening programme. Donal Óg claimed that criticism of the rehearsed defensive styles of Davy Fitz and Derek McGrath – dressed up in charges of 'disrespecting the traditions of the game' – is 'part of the last remnants of British culture on these islands'. He added, 'The British, they founded a lot of games, but they struggled to accept and adapt to the wider influences in their games. What I mean is the long ball to John Bull, Jack Charlton-type spirit. I'm delighted the modern player has moved on.'

Derek McGrath criticised *Sunday Game* panellists for their ignorance of his style of play as Waterford manager, that 'what would be espoused and pontificated from these seats I'm sitting on now is looking like a public forum of self-indulgence'.

Ken McGrath tweeted in response, 'Absolute nonsense. Egos gone out of control.'

25

2010s

CONCERNED CITIZEN: MICHAEL DARRAGH MACAULEY

Team spirit is an illusion you only glimpse when you win.
Steve Archibald

Michael Darragh Macauley has ways of knowing that go beyond science; a way of knowing which can open horizons beyond the world of facts, events and measurable data.

The Dublin star follows the advice of Oscar Wilde: 'Be yourself. Everyone else is taken.' On the field he is known for his bravery. Hence Joe Brolly's description of him: 'He would put his head where you wouldn't put up a crowbar.' In 2019 he was part of the Dublin team that won the historic five-in-a-row.

The 2013 Footballer of the Year is also a man with a strong social conscience. He is an ambassador for Concern Worldwide. His career is based on the empowering work that he does in the north inner city with the North East Inner City Initiative. This initiative reaches out to people in these communities that he describes as 'struggling through a river that people are swimming down and it can be a dangerous river'. His work is trying to give 'branches for these children to cling onto along the river'. Macauley explains that it is good to find role models. He strives, through his work with North East Inner City Initiative, to get as many people on a better road as possible through sustainable projects. It has a huge emphasis on educational programmes. He explains that it is really important when empowering people that, 'You don't just give them shiny things because they don't feel a part of it. Give projects.' For Macauley, he wished for a career that drives him to get up in the morning but, more importantly, one that ensures that he can sleep soundly at night.

AN EDUCATION

Earlier in his career was told to retire at 20 due to an injury which led to a two-year break from football. In that two years, he took an insurance job which taught him that he would never like to work a 9-to-5 desk job again: 'My most vivid memory of my time there was being at the photocopier one day and meeting a man who was 45 and had been with the company for more than half his life at that stage. I remember thinking to myself: "This is not going to be me."'He always got along with kids and wished to be a primary school teacher. His own primary school teacher was somebody who changed 'for the better' the course of his career. So, he went back to college at 21 to study Irish, while at the same time winning the All-Ireland. Sadly, his dad passed away the first year of teacher training. Macauley was working in a school in Tallaght filled with ideologies and 'hoping to change the world'. 'It's easy to be a bad teacher,' he muses, 'but it takes effort and enthusiasm to be a good one.'

In ancient Rome the big question was: *VIis mutare aliquid magis excitando tuum?* Do you wish to change to something more exciting? Macauley had his own version of this question. After his stint in the classroom, he became a sports and engagement manager with the North East Inner City Initiative and got the perfect outlet for his social conscience.

SHOW SOME CONCERN

As a Concern ambassador, Michael Darragh brought joy to Syrian refugees during an eye-opening visit to war-torn Iraq. There he met families who had only just become refugees after airstrikes by Syrian government and Russian forces killed 20 civilians. Macauley recalls the plight of young Syrian refugees:

'It's heart-breaking to hear their story and, unfortunately, their story is ten-a-penny over there. People have been hearing about the Syrian crisis for ten years now and I don't think they are really reacting to it at all. I'm just trying to raise awareness that these kids were just like kids anywhere in Ireland. They need our help.'

He told the heart-breaking story of one of the families he met to illustrate the bigger story. 'The family spent their last five years kept in captivity by a well-known terrorist organisation. These are ten-year-old and 15-year-old boys who grew up like that. Their father has been missing for five years. They have one meal a day. They're sleeping in one blanket in the heart of the winters.'

The refugee camps he visited had extremely limited educational and recreational facilities, but the children still managed to recruit the Dubliner into leading some much-needed sports activities. The excited children were thrilled as the Ballyboden man played football, volleyball and other games with them. The sun shone down on the games – but this good weather was not set to last for long. Within days, heavy rain fell and lasted for the next four months.

Concern Worldwide chief Dominic MacSorley praised the footballer for using his platform and influence to spotlight the most vulnerable people around the world. He said: 'Michael Darragh has gone above and beyond to support us since he became ambassador in 2018. From generously donating a pair of his All-Ireland final-winning boots to meeting people in some of the world's most hard-to-reach places, he has always been willing to help. Michael has shown he is not only a champion on the pitch, but he is also a champion for those in the greatest need too.'

In the Barderash camp, where 14,000 refugees were living, Macauley and Concern employees watched mothers and children queueing for kerosene and blankets that would help them survive the upcoming winter. The Dublin star highlighted the hardships and challenges these young people faced on a daily basis, despite the brief moments of reprieve they had during his visit. He has also urged the Irish public to help the struggling people he met and the thousands of others who are also based in camps around Iraq.

As he watched this tableau of terror and horror unfold, Macauley felt that keeping aloof ultimately involved complicity. If he was not part of the solution, they would be part of the problem. Characteristically he did not allow himself the luxury of simply wallowing in moral indignation. As always, he sought a practical response recognising that those in the court of suffering required specific assistance.

In his song *Anthem*, Leonard Cohen describes 'a crack' that 'lets the light in'. In this place of abject, back-breaking, gut-wrenching neglect Macauley and the Concern staff were those cracks that let the light in. The code of their humanity was that not even great deprivation can shackle the human spirit. His is an approach akin to the community development model in the developing world pioneered by Paolo Freire, whose experiences in Latin America made him acutely aware of the attitudes of the would-be 'helpers' upon those who were seen to be in need of 'help'.

Many children are neglected with no hope of ever gaining a proper job. Macauley desperately wants to teach them the skills that will increase their chances of securing employment and give them the opportunity to become self-reliant. Theirs is a lost childhood and their only hope is the opportunity to go to school. He endeavoured to help the children to grow and to recognise their potential, and to offer the children in his care the opportunity to become self-respecting, self-reliant adults, capable of effecting positive change in society.

Macauley's strategy is very much one of empowerment. He is the personification of an old ideal:

> Go with the people
> Live with them
> Learn from them
> Love them
> Start with what they know
> Build with what they have
> But with the best leaders
> When the work is done
> The task accomplished
> The people will say
> 'We have done this ourselves.'
> (Lao Tzu, China, 601–531 BC)

Macauley's mission with Concern strikingly dramatises the poverty of the modern world, perilously ruled by self-interest and economic power. His power is in the capacity to stir our resolve and strengthen the collective will to change. He never doubts that a small group of committed people with ideas and vision can change the world. Why? It is the only thing that ever has. He embodies what is best in humanity because he lives by the motto that giving, in its purest form, expects nothing in return.

PART IV
The Big Issues

In June 2020 after the horrific death of George Floyd, the Black Lives Matter movement gripped the world. Former Dublin great Jason Sherlock reminded the Irish public that racism was also an issue in Irish society as a whole and the world of Gaelic Games in particular.

After Galway beat Waterford in the 2017 All-Ireland hurling final Conor Whelan, a cousin and teammate of the late Niall Donohue and 2017's Young Hurler of the Year, held a flag with Donohue's name on it minutes after the final whistle sounded in Croke Park. Under it lay the quotation, 'There are three things that we cry about in life; things that are lost, things that are found and things that are magnificent.'

Connotations of pride, resilience and strength make admitting vulnerability difficult. Donohue's clubmates described him as a player that teammates grew taller and brighter around, yet Donohue felt shrinking and dark. Learning from Donohue's parting allows us to use sport to find those who are lost. GAA stars like Aisling Thompson discussing their mental health battles allows others to appreciate that even the most powerful can feel powerless. The GAA helps the heartbroken find solace, and for Gaelic Games to have this ability is truly magnificent. It gives members a sense of purpose, the support of a community, an opportunity to come together, and a link with generations past.

Nelson Mandela praised sport's unique power to bring hope and peace where before there was only despair. The 2017 All-Ireland gave Galway a chance to honour those like Niall Donohue, provoked by sport to remember times of raw joy and emotion with those no longer with us, but Donohue's life gave these players perspective; a realisation that life's magnificence lies in relationships, health and happiness and although sport can enable these, it should never surpass them.

In the past the GAA was all about the games, but in recent years players have come to the forefront of the national debate about a proliferation of important social issues. They have given great leadership and have ushered in a new chapter in the GAA's evolution as a national movement. In this way they honour the Association and energise the nation. This section considers some of them.

26

YOU'VE GOT TO SEARCH FOR THE HERO INSIDE YOURSELF: MARK ROHAN

Character is doing the right thing even if nobody is watching.
Eugene McGee

Sport is agony and ecstasy. It does not lend itself to grey areas. A number of sports personalities have experienced first hand the 'slings and arrows of outrageous fortune' and discovered just how quickly glory becomes anguish. Fate is not kind. Mark Rohan is Irish Paralympic royalty but in a previous life had played under-21 football for Westmeath and was a noted soccer player. When I visited him in his home in Ballinahown he told me how his life was changed forever in November 2001.

'I was on the way to a soccer match on a Sunday morning and I lost control of the motorbike coming up the hill and ended up hitting a tree in the ditch. As a result, I am paralysed and have lost all movement and sensation from underneath the arms. I broke four bones in my back and other bones in my shoulders and ribs.'

News of his injury cut a swathe of desolation among GAA fans everywhere. This is a side of sport and life that can only make you wince. It is adversity which proves the true testing ground of heroic status, as only a true hero can smile through a vale of tears. Mark had to face a huge psychological adjustment.

'Immediately after the accident I went to the Mater Hospital for ten days. I suppose at the time everyone was telling me "you'll get the power back" but after that I went to the National Rehabilitation Centre in Dun Laoire and that's when it started to sink in.

'At the start I was getting a lot of infections. After seven weeks they let me home for Christmas. It gave me a hope. One of the things about being in Dun Laoire was that although I knew I was unlucky to be there I was lucky in comparison with so many others. I was lucky to have my hands. There's always a lot of people worse off than you.

'In January I started getting back to physio and learning how to dress myself and learn things like bladder care and bowel care and that was the start of it. I spent six months there, with occupational therapy every day and learning things like pushing a wheelchair down the road and managing to cross it and noticing things that able-bodied people don't generally notice and getting used to that.'

Mark presents a brave face to the outside world. What is striking is the contrast between his language and his content: a cheerful voice relating a story of extreme pain. Any despair his story might generate is relieved by the spunk of the narrator. There is also a deep gratitude that his brush with mortality did not deny him the opportunity to finish off important business, the rest of his life.

YES, WE CAN

Mark has embraced a 'can-do' philosophy.

'I always set myself a goal. After spending six weeks in bed I was looking forward just to getting up, even it was only in a wheelchair. Then I was looking forward to coming home for good and then getting back into the swing of things. I suppose if you dwell on things too much you'd get down but you always have a goal to aim for and that gave me a focus. You can't really get down because that stops you from moving on.'

Mark has been fortunate in one respect.

'My friends were brilliant. For a period of about four months there was someone in to see me every night: either friends or my parents and that was great. The big thing, though, was that they didn't look on me any differently than before the accident.

'There is so much work to be done for disabled people. For a person confined to a wheelchair like me it was almost impossible to gain access to a lot of places unless they have been built in the last few years. When I take a trip around Athlone on the wheelchair, there are very few places which cater adequately for the disabled or those confined to wheelchairs. Places of entertainment are very important for all sections of the community. We all need to get out and enjoy ourselves, and yet again, when I think of all of the entertainment spots in Athlone, few of them cater for wheelchairs. Being disabled or confined to a wheelchair does not mean one loses appreciation of entertainment, but when the facilities are not there, it's hard.'

Another recurring source of irritation to him is the failure of footpaths to encourage disabled people out.

'There was so much talk a few years ago about integrating the disabled. Yet, so little appears to have been done and it is only when one is sitting confined to a wheelchair that the truth hits home about the lack of progress in this area. I was very lucky insofar as my family lived in a bungalow with doors wide enough for the wheelchair. Most people in towns live in two-storey houses and are not so fortunate.'

Mark presents a brave face to the outside world, though the determination in his personality is a strong suit. What is striking is the contrast between his language and his content: a cheerful voice relating a story of obstacles and disappointment. Nowhere is the truth of Hugh McIlvanney's observation more apparent: 'Sport, at its finest, is often poignant, if only because it is almost a caricature of the ephemerality of human achievements.' Any despair his story might generate is relieved by the spunk of the narrator.

'I can't make any sense of what has happened to me, though people speak about God working in mysterious ways. I am reluctant to give advice to people who are disabled because every disability is different, and every spinal injury is different. What keeps me going is that I know I am lucky to be alive. What I would say to anyone who is confronted with adversity of any kind is to keep their head up and have goals to aim for.'

27

THE CLASH OF THE ASH:
TIM MAHER

The GAA is who we are.
John O'Mahony

Accessing vast experience and wisdom, Tim Maher's world is amplified to patterns and echoes from more distant horizons.

Hurling is woven into Irish history. The roar of the crowds, the whirr of the flying sliotar and the unmistakable and unique sound of the ash against ash has enthralled sport fans for decades. However, in recent years hurling has spawned a fast-growing game in the world of disabled sports: wheelchair hurling. The man behind this new game is Tim Maher.

'As principal of the school attached to St Mary's Hospital in Baldoyle, I introduced wheelchair hurling as part of the PE programme. I got the idea when I saw the students playing a lot of games with a ball and rackets. I decided it would be worth experimenting to see what would happen if we substituted hurleys for rackets. When I first suggested the idea, a number of people thought I was going a bit soft in the head, but I was determined to give it a go. Obviously, I was keen to modify the game slightly so that there was no safety risk to the students.

'The game took off and is [still] going from strength to strength. We started it off just in the school here but then the idea spread, and we started interschool competitions. We held a blitz which featured six schools: Ballinteer Community School; ourselves; CRC Clontarf; Enable Ireland, Sandymount; Marino School, Bray and Scoil Mochua, Clondalkin. Both boys and girls play the game as equals.

'I think Joe Canning himself would be impressed by the skills evident in this game. It is also noticeable that it is great for developing the students' co-ordination.

'There are so many benefits to the game. The most obvious one is that the pupils get great fun and enjoyment out of it. They also learn a lot about teamwork. Now that there is a competitive outlet to the game, they also learn about winning and, equally importantly, about losing.'

28

GLORY DAZE: KATIE LISTON

All that we love deeply becomes part of us.
Helen Keller

In life, too often the urgent trumps the important.

But not for one woman.

As one of the greatest Kerry footballers of all time, Katie Liston's place in the GAA annals is assured. Because of her surname she was constantly asked if she was related to the 'Bomber'. When opponents asked her in her playing days she always told them she was because she felt it gave her a psychological advantage. The reality was otherwise.

However, now as a lecturer in the Sociology of Sport at the University of Ulster, her extensive research has helped put the issue of concussion on the agenda in the GAA and beyond.

The media can assert huge amounts of pressure on sports stars in today's world. With social media now ingrained in society, it is impossible to hide from the headlines or the taunts of the public.

Joe Canning gives a telling illustration of the pressures on players today: 'There is a massive difference between winning and losing.' He went on to explain that even losing by a point can have you portrayed as a villain in the papers and that 'perspective is often lost'.

The fans and journalists can lose sight of the fact that the players tried their best and are hurting the most inside. Defeat is a hard pill to swallow and even harder when it seems everyone is against you. In order to prevent this from happening, Joe attempts to perform to an exceptional level every game in order to 'shut them up' and has had to do so from a young age. This can be seen as motivation or a system that forces athletes to try to perform to unachievable standards week in, week out.

YOU DON'T KNOW JACK

Katie Liston talks of how Olympic athletes were beaten with sticks if their performance was deemed insufficient. Take Jack Wilshire, for example. He was thrust into a senior professional scene at Arsenal at just 16, exposing him to all kinds of new challenges, such as tougher opponents and mass attention from the media. It is instances like these that prove athletes must be nurtured in a way to aid their well-being and maximise growth in all aspects of life.

Katie Liston points out the existential crises at the heart of the concussion crises: competitive sport involves an active process of socialising into a culture which normalises pain and injury. Pain is a daily cost of being an athlete and only once this pain fully inhibits your ability to play is it an injury.

What Katie incisively exposes in many ways is the social issue of a 'man up' culture which has festered itself in sports such as NFL, rugby, and increasingly Gaelic football and hurling. Katie quite rightly points out the fact that the only other field apart from the playing field where such machoism would be celebrated is the war field. Think of the under-ten coaches telling the star forward to 'play on and see how you go'. The Irish tendency to say 'I'll be grand' combined with the negative stigma surrounding those who discuss their injuries creates a vulnerable environment for someone who is suffering concussion. We label players as 'soft' when they sit out due to injury and make heroes of those who play through extreme and risky pain.

Liston promotes changes in the law, education, research and management to help tackle this issue. The necessary change is a change in attitude. Education provokes players and coaches to take a more holistic view.

Katie has documented that concussion is a frequent injury, but many of us do not realise how serious an injury it is. Concussion is 'velocity brain shaking'. Liston condemns the poor duty of care shown by managers of sports teams who do not take the injury seriously enough. There is a clear relationship between competitive sport and health. There is a paradox in competitive sport relating to health and this is something that must be addressed. Liston states that there is a sense of 'play on', 'we need you', when it comes to sports. It is second nature to sportspeople to be told that they must play on after suffering a concussion. Concussion can seriously affect the player and if not dealt with in a correct manner, the player can suffer life threatening injuries.

MIGHTY MANNION

Former Roscommon footballer Karol Mannion is one of the few players who have courageously gone public about his experiences with concussion. He listed the effects: brain function problems, headaches, concentration problems, memory problems, among others. Some of the more serious side-effects include slurred speech, ringing in the ears, fatigue. Concussion is not an injury that is to be taken lightly. It is a serious problem that coaches and managers need to deal with better. It is no longer acceptable to encourage their players to overcome the pain and continue playing. Concussion poses many health risks that managers need to be made more aware of. Ethically it is wrong to put pressure on our sports stars to perform after having suffered a serious head injury. Liston comments that 'the balance between performance and health is less than even'. Concussion camouflages its location: the brain, one of the most important organs. We must not pressurise our players to accept unnecessary risks to their health. We have pushed the limits enough when it comes to ethics and duty of care.

In sport, a player is only deemed injured when they can no longer play. If you complain, you are often given the nickname 'Sick Note', as Spurs' Darren Anderton and Arsenal's Abou Diaby experienced. A lot of the time it is only when the injury is obvious that people will accept your desire to stop and offer you genuine help.

With concussion it can be more difficult to detect the true extent of the damage. Katie Liston describes brain injuries as 'invisible'. Her case studies highlight the anxiety players face due to their concussion damage sustained from sport. She describes it as being 'drunk and hungover at the same time'. However, because they did not need a wheelchair or a cast, people often thought they were fine. Katie Liston leads the way not only in the GAA but in society at large in raising awareness about concussion.

29

KNOW WHEN TO FOLD THEM: OISIN McCONVILLE

Do not overlook tiny good actions, thinking they are of no benefit; even tiny drops of water in the end will fill a huge vessel.

Buddha

Oisin McConville is no stranger to burdens. There was time when a host of invisible demons was beating him with rods of fire. That is his past, not his present.

Sport is an escape for so many people and for Oisin McConville it was no different. Submersing ourselves in sport provides escapism. Growing up in a nationalist Northern Irish village in the 1970s, McConville recollects that football provided an escape from the Troubles. The GAA was radicalised in times of conflict as a key weapon of cultural nationalism, therefore arguably the GAA was more of a wing of the conflict than an escape from it. Oisin describes himself, as a young boy, as being very scared of the violence around him and in order to remove himself from the fear of day to day life, he threw himself into sport.

The Armagh legend shook the GAA public when he first spoke of the escalation of his gambling addiction from recreational to the pathological. He used teammates and family for money. He moved bookmakers and concealed his emotions to avoid exposure. He was far from self-fulfilled despite the honour others bestowed onto him. A prominent feature of a successful athlete is their proud nature, upheld by others for their strength and achievements. The surge and normalisation of online gambling mean it is an addiction that a teenager could pursue in a classroom.

McConville began his gambling addiction at the age of 17, at which point he was visiting the local bookies at Crossmaglen three times a week, and by the time he was 18 he was gambling every day. Oisin describes the bookies in those days as 'a smoke-filled room at the back of a pub'. He aspired to be like the 'high rollers' who gambled there, as he naively believed it was an easy way to make quick money. As years went by, his addiction got worse. He admits that the only place where he felt in control was on the football pitch and in the bookies. In today's society the rise of online gambling apps has led to problems of addiction and over-spending, particularly among young people. There are numerous reasons for the rapid increase in gambling options: the creation of new technologies has provided a global platform for internet-based gambling, the ease with which gambling can be used as a source of income and the lack of gambling laws in Ireland. There is no doubt that the greater exposure and accessibility ensure young people have access to gambling products and betting apps which significantly increases the prevalence and risk of addiction.

McConville describes himself as a people pleaser. Because he owed so much money, he became paranoid and suffered from social anxiety. He wanted to portray to the outside world that he was still the cock of the walk, that he had everything going well for him. He did not want people to discover how he was truly

© Ray McManus/SPORTSFILE

GONE TOO SOON
Roscommon players link arms after the tragic loss of Ger Michael Grogan in 2002.

GOING FOR GLORY Harry Minogue ensures that the next
generation of GAA fans will have a smooth passage.

© Shane Minogue

QUEEN OF THE ASH Kilkenny legend Ann Downey patrols the sideline.

CATCH OF THE DAY Kieran Donaghy soars over Kildare's Mick O'Grady.

MY BALL Kilkenny's Huw Lawlor climbs higher than Tipperary's Séamus Callanan.

IT'S A LONG WAY TO LEITRIM! Zak Moradi has travelled far to star for Leitrim.

© INPHO/Donall Farmer

THE LIFE OF BRIAN Clare's talisman Brian Lohan in characteristic pose.
Here making life difficult for Offaly's Joe Brady.

THE KEYS TO THE KINGDOM
Tommy Walsh launches another
Kerry attack.

THE BOY IN BLUE
Michael Darragh Macauley goes for goal.

© INPHO/Bryan Keane

© INPHO/Ryan Byrne

© INPHO/Donall Farmer

SUPERMAC Oisín McConville lines up another score for Crossmaglen
despite the efforts of Garrycastle's Enda Mulvihill.

BRILLIANT BERNARD
Bernard Flynn evades Cork's Tony Davis in the 1987 All-Ireland final.

© INPHO/James Meehan

MAYO'S MENACING FORWARD
Martin Carney seeks a pass.

TUAM STAR Ja Fallon attempts to escape Meath's
Caoimhin King and Anthony Moyles.

THE MAESTRO Mick O'Dwyer gives his Wicklow team
a rousing pep talk before they face Cavan in 2010.

FERMANAGH FACE FOES
Pete McGrath instructs his
Fermanagh charges in 2010.

TAKE MY POINT
Ciarán Barr gives the instructions in
the Leinster under-21 semi-final.

FOR THE PRIDE OF THE PARISH
Karol Mannion is goalbound as Western Gaels' Dermot McGarry fears the worst.

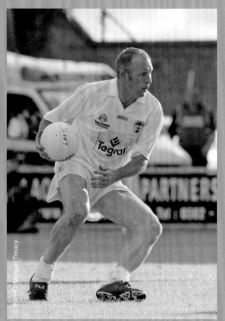

© INPHO/Morgan Treacy

© INPHO/James Crombie

THE STRIFE OF RYAN
Kildare Immortal Glenn Ryan in defiant mode.

THE LYNCH-PIN
Limerick's Cian Lynch drives the Shannonsiders forward.

MIGHTY MACS
Waterford's Ken McGrath leaves Cork's Niall McCarthy in his wake.

© INPHO/Cathal Noonan

© INPHO/Cathal Noonan

THE PURPLE AND GOLD
Wexford's Ursula Jacob gives it a lash.

© INPHO/James Crombie

MURPHY'S LAW
The peerless Juliet Murphy takes the fight to Monaghan.

ARE YOU RIGHT THERE MICHAEL?
Michael Murphy claims the ball from Meath's Padraic Harnan.

SIMPLY THE BEST
Offaly's extraordinary forward Matt Connor glides through the Longford defence.

© INPHO/Oisin Keniry

© INPHO/Billy Stickland

feeling; that behind closed doors, his life was falling apart. Not only was his addiction losing him money but also friendships, relationships, self-respect, self-esteem and integrity.

During this time his main focus was on how he was going to get money to place his next bet and how he was going to pay back the loan sharks. McConville acknowledges how he belonged on the football pitch; it was a place where he could express himself and was valued. However, in the outside world he believed he was worthless. Sport gave McConville the framework to become one of the football greats of our time, winning the All-Ireland Senior football championship against Kerry in 2002 and putting in a classy performance while knowing at the back of his mind that he was drowning in debt.

'I would always stay on the pitch because I knew once I left I would gamble again,' he recalls. A call-up to your county squad is an honour for anyone, but he saw it as a mask, that he would be seen as 'Oisin the footballer' and not the gambler. On the pitch he had self-control, discipline, fulfilment and comradery, the very virtues he sought off the pitch when he was consumed by a vice provoking addiction. Although GAA provided solace and structure, it also provided a mask and purpose to hide behind, potentially preventing him from addressing his issues sooner.

In 2005, McConville went into treatment for 13 weeks and he describes it as the best 13 weeks of his life. One of the people who helped him on the journey was Sr Consilo Fitzgerald, who in 2003 pipped Tom Crean and Mick O'Dwyer in Radio Kerry's listeners' pole of the Greatest Kerry Person of all time because of her lifelong commitment to those with addiction. Initially Oisin was troubled that he would struggle with the religious and spiritual dimension of her service. She put him at his ease with her comment, 'Religion is for people who don't want to go to hell. Spirituality is for people who have been to hell and back.'

He recalls how during this time his coaches lacked emotional empathy and support for his mental health issues and instead questioned him about when he would be back training. His managers had no interest in the underlying cause of his problems.

To compound his problems he discovered that a betting company, Bar One Racing, were sponsoring his club side Crossmaglen. McConville declares how difficult this was for him, how his only escape from his addiction, the club team, was now collaborating with the industry which created his demons. This forced him to make a very difficult decision of whether to continue to wear the jersey or to turn away from football completely. Ultimately he decided that, for his own mental health, he should remain playing even if he did not agree with what the club and its sponsor were representing. In 2018 the GAA, at its annual congress, banned betting companies from sponsoring any of its teams.

McConville states that team sport participants are three times more vulnerable to gambling addictions. Sport's link to gambling is not a recent phenomenon. Even before the birth of Christ, the Romans were betting on chariot races. Immediacy and unpredictability are what make sport captivating, however these features are synonymous with gambling. Sport provides an outlet for adrenaline seekers in a confined area with rules, but does sport give individuals a competitive, invincible and addictive personality that can be destructive in other areas of life? McConville explained how from a young age his status as a sporting star on the corridors at Saint Patrick's Armagh fuelled this sense of indestructability.

He praises today's more holistic coaches, with 99 per cent of GAA clubs having a health and welfare officer, with welfare officers like McConville himself at the forefront of the GAA's new drive to tackle mental health and addiction head on.

DISTANT SHORES

In 2019 Oisin McConville travelled to Gaza and the West Bank with Trócaire.

'I suppose it might be unfair to make a direct comparison to what was going on in Cross, but there's loads of similarities. I would feel that growing up in the era I grew up in, it was just the norm. I suppose the norm was bombs and shootings and killings, the windows being blown in, all that sort of stuff. I didn't realise that wasn't the norm until I was 11. I definitely think it had a profound effect on me at some stages.' On this cliff edge of adventure, he travelled to the Occupied Palestinian Territories with Trócaire to highlight their Christmas Appeal, which helped to support families who are living in conflict zones around the world.

'It was what I expected and maybe just another little layer on top of it. Some of the things that were actually quite nice about it, the kids are so happy, they don't know any different.

'I remember we were driving to a family that had lost seven members in an attack. When we pulled up outside, there were four, five, six kids playing marbles on the street and, honestly, they were oblivious to the cars. The cars had to avoid them. I remember playing football in the road and when the traffic came you pulled back and the car goes past. But there's something very innocent about the way they were going on. Those kids seemed to be, on the face of it, very, very happy but the reality for a lot of them is much worse than that.

'I probably come back feeling a lot more politically about it than I had done. These guys can hardly walk 100 metres and there's somebody harassing them. We went up into the hills, there was a Palestinian family who had got their land back through a lawyer that is being helped by Trócaire. She had got the land back, but they were all going up to show us that there was settlements there, and there was an outpost

– so basically they were putting down caravans or tents or whatever so that the next thing is to start building on it.' The harassment that the locals were subject to had echoes of his own experiences when travelling to Armagh training in the 1990s, with a proliferation of checkpoints on the way.

'Everyone was collected at Cross at half six, and we would have been in Lurgan at half seven. We left Cross one day and we were stopped six times on the way because they knew what the route was. When they took the bags out of the car, they threw on the ground what was [in them], they didn't put the stuff back in the car. We arrived at quarter to 10, we had a cup of tea and we went home again.'

30

HARD TIMES: BERNARD FLYNN

Even in our sleep, pain which cannot forget
falls drop by drop upon the heart
until, in our own despair, against our will,
comes wisdom through the awful grace of God.
                                        Aeschylus

Coffee as strong and black as sin were called for because of the radical change in Bernard Flynn's circumstances.

Increasingly it seems that the GAA personalities of today live by the motto that while silence may often be misinterpreted it can never be misquoted. Bernard Flynn is cast in a different mould. He knows the secrets of pain. Although he carries many physical scars from his efforts on the pitch, the mental toughness he acquired playing for Meath would equip him with the emotional resources to face the big battles off it.

TIME TO SAY GOODBYE
Injuries would eventually take their toll.

'I had a lot of injuries and I retired from the county in 1995 and the club in 1998. My knee had been severed. I had arthritis. I was getting cortisone injections – some that Seán Boylan knew about but many that he didn't. I always felt I needed to do more to be sure of holding my place on the team.'

As a defence mechanism against this insecurity, Flynn overdid things and would pay a high price in later life. But then, answering questions that others would rather were not asked, he dragged up some hidden reserves of energy and determination to begin again like a surfer hitting a good wave.

'In 1990 I went to Australia with Eugene McGee to play in the Compromise Rules series. I had a dozen or so pain-killing injections on that trip. In 1995, I was getting an injection a week or at least every second week. There was somebody I was using that Seán knew nothing about because I was afraid of my living life of losing my place. Apart from the injections I was also shovelling tablets. I was always looking over my shoulder with Seán and Pat Reynolds in particular. I have massive respect for them, and we got on great, but I think I mightn't have been their type of player. I genuinely felt that if they got the chance, they were going to drop me. That kept me on my toes, but it probably knocked my confidence a few times and maybe I held back a bit more than I should have, but I have to take responsibility for that because it was up to me to sort it out. We had so many great players – Mattie McCabe, Liam Smith and Finian Murtagh – who were waiting to take my place.'

Eventually Flynn's creaking body was telling him loudly that he could no longer be reckless with his long-term health.

'I went to the former Dublin great Dr Pat O'Neill – Gerry McEntee arranged it for me – and Pat told me very starkly that if I continued doing what I was doing I would be in a wheelchair before I was 50. I think Seán was a bit miffed that I went to Pat without consulting him first because he thought he could have managed my condition using herbal medicine. I suffered a number of bad years after that.

My whole knee was cut in half and, although it was reconstructed, I was never the same again. I got a hip replacement and, although it was not a complete success, it has helped. The killing part was that just a year after I retired, Seán won the All-Ireland again with a new Meath team. To miss out on that was heart-breaking. It was Seán's greatest achievement, winning that All-Ireland with a new team, especially as, with all due respect, he did not have the glut of star players that Mick O'Dwyer had. It was unbelievable what he achieved with some of those players. The one thing I do regret is that I didn't mind myself.'

TAKE CARE OF BUSINESS, MR BUSINESSMAN

Flynn would face his most severe character test away from the intimacy of the Meath dressing-room. Post intercounty football he decided it was time to make things happen.

'I got a poor to average Leaving Cert but I had the drive within me to make a go of myself. I went into business with Michael Dempsey, who had been manager of the Laois hurling team for years before becoming Brian Cody's right-hand man. He was my best man and is my daughter's godfather.'

In business, Flynn went all out.

'We went into the pub and night club business in Laois and what I made through that allowed me to start my interior decor business in Mullingar. I gave up my good job after talking with my wife Madeline. We both wanted a fresh start. We met in a night club when I was in my late teens. She thought I was the most horrible man she had ever met. She genuinely didn't like me, but I pursued her 'till she did.'

GREAT EXPECTATIONS

Flynn's new venture began with high hopes and for a decade it looked as if no dream was too big.

'I always had an entrepreneurial mind. In 1995 I bought my first property, and until the crash in 2009 I developed a good portfolio and a really good business model. I would work in my retail business by day and in the evening with my own hands would literally rip them apart. The value was in doing them up myself and then I would lease them out, and I built up a substantial rent portfolio of around a million a year while still running the retail business.

'I had no mortgage. I was proud to buy my own home for cash in 1999, a house my wife loved. There was plenty of equity as the bank valuation confirmed. When the crash started, I didn't get out in time. I put up my last few properties I bought in 2005, 2006 and 2007 with which I put up my family home as a guarantee and that was my big mistake. The bank called in their loans in 2010. My wife really rolled up her sleeves but there were three terrible years between 2009 and 2011.'

The financial problem morphed into a series of legal problems.

'I had 24 legal cases from small ones to big ones pending at one stage. Myself and Madeline opened up the sitting room and we got files left, right and centre out. We had faced losing everything overnight. We would spend three or four hours a night, five nights a week, on paperwork when the kids were gone to bed. It was a nightmare. It took its toll. People were saying that I looked terribly bad, but I am a very resilient person and had to be strong.

'In 2010 they put in the receivers. It was when I got my hip replacement. My life was wiped and finished and, to add to everything, my retail business was gone as well. I was owed a fortune and couldn't carry it. My back was to the wall and it was very traumatic. I went into some dark corners and it was hard to come out of them. My wife, Madeline, is a very strong woman and that is the only thing that saved me.

'I had no background in college. I had no one to mentor me. Everything was on my own, but I built a good business working with the bank. I have to hold my hand up and say I made mistakes but everything I did I ran it by the bank first and we did this together. Did I borrow money? Yes. Did I take a chance in business? Yes. I also employed ten or 12 people in my retail business, and I reckon I spent over a million in sub-contractors in the local area on renovations for my business.

'The biggest resentment I have is that the bank sold all the properties I had worked so hard on. I had lost everything and all I asked the bank was they would share in the mistake we had both made but they wouldn't do that.'

Flynn was caught up in a frazzle of anxiety.

'I didn't sleep much for two or three years because I would get up in the middle of the night and work on strategies to try and claw my way out of the hole I was in. At one stage I told Madeline and my parents that I was thinking of moving my family abroad for a fresh start.

'The darkest days were spent trying to cope with the debts. I spent a quarter of a million on legal fees till I could pay no more. Now Madeline and I run our own cases. We've got the debt down. I had a wife and three young kids to provide for. My attitude was: do I lie down and die, or do I fight back? I wasn't as mentally strong as a player for Meath as I should have been but living with those great men made me mentally strong.

'I had no degree and I was unemployable. I had never gone to college because at that stage I only had one ambition, which was to play senior football for Meath. The only thing that put food on the table was that I did some media work. Every euro that came in was so important. I did some coaching with Nobber because the late Shane McEntee asked me and then with Westmeath at under-age level and later with Mullingar Shamrocks, but I never charged a penny for any of them. Now the big challenge is to try and save my house.'

IN THE EYE OF THE STORM

There is a strong undercurrent of anger in his voice, though, as he describes the way the financial community has effectively washed its hands of the mess it had some responsibility for creating. Even at the start of his business career he had some memorable clashes with the banks.

'I remember a bank manager in 1994. I was overtrading and my business was going badly. He was overbearing, arrogant and disrespectful. He treated me like dirt and spoke to me in a very derogatory way and was refusing to support me. I grabbed him by the throat and pulled him across the table. I opened up an account elsewhere.'

Like an alien from outer space Flynn and his wife Madeline would have to try and navigate themselves into a whole new world. It was then that the mental toughness nurtured in Meath training sessions in Bettystown really kicked in.

'The first time in commercial court was hard. When the tsunami came and took everything, I wasn't siphoning off my money to the Cayman Islands. Did I think of doing something stupid? It would have flickered through my head. Have I stopped others from buying a rope? Yes.'

A NEW SHOPPING LIST

It would have been easy for him to feel overwhelmed. This quiet, peaceful corner was home to tens of thousands who were trying to pick themselves from the mangled wreck of the Celtic tiger. There were many moments of indignity on the way.

'I was in with the bank at a time when I was in a bad place. My wife had sold her jeep and I had sold my car to make a few bob, and was hanging on by the fingertips. A junior official came in and he insulted me. He asked me how I spent my money down to the last euro. This cheeky pup was telling me I had to cut back on bread, milk and meat. It was the way that he spoke to me that really made me want to bust him, but I knew it would cost me and I'd end up in court. So, I tried a different tack and asked him how he spent his money. When he wouldn't, I pushed and said: "I have told you everything about how I spend my money, now you tell me how much you earn and how you spend it." But he wouldn't and was so dismissive of me. Eventually I was allowed enough to live on and to provide the basics for my wife and kids.

'That was the bleakest point of all. I will never forget walking out of that meeting because I had never felt so low. I was making every effort to tighten up and I had no problem with the idea but to humiliate me in that way was, it seemed, the way of all the banks at the time.'

WITH A LACK OF A LITTLE HELP FROM MY FRIENDS

Murky memories scamper through the mists of his recent past. The code of loyalty he acquired with Meath would come back to bite his ass in financial terms.

'I could have finished a close friend's career if I disclosed some of his activities in some of my business dealings. My barrister told me if I was to do that, I could have won the case. Against all advice I didn't because the person would have lost his pension and possibly his job. I thought so highly of this person. I just couldn't do it. I was loyal to a fault even though I knew it would cost me a lot in a time when I couldn't afford to be losing money. He held on to his job and his pension but I was very disappointed in his attitude thereafter. It hurt a lot.

'When I had money, I gave it to friends. The big thing I learned was who my friends were. There were a few people who really disappointed me but that's life.'

INSPIRATION FOR ALL SEASONS

The turning point was poignant, powerful and permanent.

'Jim Stynes became a close friend of mine when I went to Australia with the Compromise Rules in 1990. I knew he was dying, and I wanted to see him when I was right in the middle of my own crisis. A great friend of mine, Freddie Grehan, paid for myself and my son Billy to fly to Australia in December 2011. Jim and his family had probably spent 17 out of the previous 20 Christmases with us. I can't adequately explain what I got out of that trip. It was life changing. He was very frail and had lost his peripheral vision and was broken into pieces in many ways. He cried and was a bit emotional as he hugged me. We went to a restaurant, but he couldn't eat. He just sipped a whiskey. He kind of broke down and opened up about all the things he was going to miss out on, like seeing his kids growing up. As I said goodbye he wrote a little note for me on a jersey and gave it to me. I have no pictures in my house of my football career but the one thing I have hung up is that jersey. When things were bad, I just looked up at the jersey and his note. I had been struggling a bit, but all of a sudden my problems seemed minor. After I came back from Australia, I was a new man and nothing fazed me.

'I mind myself better, have a great family and am in a good place except financially. As Jim Stynes said to me: "It's only f**king money, Flynner."'

A HELPING HAND

Given the amount of pressure Flynn and his family have been under, he would have been forgiven for becoming insular. Behind the scenes, though, he has been working busily but quietly in the corner of the world where there are no cameras, no press and there is no appearance fee. The objective is simple to state but more difficult to achieve: to try and rescue the GAA greats of the past who have fallen into the abyss.

'I fractured both legs, had my knee severed, broke my collar bone and broke my sternum bone. Gerry McEntee told me, no matter what, I should keep up my VHI because I would have been banjaxed otherwise. My own experiences have given me a real feel for those players who are now in a bad way because of injuries but who can't afford to have them seen to. We had a gold event which raised €250,000. I started the GAA legends and I helped raise a million euro for charity of which I am proud.'

There is an air of expectation as he takes a familiar role, centre stage. He talks in his soft accent about issues with all the confidence and authority of a man firmly established as a leading figure on the national stage. Yet what struck me most forcefully was the way his eyes sparkled as he talked about the future. He exudes a decency and warmth not always associated with celebrities. His has the idealism of a youth and there was not the slightest trace of cynicism or disillusionment, though there were hints of a steely resolve behind the mild, almost innocent exterior. He is evangelical about a new venture, which is taking up a huge chunk of his time and energy.

'I resigned from the GAA's past players committee. I want to make a difference and one of my big passions is helping the past players. Sadly, there are a number of former players who have fallen on hard times and if we could help even four or five of them a year, I would be happy. It must be done.'

He has managed to give a little hope to all the former greats he cares for, and a little hope is a powerful and precious commodity.

WHERE DO WE GO FROM HERE?

Flynn measures what he values rather than values what he measures.

'I'm over 50 now and I have no pension. My wife, who had believed in everything I did, has the threat of losing the home she loves constantly hanging over her.

'I see my glass as half-full. I look on it as half-time in a match. Now it is up to me to rescue the game in the second half. I'm enjoying life a little bit more with an awful lot less.'

31

THE LOST LEADER: GER MICHAEL GROGAN

Our dead are never dead to us unless we have forgotten them.

George Eliot

The unthinkable had become the thinkable.

It was like a trapeze act without a net below. The adrenalin was really flowing, and my heart beat a little faster.

My mind was crowded, as though there were a critical fact teasing me at the periphery of my brain, a detail I ought to be thinking about, a memory I ought to be seizing, a solution to a problem that seemed just beyond my grasp. The tension in me reminded me of the aftermath of a thunderclap: full of sound and yet intensely silent.

The news was beyond our worst nightmares. Even the most loquacious was struck mute. Words were patently inadequate because we were unable to speak of the unspeakable. I discovered that anxiety attaches itself and then it burrows inside and makes a nest and lingers like an unwelcome guest. It eats whatever is warm in the chambers of the heart, and then settles in seemingly pervasively. You could cut the tension with a knife. My brain was like a washing machine, turning and spinning.

Hope was a kind of sacrament that was not shed lightly, but there was no hope that morning.

We live in a strange world which, at times, is very difficult to understand. We have a habit of getting our priorities all wrong. This thought struck me on 10 March 2002 when we heard the shocking news that Ger Michael Grogan had died in a traffic accident. It is still difficult to comprehend that this young man who gave new meaning to the phrase 'larger than life' is no longer with us. Ger Michael was an outstanding fielder of the ball and a versatile performer. But it was another quality that meant he stood out from all his colleagues. He was blessed with a maturity that stretched way beyond his tender years. For his father, Christy, his son's death is the wound that will never heal, although there is little drama about him, no apparent depths of intensity or unful-filled longings that are evident on the surface, at least.

He stood there, beside me but soaked in solitude as we visited where Ger Michael took his last breath. His eyes were lowered as if he was making an offering on the altar. Grief spread over him. Again. Ripping the breath from his lungs. Yet within a few minutes he finds the words again.

'It was actually one of the proudest days of my life when he came on wearing the primrose and blue jersey of Roscommon in Castlebar in the All-Ireland quarter-final against Galway in 2001. It is hard to believe that was 20 years ago, and the 20th anniversary of his death is coming fairly soon.'

The only tiny crumb of comfort for Christy is that in his tragi-cally short time on earth Ger Michael achieved more than most will ever manage.

'Thank God he achieved his lifetime ambition by playing for Roscommon. Few of us get that chance to live out our dream.'

To outsiders, these top-level competitors are not of this world but Ger Michael lived and breathed the game. He knew why second best was just not good enough. He knew that it is the small things that make the big differences.

'He was just 23 at the time, six foot six, 15 stone weight and both he and I thought it was going to be the start of a long career for himself representing Roscommon at county level.'

Ger Michael's former Roscommon teammate, Karol Mannion, was a big fan.

'He had made his mark, but I am convinced he would have gone on to be a brilliant player for Roscommon. He had everything you need to get to the top: the size, the power; the talent and, above all, the confidence.

'My abiding memory of him is a county semi-final. I was playing for St Brigid's and he was playing for Roscommon Gaels. He was their full-forward and was marking Seámie Óg McDonnell. The first ball that came in between them, Ger Michael caught it and stuck it over the bar. He turned to Seámie and said: "That's the first of six." After that Seámie was literally marking him so tightly that he ripped his shorts and five minutes later Ger Michael had to leave the field to get new shorts!'

THE END OF INNOCENCE

Death always sends a chill through the bones. Each death is a painful reminder of the ultimate and unwelcome end for us all. It is all the more harrowing when a young person dies and all the promise of a young life is taken away, as Christy knows all too well, with his son, sweet as love in his memory.

'At about 3 a.m. my other son Chris called to my house and told me Ger Michael had been involved in an accident and I knew from the tone of his voice and his demeanour that it was serious. Himself and a friend of his were returning home from the town and crashed. My son was a passenger and the driver was injured but thankfully he recovered. Nurses and doctors were doing their utmost to resuscitate him, but it wasn't to be. My wife and I, our son and our daughter were hoping against hope that he would recover because he was such a fine, strong lad. I watched him take his last breath and this is something I will never forget.'

Christy was no stranger to giving bad news but hearing this traumatic tale was something else.

'I had been a guard for over 30 years. I recall one night on the Longford–Dublin road where three young people were killed by a drunk driver, two instantly and the other a few days later. I had to knock on their parents' door at three, four and five in the morning. It was very sad, and it left an indelible mark on my mind, but I'll tell you something, when it comes to hearing that news yourself it is on a whole different level of emotional devastation.

'My eyes met my wife's. The fellowship of the besieged was firmly established. I knew instinctively that all that was keeping her going was the thought of joining Ger Michael in a higher, more perfect world.'

As the crowd gathered Ger Michael's many qualities were dissected. He was a very astute judge of people. Seldom did he rush into judgement. Rarely, if ever, did he judge by appearances. He always probed beneath the surface. He had the happy knack of dissecting what people said with the precision of a surgeon's knife. Christy remembers:

'Although he was not a great television fan, he watched the news religiously. God, I wished I could buy back just another ten minutes with him. Later I heard someone describe him as "a horse of a man". Down here, that's a great compliment.

'I waited until the mourners had departed to be alone with him for a final moment. I prayed to buy him some shares in the hereafter. Now I know why "Goodbye" is the most painful word in the English language. Parting is no sweet sorrow.

'Now, coming home will always be a sad occasion for me. The time came to return to the world of work. I called in to say goodbye to Ger Michael's friends. How could some place so familiar become so alien? His ghost whispered from every corner. Every piece of furniture has its unique memory of him. I discussed incidents and accidents with his mother. When it was time for me to go, neither of us could find the words to convey our feelings. But really there was no need just then.'

As always, the people of Roscommon rose to the occasion to show their solidarity.

Ger Michael's funeral was like no other. Most funerals are a burial of something or someone already gone. Ger Michael's death pointed in exactly the opposite direction and was therefore the more poignant. Normally we bury the past, but in burying him, in some deep and gnawing way, we buried the future.

'For the first week we were distracted by all the people coming to console us, but then the grief caught up on us and we cried to the point of exhaustion. I couldn't sleep because the pain was indescribable. The most heart-breaking thing was knowing that he would never walk through our door again. That is something I could never get over for a long time and, to be honest, I still haven't got over it.'

His son's sudden death was like landing on an alien planet for Christy.

'I was not sure if I could survive without him. I thought I could never love again, but I soon learned that love can live long after death. It is a second time love, like a summer shower, the leaves having retained the rain, rain on the unsuspecting head as though it had rained again.'

The rich architecture of Christy's faith sustained him in his darkest hour.

'I know Ger Michael is up in Heaven with our good God looking down on us. I know he has the light of God shining on him and that gives me great consolation.'

In 2010 a monument was erected to commemorate Ger Michael.

'It was a moving moment for me. It is difficult to comprehend that this young man is no longer with us. We live in a fast-changing world and in the swirling tide of history it is easy for things and even people to be forgotten. This memorial will ensure that Ger Michael is never forgotten.

'Unfortunately many other former Roscommon footballers have died suddenly or in tragic circumstances, notably Dermot Earley and Conor Connelly, but what singles Ger Michael's case out for me that he was the only player who I know of who died while he was a current Roscommon player. So that was the inspiration to ensure that he was remembered in this way. The monument says of my son: "Gone too soon." No truer words were ever spoken.'

THE BEAUTIFUL GAME

When I told Dermot Earley of Ger Michael's death he read the exquisitely evocative poem *The Beautiful Game* in tribute:

> Less than a minute remains on the clock,
> As I tighten my lace and turn down my sock,
> One last chance, and it's all down to me,
> It must be a goal, for we need all three.
>
> I step up to the ball and look towards the posts,
> Is that the crowd I hear, or is it the ghosts
> Of men who before me have faced the same test,
> And never once failed to give of their best

THE LOST LEADER

My father he gave me the love of it all,
When he guided my feet to strike that first ball,
A hurley or football it's the same thing to me,
It's playing the game that matters you see.

From boys in a field to the crowd's great roar,
There's never been anything to excite more,
From the day I could run till the day I can't walk,
And even then, about the game I'll still talk.

The few steps to the ball now seem like a mile,
But a well-placed shot and I'll be carried in style,
On shoulders of teammates expressing their joy,
It's a dream that consumed me since I was a boy.

My feet pound the ground, my foot sends the ball,
It sails through the air over men who are tall,
Then dipping and curling it finds the goal,
And just for the moment I'm in touch with my soul.

A whistle blows hard and I awake from the dream,
I'm watching my own son play for the team,
And maybe one day they'll announce His name,
As he steps out to play ... The Beautiful Game.

(Author Unknown)

Ger Michael was a hero in the true sense of the term because when he performed well, *do lioigh an laoch san uile dhuine* (the hero in all of us was exulted).

The truth is it is more important to be a great man than a great player. Ger Michael was both. His presence will linger with us forever. The grooves in the mind hold traces and vestiges of everything that has ever happened to us. Nothing is ever lost or forgotten – a ruin is never simply empty. It remains a vivid temple of absence. His loss will always be keenly felt by his family, as Christy constantly acknowledges:

'Not a day goes by when we don't think about him. There is a gap in our lives that will never, ever be filled.'

Grief is the price we pay for love.

The greater the love – the worse the pain.

It was difficult after what he had just said to know how to make further conversation without it sounding like inconsequential and even insensitive small talk.

With apologies to John Donne, the Gaelic Games family is a volume. When a great player dies all the pages are not tossed aside but translated into a new language. In the fullness of time God's hand will bind our scattered leaves into that library, where every book will lay open to one another. All football fans in Roscommon and beyond are the curators of Ger Michael's memories.

Ar dhéis Dé go raibh a anam.
He left the world better than he found it.
He left us better than he found us.

PART V
Dual Stars

There have been 18 players who have won All-Ireland senior medals on the field of play in both hurling and football. Eleven of these are from Cork, including such luminaries as Jack Lynch, Jimmy Barry-Murphy, Brian Murphy, Ray Cummins, Denis Coughlan and famously in 1990 Teddy McCarthy.

Folklore abounds about the first Cork player to become a dual All-Ireland medal winner, Billy Mackessy, who was also a renowned publican. An enterprising Leesider who was short of a few bob had a penchant for poaching free drink in the hostelries of the city. One day he sauntered into Billy's pub with another chancer and in a near whisper asked Billy how many All-Ireland medals he had, to which the reply was 'two'. The quick-witted duo then went to the other end of the bar and told the bartender that they were due two drinks 'on the house'. The barman gave them a puzzled look. The resourceful drinkers then confirmed their entitlement by shouting down the pub to the owner, 'Wasn't it two you said, Mr Mackessy?'

This section comes at dual stars from a slightly different angle in that it profiles people who have starred not only in different codes but in different counties.

32

THE HOMES OF DONEGAL: MARTIN CARNEY

There's no place on earth like the homes of Donegal.
Seán MacBride

We are not what we look at. We are what we see.

Martin Carney's senior intercounty career lasted 20 years. He came to national prominence when he was part of the Donegal team that won the county's first Ulster title in 1972. He also played his part when Donegal won a second provincial title in 1974. Crucial to Donegal's breakthrough was Brian McEniff.

'We played Leitrim in the league in Carrick-on-Shannon. I think the score was 4-13 to 1-3 to Leitrim. Brian McEniff was player-manager of Leitrim at the time. He got us into a room in Bush's hotel in Carrick-on-Shannon and said, "Right, boys. The only way we can go is up. Today was the lowest we could possibly go. The championship is coming up soon and are we going to make an effort for it or are we not?" We all made a vow there and then that we would all train hard for the championship and we did.

'I know Brian as a friend and as a club mate. He didn't

understand other than trying to win. His ambition to succeed was not part of the Donegal psyche to that point.

'We beat Down after a replay and Tyrone in the Ulster final. It was kind of a fairy tale after so bad a start to the year. As it was Donegal's first ever Ulster title the whole county went wild. It was like winning the All-Ireland. We had a great week afterwards! The celebrations probably affected us in the All-Ireland semi-final against Offaly, the reigning All-Ireland champions. We were playing very well up to half-time, but we gave away a very bad goal to Kevin Kilmurray. Even though we lost we were probably happy enough with our performance because Ulster teams weren't doing well in Croke Park at the time. I'd say Offaly got a bit of a shock that day.'

Donegal were brought down to earth with a bang the following year.

'In 1973 we were beaten in the first round of the championship by Tyrone. Tyrone were a coming team and went on to win the title. Ulster was always a graveyard for reigning provincial champions.'

In 1974, though, Donegal were back on the glory trail.

'In the Ulster championship we beat Armagh and Monaghan in the semi-final. We beat Down in the Ulster final in a replay. At one stage in the second half we were eight points down with about 22 minutes to go. We were lucky enough to get two penalties and the late Seamus Bonner took both. There wasn't much pressure on him for the first one because we were eight points down and he thought if he scored it would make the score respectable but if he missed we were getting hammered anyway and it didn't matter much. There was much more pressure on him for the second one because we were three points down and it was to tie the match. Thankfully both penalties went in and we got another goal in the last few minutes to win by three points.

'It is always disappointing to lose when you are one step away from playing in an All-Ireland. The biggest disappointment was losing to Galway in 1974. We were very unfortunate. At one stage Donal Maughan and Patrick Shea went up for the one ball and collided with each other. John Tobin stood back and as they were falling down he was collecting the ball and racing through to score a goal.

'John Tobin's career as a player is probably defined by the disappointment of the 1974 All-Ireland defeat to Dublin. Yet when we played Galway in the All-Ireland semi-final that year John led us on a merry dance. He was a gifted player with an amazing body swerve. People often forget that those games lasted 80 minutes and were very severe on the body. I was playing in midfield that year and I know!'

MAKING HISTORY

In 1989, Brian McEniff took charge of training Donegal again.

'His dedication is total. He never missed a single training session in the 1992 campaign, and this encouraged the players to do the same. His willpower rubbed off on the players. He's also got incredible enthusiasm and that's infectious. His finest hour came in 1992 when he masterminded Donegal's All-Ireland 0-18 to 0-14 triumph over red-hot favourites Dublin.

'Donegal had been so unimpressive in the All-Ireland semi-final against Mayo that nobody gave us a chance against Dublin. I think that gave the Dublin players a false sense of security. The media really built them up and I think the Dubs started to believe their own publicity. That's a dangerous game. In contrast there was no hype about us because we hadn't done anything to deserve it. None of our fellas were going on radio shows blowing their own trumpet.

'You can't win an All-Ireland without leaders on the pitch and we had four of them in 1992. Anthony Molloy, Martin McHugh at centre-forward, Tony Boyle at full-forward and Martin Gavigan at centre-back were all leaders in different ways. Molloy was a superb leader. He could catch a ball in the clouds and that would lift the team. If you could get past Martin Gavigan you were doing well. Tony and Martin could get you a score from nowhere.'

Martin Carney had a privileged seat when Jim McGuinness steered Donegal to their second All-Ireland triumph in 2012. He was on co-commentator duty for RTÉ television. His post-match summary earned great plaudits: 'From their tip of Malin to the southerly point of the Drowes river; to the hills, the valleys and the towns along the majestic coastline; through the wild wilderness of the Bluestacks – this will be celebrated like no other.'

CHANGING COLOURS

Carney called time on his intercounty career with Donegal at an early stage.

'The best place to know where you are from is to visit graveyards and see how many names you recognise. I loved playing for Donegal, and that is where I am from, but things were not going well for Donegal and we were destroyed by Derry in 1978. Good work was being done at underage level, which reaped a reward years later, but basically we were a mess at that stage.'

Carney's strong family ties led him to transfer to the green and red of Mayo in 1979.

'My father is a Mayo man and my uncle, Jackie Carney, trained Mayo to win the All-Ireland final in both 1950 and '51, having played on the Mayo team that won the All-Ireland in 1936. I was teaching there, and I am happy there. The first couple of years saw us losing to Roscommon in the Connacht championship, but we had a good run in the league in '81 and then suckered Galway, the National League champions, to win the Connacht final. Kerry were at their best that year. We kept up with them for an hour in the All-Ireland semi-final, but we had nothing to match them after that. On a personal level it was nice to captain the team, but I think its real value was to re-establish a little bit of worth to Mayo football, not having won a Connacht title in the 1970s.'

Although Galway crushed Mayo the following year in the Connacht final, the game did produce some moments of theatre as a by-election was taking place in Galway at a time. This was the year of GUBU, and the Fianna Fáil government did not have an overall majority, hence the importance of the outcome.

'Charlie Haughey and half the cabinet were there. There were helicopters landing in the stadium, which was unheard of at the time in a GAA match. It was more like the Epsom Derby than a Connacht final.'

After the hiding in the Connacht final Carney credits two men with Mayo's revival.

'Liam O'Neill took over as manager and he was succeeded by John O'Mahony. They were very contrasting personalities and could never have worked together, but what Liam put in place John built on. Initially, though, Liam was to benefit from John's work with the under-21 All-Ireland-winning side in 1983 in the form of a number of new players. We won a Connacht title in '85 and found ourselves playing Dublin in the All-Ireland semi-final and then the replay. It was thrilling stuff and there was a real buzz in playing Dublin, with all the noisy atmosphere and theatre they bring. If we had played Kerry there would have been none of that because Kerry don't travel to All-Ireland semi-finals. We could have won the drawn game, but they were that bit steadier in the second game. I am not doing an Arsene Wenger, but I didn't see what happened to John Finn when his jaw was broken, but he was a real mess in the dressing-room at half-time in the first game. It was a testament to his stubbornness that he went out and played in the second half, though I wonder how he was let out to play when he clearly wasn't fit.'

In 1988 Mayo were back in an All-Ireland semi-final, losing to Meath.

'This time, though, things were a bit different. Up to then Mayo had always been a rollercoaster, from one extreme to the other. We were either fully up or completely down, but John O'Mahony kept things grounded. We won the Connacht title again in 1989, when Liam McHale literally owned the ball and gave one of the great individual displays. We also had Seán Maher in the side, who was a very under-rated player, and he gave us that enforcer rather than a creator presence we badly needed. Anthony Finnerty famously described Jimmy Burke's goal that year as "the push-over goal". It kind of bounced off him.

'For a county that had not won an All-Ireland final for so long, there was such an outpouring of goodwill and an incredible longing to win. Johnno tried to control it as best he could, but a lot of local interests were looking for a slice of the action. When we scored the goal, I can recall looking down the Cork bench and seeing the sense of shock. They were as brittle as us in a different way, but John Cleary and Michael McCarthy took over and they deservedly won. Although we lost, the team was feted and there was plenty of back-slapping that created its own problems and the team was distracted the next year and the opportunity to build on the advances of 1989 was lost.'

Why have Mayo failed to win an All-Ireland since 1951?

'I can't answer that. Part of it was that for a long time we were too nice and could get bullied, though that changed since John Maughan's time. History and emigration were also contributory factors.'

Although best known in recent years as a pundit on RTÉ TV and Today FM, Carney was also involved in John O'Mahony's back-up team in Mayo, with responsibility for 'stats'. What was the secret of O'Mahony's success?

'He is very loyal and trusts people and expects the same in return. His man-management skills were probably best shown in Galway in the way he got a lot out of players, especially those that might have been seen as a little difficult, like Michael Donnellan. Likewise in Mayo, he handled Padraig Brogan well in all the circumstances. He could convince the likes of Seán Maher that he was a peerless midfielder, although that would not have been the popular belief in Mayo, but Seán had a massive influence. He is also extremely organised and had a finger in every aspect of the organisation; and he was prepared to leave no stone unturned. He is also a good human being.'

As a member of the Football Development Committee, Carney was one of the instigators of the new championship structure.

'We provided a badly needed facelift for the championship with the qualifier system. At the moment, I think the area needs to be revisited again because the club is losing out too much.'

33

THE GIRL WHO PLAYED WITH BOYS: NICOLE OWENS

Ladies football is a jewel in the GAA's crown.
Laois legend, the late Lulu Carroll

The emergence of a charismatic Cork team, their thrilling rivalry with Dublin and the soaring attendances, have seen ladies' football enjoy a much higher profile than camogie in recent years. The great rivalry that has developed between Cork and Dublin has had an unintended consequence. In Autumn 2017, RTÉ television transmitted a documentary *Blues Sisters* which gave the inside account of Dublin's incredible All-Ireland-winning season that year. Former Galway goalkeeper Pat Comer, who created the famous GAA documentary *A Year Til Sunday*, was part of the *Blues Sisters* production team and he became a regular at Dublin's training sessions and games throughout the season. One of the stars of the programme was Dublin's All-Star forward Nicole Owens, who courageously shared her own story of her battle with depression. Her interview generated exceptional interest and Nicole has gone on to become a leading mental health campaigner on the national stage. It is as if she lives by the motto: if you live without making a difference, what difference does it make that you lived. In November 2018 she attended a conference at her alma mater, Trinity College, and spoke of her experiences and her philosophy.

So, when and how did her condition manifest itself?

'It was part of my story growing up. Another part was the silence I carried around. As a teenager, struggling with my sexuality, depression manifested because I didn't have a way to verbalise those feelings. To speak about them to anyone meant I'd need to address what was fuelling the problem.

'My way of handling it was to spend periods of time alone when I'd be very upset. This only happened every couple of months, so I could manage. Eventually, it got to a stage where every day I was waking up with instant dread. When I got really upset over some-thing completely innocuous in college people began to notice, so I had to open up. I turned to my mum. She's a pathologist so it's hardly her area of expertise, but she had a lot of resources to draw upon.'

A major concern for Nicole is to speak out so that she might be able to help young women who find themselves in a similar situation.

'There are certainly more visible gay female athletes. Actual role models. Sport in Ireland, particularly GAA, does not have any visible gay male players and that's a real shame. My teenage years were a constant struggle to cope with who I am. Imagine how that feels. Looking back, I wish I'd spoken about it sooner. There were so many years of worry. Since I opened up, the reaction from friends and family, strangers even, has only been positive.

'It's been normalised in my circle of friends, but when, age 15, 16, I held it all in. Someone would make a flippant comment about this or that being "so gay" and it felt like a punch in the heart. I carried that pain around far too long. The cure is simple, honestly, just say who you are. That's why the day of celebration is called "Pride". It's liberating. Frightening at first but liberating afterwards.

'When I stared down my problems, it wasn't as terrifying as I presumed. Turns out the real terror was doing nothing at all, until it became too much to handle.'

Then came the watershed moment. Negative thoughts had entered her head and she needed help.

'One day, it kind of came to a point where I broke down in a lecture and my poor mam had to leave work and bring me home. At the time I had been kind of having dangerous and really negative thoughts and I realised I needed to talk to someone. It's something that people don't really ... I didn't really have the classic signs in terms of I still loved playing football, but at the same time [I was] deeply, deeply unhappy.'

She had to confront her own preconceptions.

'At the start, my attitude to medication was "no way". I went to a clinical psychologist, but I was resistant to pills. It was an ignorant view to the role they play but therapy alone could not bring me to a good place, so I went back to my GP and I've only had positive experiences since taking regular medication these past years.

'These are my experiences. Therapy can feel like a very "touchy-feely" method of dealing with depression, whereas I'm a very logical person who likes to employ actions to tangibly address a problem. Cognitive Behavioural Therapy (CBT) is a way of breaking down triggers, looking at what has me feeling down.'

As a girl Nicole literally stood out on the playing field.

'I used to play against the boys. Running out, spectators would be laughing and pointing at the guy marking me. Big mistake. It only put pressure on him, especially when I started playing well, and these comments were unwise, as they fuelled my desire to play better. My opponent was the nearest victim. I was ten.'

To misquote Bob Dylan, in ladies' football "the times are a' changing".

'Gaelic football is the fastest growing female sport in Ireland. There are hundreds of girls down at the nursery in my club St Sylvester's every weekend – which is great – but the value I got from playing against boys up to under-12s, when redirected towards the Dublin girls development team, has me split on gender segregation. I benefited from playing with boys. The coaching was way more advanced. The skills gap remains but that is slowly changing. My generation of players have a role to play in this.'

34

THE BEST OF THE WEST:
CIARAN FITZGERALD

But hark a voice like thunder spake. The West's awake.
                                                    Traditional

His wide smile catches the heart off-guard.

The beauty of television coverage of sport is that it can occasionally capture an image which offers a telling insight into a sporting hero. For the Irish rugby fan an enduring image will always be Ciaran Fitzgerald's efforts to rally the Irish team as they appeared to be letting the Triple Crown slip from the fingers in 1985 against England in the wake of their dazzling and stylish victories away to Scotland and Wales. Even those who had no experience of lip-reading could clearly make out his plea from the heart, as he temporarily put aside the good habits he acquired as an altar boy with the Carmelites in Loughrea. 'Where's your pride? Where's your f**king pride?'

TEENAGE KICKS
His record speaks for itself – Triple Crown and championship in 1982, a share of the championship in '83 and the Triple Crown

again in 1985. Fitzgerald, though, was a rugby virgin until his late teens. 'As a boy growing up in Loughrea the only social outlet available was the boxing club. I won two All-Ireland boxing championships. My heroes, though, at the time were the Galway football team who won the three-in-a-row in 1964, '65 and '66, and I attended all three finals.

'At Garbally, my main game was hurling. The highlight of my hurling career was playing in an All-Ireland minor final against Cork in 1970. Our team had been together from the under-14 stage and featured people like Seán Silke and Iggy Clarke. Initially I played at half-back but for some reason for one match they moved me to the forwards and I scored three goals.

'The problem was that when I played at full-forward in that All-Ireland final I was marked by Martin Doherty, who subsequently made it big with the Cork senior team. Big was the word for Martin. I would have needed a stepladder to have competed with him in the air! I was moved out to centre-forward but who followed me? Only Martin. He destroyed me. That Galway minor team went on to win an under-21 All-Ireland and most of them formed the backbone of the senior All-Ireland-winning team in 1980. After I left school, though, rugby became my main game.'

35

THE SUNDANCE KID: JP McMANUS

I backed the right horse, but the wrong horse went and won.
H. A. Jones & H. Herman

A man was condemned to share a cell for one night with a deadly snake coiled taut in the corner. The man dared not sleep, move or even breathe deeply for fear of attracting the snake's attention. As dawn lit the horizon, the man relaxed. In the full light of day, he saw that the snake was but a length of old rope. Many people have hundreds of lengths of ropes thrown in different corners of their minds. Then their fears begin to work on them. They grow into monsters. JP McManus is not such a man. As a punter he is feared and fearless.

In the 1970s JP established himself as a legendary figure with his successes in the betting ring at Cheltenham and elsewhere to such an extent that top sports journalist Hugh McIlvanney wrote a piece about him in *The Observer* in which he called him 'The Sundance Kid'. The name stuck and he was catapulted to an elite status in Irish sporting folklore.

His Roscommon-born father, Johnny, moved from Dublin to Ballygar before eventually settling in Limerick in the early fifties.

Johnny always kept a few young potential showjumpers. He liked to bet on the horses – always a pound at a time. He also read a lot about horses. It rubbed off on JP insofar as he came to love horses; and also the thrill he got from collecting when his fancy won. The earliest bet he can remember was on Merryman II when he won the Grand National in 1960 at 13–2 when he was nine.

His punting was a handicap to his academic advancement. He tells a story from his schooldays about a history exam which was due to start at 2.30 p.m. but the problem was that he knew that after 45 or 50 minutes a Brother would come to stand at the door to ensure that no one slipped out early. He fancied a horse very much at Limerick. He managed to get out of the room before the Brother took up duty and cycled like mad to the racecourse only to arrive at Greenpark just as his fancy was passing the post – a winner!

After he left school, he moved into his late father's plant hire business. One of his duties was to clear the site for the house that he subsequently lived in. Realising at an early age that the path to fame and fortune was not to be found driving a bulldozer, he decided to become a bookmaker, having dabbled in betting since his school days. Much of his teenage years was spent in Alf Hogan's betting shop in Limerick when the tax was a shilling on single bets and nothing on multiples. Income tax is the mother of invention.

He went broke twice as a bookie shortly after he started and had to return home. The second time he went back, his mother gave him the loan of a few hundred pounds. He told her, 'If I take it and Father gets to know about it, he won't be too pleased,' as the last thing he wanted JP to be was a bookmaker. She told him, 'He won't know anything about it.' JP took the money, and he later reflected:

'I suppose I had more respect for it [his mother's loan] than for any money I ever had in my pockets. The odd thing is that I've never been broke since. Sure, I was often, very often, very short of money but there is all the difference in the world between having a little money and having no money at all. Once you've been flat broke and somehow come through it, you certainly come to respect money and you certainly never want to be skint again.'

He considers himself a professional gambler whether he is punting or making a book but not an addictive gambler. In 1975 he purchased his first horse, the Con Collins trained double Irish Cesarewitch winner, Cill Dara. Since then he has supported many trainers like Eddie O'Grady, Christy Roche, Arthur Moore, Enda Bolger and Donald Swan. Asked how many horses he owned he replied, 'Too many slow ones!'

The raising of the betting tax rate from five per cent to 20 per cent in the early 1970s prompted McManus to stop betting in SP offices and concentrate on the course.

He later moved to Geneva to head a currency-dealing operation. His close friends include Dermot Desmond and John Magnier, and the three have been described as a 'super-rich holy trinity'. All three were rumoured to have made a killing in correctly anticipating the Mexican peso devaluation in 1995. Desmond was one of the Sundance Kid's partners in the reported £38 million purchase of the Sandy Lane Hotel in Barbados. Estimates of his wealth vary but an indication of the depth of his pockets came in October 1998 when he offered a £50 million donation to the Irish government towards the cost of a new national sports stadium. Little wonder then that in racing circles he is considered the richest man in the sport, outside the sheikhs and Robert Sangster.

WITH GODD ON OUR SIDE

His first Cheltenham winner came in 1982 with Mister Donovan in the Sun Alliance Novices Hurdle at 9–2, trained by Edward

O'Grady and ridden by TJ Ryan. In an interview after the race he said, 'I didn't have a very good day the opening day, but I wasn't too bothered, as I was pretty confident I would get it all back on the Wednesday. I expected we might get up to 14–1 but the word got out about Mister Donovan's ability and I had to take far less than those odds.'

The following year he won again with the Edward O'Grady-trained Bit of a Skite. In a rare interview he said, 'I didn't have a bob on him. A fortnight before the race one of his feet got a bad infection and the blacksmith had to cut a large hole in the front of his hoof. For 11 days the horse just worked in Joan Moore's equine pool. In fact, the morning of the race the hole was filled with Polyfilla just for cosmetic purposes. We couldn't back him. Sure, who cares now anyway?'

The winning jockey was Frank Codd but according to the race-card it was Frank Godd. One Irish punter blissfully unaware of the injury was tempted by the odds of 5–1 on the logic of, 'How can we get beaten with God on our side?'

JP seldom bets on his own horses. 'Once the bookies think I'm having a cut with one of my horses, the odds they offer are quite restrictive.'

THE FIRST CUT IS NOT ALWAYS THE DEEPEST

While amateurs tend to scale back when on a winning streak, professionals tend to double up. Love hurts. So do heavy losses at Cheltenham, and the Sundance Kid has had setbacks on the way, notably a bad Cheltenham in 1976, especially the failure of Brown Lad to win the Gold Cup.

JP's popularity with racing fans can probably be attributed to his capacity to handle both victory and defeat with equanimity. Irish fans support JP in Cheltenham because they hope they can share in his success if they follow his lead. Over the years JP has put together a very strong team of horses – not just in Ireland but with a great Cheltenham hero Jonjo O'Neill in England.

Like most punters McManus loses as well as wins. He just does it on a larger scale. One example of this approach is the story about his fortunes during the Festival in 1994. He was said to have lost £30,000 after backing one of his own stable, Gimme Five, to win. The next day he returned to back Danoli to the tune of £80,000, which saw him take in double that amount. With characteristic understatement he was widely quoted as saying, 'That put the wheels back on the bike.'

Istabraq's Champion Hurdle wins were some of JP's biggest wins in Cheltenham. Given his penchant for naming horses after Limerick hurlers a number of people speculated that a man named Istabraq must have played for Limerick in their All-Ireland success in 1973! Apart from his Cheltenham triumphs, a particularly satisfying Istabraq win for McManus was his victory in the £50,000 James McManus Memorial Hurdle in Tipperary in October 1997 – a race named after the winning owner's father.

YOU'VE GOT A FRIEND

McManus paid £13,000 for charity, for the racecard of his great friend, the voice of racing, Peter O'Sullevan's final BBC commentary in the 1997 Hennessy Gold Cup. Peter spoke to me about his relationship with one of Limerick's most famous sons.

'He's a great friend. He's poured me many a glass of Haut-Brion! I have to say that I had the great good fortune in the early years of our friendship to get on well with his mother, which is very important for a journalist ringing his home and trying to eke out an interview from him! I admire him enormously for his capacity to take defeat and success equally well. He has a marvellous approach.

'He does a lot of things on the quiet to help people. Of course, he funds a huge number of projects in Limerick in particular.

'JP told me once that the trouble with Cheltenham and jump racing is that you wish half your life away. From September, October, you're wishing it was Cheltenham time and the travelling is usually better than the arriving. Anticipation is the keenest pleasure.

'Of course, things don't always go according to plan. One of his Cheltenham winners was Bit of a Skite. JP had been talking with great confidence about the horse for most of that season and I had planned to have a sizable wager on him, but then the horse got injured and he dissuaded me from having a bet. The next time I saw him was in the winners' enclosure with the horse he had convinced me not to back! In fairness he felt worse about that than I did.

'What really ignites Cheltenham is the unique partisanship between the Irish and the English. Mercifully it's a friendly rivalry between the two countries. The English and Irish meet on common ground with a shared appreciation of the horse. The English applaud with equal enthusiasm when the Irish win.

'JP McManus is not patriotic when it comes to betting. He makes his decision on who is most likely to win. Okay if it is an Irish horse it's a bonus but in betting terms it doesn't make any difference.

'Remember that JP is not betting for fun. He's not in the business simply for the thrill of having a go. If he doesn't keep ahead of the field, then it's all meaningless. The business is about picking winners at the right odds. That is why reading the form book is so important. You must be able to weigh up the race, take the conditions into consideration and, most importantly, feel you are getting value for money. If he fancies a horse sufficiently it won't bother him that he is not the favourite, though he'll obviously be very keen to find genuine reasons why a horse can drift in the market. You can't put any faith into rumour.

'Another trap he generally avoids is ante-post betting. He's got to know the state of the ground before he really makes up his mind. He told me once that as a rule of thumb punters usually do better when the ground is soft. When it's fast at the festival meeting, you've got to be extra careful. The records show that, he tells me.

'Of course, for the bookmakers, Cheltenham is a great luxury. Everybody wants to bet because the festival has an enormous amount of atmosphere. Cheltenham inspires the likes of JP McManus. It draws them like a magnet. The trouble with English racing for people like JP is that there aren't enough bloody non-triers. Personally, I blame the Jockey Club!'

The laugh in his voice betrayed his own membership of that august body.

THE GOLDEN VOICE

Peter O'Sullevan had it. Dan Maskell had it. Bill McLaren had it. Michael O'Hehir had it. Micheál Ó'Muircheartaigh has it in abundance. The 'it' is hard to define but it has to do with their power to make the sport they love accessible to all. The ingredients are in-depth knowledge, a love for the game that knows no limits and an unfailing ability to convey the flow of a match to equally satisfy the needs of the cognoscenti and those at the opposite end of the spectrum of sporting knowledge.

Micheál is best equipped to explain how JP has brought hurling onto the racecourse.

'JP is from Limerick and he loves Limerick hurling. Limerick had a great side in 1973, with the likes of Pat Hartigan and Eamonn Grimes. They had to be to beat that wonderful Kilkenny team to win the All-Ireland. Of course, they pulled off a master-stroke, deciding out of the blue to play Éamonn Cregan, possibly the greatest forward Limerick ever had, at centre half-back, to counter Pat Delaney. That win must have made a big impact on JP.

'JP's very friendly with people who used to play for Limerick. He's called his horses after famous Limerick hurlers like Joe Mac, called after Joe MacKenna – the horse that didn't win in 1998! Another horse was called Grimes (both were trained by Christy Roche) after the Limerick man who captained an All-Ireland-winning side in 1973 – someone told me he did best on fast ground. A third got his name from Limerick's great full-back, a man whose playing career was sadly ended by an eye injury, Pat Hartigan. And, of course, McManus's horses race in green and gold colours after his beloved South Liberties club.'

36

THE WICKLOW WANDERER: MICK O'DWYER

We would have won at least three All-Irelands without O'Dwyer because we had so many talented players but we would not have won eight. He kept us wanting to come back for more.

Pat Spillane

He is of a generation that trusts their eyes. They can tell what's coming by lifting their faces towards the sky and seeing the formation of the clouds.

Mick O'Dwyer is universally acknowledged as the greatest Gaelic football manager of all time because of his achievement of winning eight All-Irelands with Kerry, two Leinster finals with Kildare and a Leinster final with Laois.

In 2007 he marked the occasion of his seventieth birthday by becoming manager of Wicklow, where yet again he sprinkled his magic dust. Despite a rare health setback, O'Dwyer continued to coach the squad during the summer of 2007 and transformed them from being ranked the second-worst team in the country to the dizzy heights of a place in the top 12 in 2009. He did so by using a simple philosophy, believing what is complicated is rarely useful and what is useful is rarely complicated.

Pat Spillane was impressed.

'Wicklow had been waiting for a taste of success for a long time. So the odds were against Micko from the start. I was not at all surprised, though, that he did something with them. He even brought them to a Tommy Murphy Cup. Okay, so there were some smart alecs who dismissed it as the Tommy Cooper Cup. Fair enough, I admit that I was that smart ass!

'I have heard it said that what Micko did with Wicklow ranks as his greatest achievement in management. That is a huge claim, but it is one that has some merit. To turn them into a team that were in the top 12 in the country must rank as the GAA's equivalent of the ugly duckling who was turned into a swan. I take my hat off to him.'

ANATOMY OF SUCCESS

Few people are better equipped than Spillane to explain why Micko brought such success to Wicklow.

'Micko is old school. I love that about him. I must bemoan our tendency to ape everything in other sports. People know Matt Williams now because of his work as a rugby pundit on TV3. When he was the Scottish rugby coach, Matt had the number 27 inscribed on the training gear of all his players to signify that they eat, drink and sleep the game 24 hours a day, seven days a week, 365 days a year. If you add up all those individual digits you get 27. How did that work for him? Scotland flopped and he quickly lost his job.

'One year (2004), Ireland lost its opening Six Nations rugby match to France. Irish coach at the time Eddie O'Sullivan spun the result very well. He said Ireland took a lot of positives out of it. The statistics showed that:

- Ireland won 22 lineouts; France only won 7.
- Ireland won six mauls; France only won one.
- Ireland won 56 rucks; France only 50.
- Ireland won 33 balls in the opposition's 22; France only won 10.
- Ireland spent 49 minutes, 2 seconds in the opposition's half; France only spent 35 minutes 52 seconds in our half.
- Ireland only made 16 errors; France made 19.

'With those impressive statistics, Ireland must have won comfortably. No. Ireland lost by 18 points. Eddie's spinning wasn't finished yet. He pointed out that we finished strongly, and we never gave up.

'Subsequent events proved Eddie O'Sullivan was right to be optimistic because Ireland won the Triple Crown. The reason why I was annoyed about his comments after the France game is that it reminded me that we are a great nation for moral victories. It is something that I'm always harping on about because I think our eagerness to celebrate moral victories is detrimental to the possibility of us achieving the ultimate success. We took a huge moral victory out of winning the Triple Crown that year but to me the key fact was that we only finished second in the championship.

'What was even worse was the way we celebrated, limping out of the soccer World Cup in both 1994 and 2002. Who will ever forget when Albert Reynolds was photographed with big Jack when the team returned from USA '94? It was like Charlie Haughey and Stephen Roche in 1987 all over again. Then off for a damp squib of a concert shown live on national television in the Phoenix Park, with acts of dubious musical talent and reputation. Then in 2002 it was back to the Phoenix Park again for another celebration live on RTÉ and for Joe Duffy to ask Damien Duff about his Padre

Pio medal. On both occasions we were being asked to celebrate defeats to Holland and Spain, respectively.

'Forgive me if I'm cynical, but I come from a county where success is delivering a trophy at the end of the day and anything less than winning the trophy is failure. It sums up the psyche of Kerry footballers – which is that second best is not tolerated. When you do tolerate second best, you accept failure that much easier. Mick O'Dwyer is someone who is never happy to be second best and he brought some of the mentality to Wicklow.'

MONEY, MONEY, MONEY

There were rumours that O'Dwyer was making a 'tidy sum' for providing his services to Wicklow. Pat Spillane was having none of it.

'Nonsense. We all know that payment to managers goes strictly against the GAA's amateur ethos! Of course, nothing is more sacred than that! I must point out to you that managers in the GAA only get expenses!

'In recent years, the GAA's relationship with amateurism has been riddled with hypocrisy. Despite the spate of rumours that have bedevilled the GAA in recent years about payments to managers, the Association has been powerless to act because of absence of proof. Former president Peter Quinn famously observed that while there were many claims that managers were being paid under the table, the GAA couldn't even find the tables!

'I am reminded of the story of the time a large amount of money goes missing. There are four named suspects: the local bishop, the poor GAA manager, the tooth fairy and the Easter Bunny. The gardai arrest the bishop. Why? The other three are figments of the imagination.

'Many GAA administrators have the attitude of Bill Clement. Bill was former secretary to the Welsh Rugby Union during the days when amateurism was adhered to rigidly and with a zeal that even the Redemptorists would have admired. One day the legendary Welsh hooker Bobby Windsor approached him. Having given sterling service for years to both Wales and the Lions, Bobby decided that the WRU should at least help him with the hire fees for the dinner suit he was obliged to wear at official dinners. So, he went to see Bill Clement. Bobby explained how times were hard in the steel industry in Gwent, and, like many others, he had been put on short time. His wife and family were feeling the pinch and every bit of extra cash could help. "So, if maybe the Union could help me out by hiring the finer suits them that would be appreciated," said Windsor.

"I'm sorry," replied Clement. "That's against the rules."

"Well, what about my shoes?" said Bobby, getting a bit agitated. "Surely, you could help me out and allow me to buy a decent pair of shoes to look smart in? These ones are falling apart." At this juncture, to emphasise the point, he took off his shoe and showed Clement across the desk how the sole was flapping at the toes. Bill thought about it for a few seconds and then quietly opened a drawer on his desk marked "Ticket Money". He took out a huge bundle of notes and untied them from their tightly wound rubber band. As Bobby was waiting for him to count out the cash, Clement chucked the rubber band over to Bobby and said, "Here, that should sort out the problem with your shoes.'"

37

THE DIASPORA: MICK HIGGINS

Mick Higgins ranks in the top 25 footballers of all time.
Eugene McGee

Cavan's famous victory over Kerry in the 1947 All-Ireland final is perhaps the most iconic moment in the history of the GAA. To borrow from Paul Simon, the nation turned its lonely eyes to New York for 'the Polo Grounds Final'. For Cavan star and Texaco Hall of Famer Mick Higgins the trip to the Big Apple was a journey home to the city of his birth.

As the leading academic Damien Kiberd has noted, many of those republicans who lost the Civil War could not bear to live on in a land which was a sore disappointment to their dreams. A number went to a real republic, the United States, where they made fortunes in business – and bootlegging. Even today if you walk the streets of New York, you see vans plying up and down with names like 'PJ Brennan, Est 1926' inscribed on their doors. The republican idea has always been linked to entrepreneurship: after all, the French revolutionaries of 1789 were the first politically organised businessmen of the modern world, keen to replace a parasitic upper class with a society of 'careers open to talents'.

The loss of such flair to Ireland in the mid 1920s was something which the fragile young state could ill afford. It became a mantra among commentators that the Irish were successful in the US in ways they never could be at home. One reason for this was that Irish-Americans continued to believe in their own culture, long after their 'sophisticated' stay-at-home cousins seemed to have given it up.

Shortly after she was elected president of Ireland in 1990, Mary Robinson coined the phrase 'the Irish diaspora' to describe the intrinsic link between Irish emigrants abroad and 'their native sod'. From the outset Gaelic Games have been one of the most formidable imaginative batteries which allow Irish exiles in the four corners of the earth to feel they continue to belong to 'home'.

The 1947 All-Ireland final was held in New York as a gesture by the GAA of goodwill to the Irish people in America. Once it was announced it aroused great interest in every county. To get there was a great prize in itself. The teams left Cobh together for a six-day trip on the SS *Mauritania* to New York, after getting their vaccinations against smallpox, which were compulsory at the time. The fact that it was the first final played abroad gave it a much more exotic quality, so it really grabbed the public imagination.

But what kind of machinations were going on behind the scenes in New York to make this event possible on the ground? A breath-taking series of hair-raising plots behind closed doors, involving moral blackmail, bribery of a kind, intimidation and blatant lie-telling allowed this event to happen. Locating the 1947 All-Ireland final, played in the Big Apple, was one of the great achievements of Canon Michael Hamilton's active career. Initially almost everyone seemed implacably opposed to the project.

Machiavelli himself would have admired the 'prompt-ings' behind the scenes that finally persuaded a controversial Central Council meeting at Barry's Hotel that it was worth carrying through. Folklore abounds of how Milton Malby's Bob Fitzpatrick's passionate speech to congress, complemented by the prop of a tear-stained handkerchief, swung the vote as he read from a bogus 'emigrant's letter'.

Many years ago, Kerry's Joe Keohane gave me the Kerry perspective.

'Before the final Kerry, Cavan, Galway, Laois and Mayo had toured in New York. Mayo, in particular, could have clocked up frequent flyer credits, thanks to the clout and cash of a judge from Bohola, Bill O'Dwyer. After he was elected Mayor of New York in 1946 the GAA had the cachet and the connections to locate its premier event in the world's most famous city.

'The decision gave new oxygen to the championship that year, as every team in the country dreamed of a trip to New York. This was most apparent in the Munster final that year when we defeated Cork in the Athletic Grounds. With the clock ticking, Cork were awarded a penalty.

'I argued with the referee for two minutes, and helpfully stood on the ball and of course almost buried the ball into the mud. When Jim Ahearne struck the ball, it dribbled weakly along the pitch. All the time I was arguing, I could see the skyline of New York getting clearer and clearer!'

For Cavan, the trip to New York was particularly welcome because in previous years they had experienced many bitter disappointments as one of their biggest stars from that era, Mick Higgins, who later trained Longford to their only Leinster title, explained.

'Initially most of our team would taste the bitter pill of defeat in three All-Ireland finals before getting their hands on the ultimate prize. We lost to Kerry in 1937, Roscommon in 1943 [after a replay] and Cork in 1945. It was a unique occasion in the history of the GAA. Lots of teams have won All-Irelands but only one has won one in New York. We took great pride in that. We knew we had made history and that we would never be forgotten as a result. To this day Cavan people are proud of us because of our achievements.'

38

FROM DOWN TO FERMANAGH: PETE McGRATH

We are no longer the whipping boys.
Anthony Daly

Fame is the mask which eats the face.

However, Joe Brolly's face remains intact.

The mist was spreading like the creeping fingers of a ghostly hand. Joe Brolly was ready to give me an audience. He had no problem playing tribute to Derry's great rivals, Down.

'Looking back at the 1970s and the 1980s, the reason why the teams from Leinster and Munster always wanted to play an Ulster team in the All-Ireland semi-final was because Ulster teams were defeated before the match even started, because of psychological reasons. Deep down they didn't believe they could win.

'We had nearly beaten Down in a titanic game in the Athletic Grounds in 1991. We were a point up at the end when they got a free 60 yards out. I was close to the ball at the time and I heard Ross Carr saying to Enda Gormley: "I'm going to drive this over the bar." Enda told him: "Wise up, you f**king eejit." But Ross sent it over the bar, and they went through instead of us, but when they won the All-Ireland it inspired us because it made us realise how close we were.'

After the high of 1993 Derry made an early exit in the championship in 1994, as Brolly recalls.

'Our great rivals Down beat us in an epic game in Celtic Park. Eamonn Coleman took them for granted because we had beaten them by 18 or 20 points the year before. Eamonn positively laughed at the notion that Down could beat Derry in Celtic Park. Mickey Linden kept them in it in the first half. Then in a classic smash and grab, they beat us with a late goal. After one game we were gone.

'Down went on to win a second All-Ireland in four years and no one could begrudge them that. They had great players. The old mantra is that forwards win All-Irelands and they had the firepower that most southern teams, even Kerry, would have been jealous of. Their manager Pete McGrath was important to their success because he allowed the players to release their full potential.'

The star of the great Down team that won three All-Irelands in the 1960s was Seán O'Neill. He is one of the greatest ambassadors in the history of the GAA. In conversation with this writer he said, 'Our tradition has been of going at it hammer and tongs, but the key thing is that we did so playing positive football and doing everything in our power to win. I really think we need to recapture the spirit because today so many teams have as their priority not to lose and to stop the other team from playing football. This is a total distortion of what our games are really about. Too many managers in recent years were focused on how not to lose but Pete McGrath was not like that.'

FERMANAGH FIND FUN
Pat Spillane is the best-known critic of Ulster football, but he wants to sing a hymn of praise to Fermanagh.

'A reason why Ulster football frustrates me so much in recent years is that a win-at-all-costs mentality seems to dominate. It wasn't always like this. Tyrone really gave us a scare in the All-Ireland final in 1986. With a great display of positive football, they had us on the ropes. Early in the second half we trailed them by seven points. And it could have been worse, had Tyrone right half-back Kevin McCabe not blasted a penalty over the bar.'

In fairness to Spillane he also is keen to acknowledge the positive side.

'When I want to think very positively of Ulster football, I do so by recalling the great town team managed by Pete McGrath that won All-Irelands in 1991 and 1994 at a time when Ulster football ruled the roost. Tony O'Reilly tells a great story about Brendan Behan. Behan turned up on a chat show on Canadian television totally drunk. The presenter was very unimpressed and asked him why he was so drunk. Behan replied, "Well, a few weeks ago I was sitting in a pub in Dublin and I saw a sign on a beer mat which said: 'Drink Canada Dry'. So, when I came over here I said I'd give it a go!" O'Reilly deftly uses that incident to speak of the need to have the kind of positive attitude that says, "I'll give it a go." That's the kind of upbeat mentality I would like to see Ulster teams coming in to Croke Park with and Pete's team had that. Gaelic football at its best is the beautiful game – played with strength and speed, with courage and skill, with honesty and humour. It has the capacity to stop your heart and leave the indelible memory of a magic moment. Think back to that Down team of Pete's in the early 1990s; a forward line of footballing artists like James McCartan, Ross Carr, Mickey Linden and Greg Blaney – in full flight they were something unbelievable on the pitch, a miracle of speed, balance and intense athleticism, thoroughbreds leaving a trail of mesmerised defenders in their slipstream, who had been as transfixed in wonder as the crowd by their silken skills.

This is why I wanted to play the beautiful game. Pete won two All-Irelands in 1991 and 1994 playing football the way it should be played, and I take my hat off to him. The icing on the cake came in 2015 with the great joy he brought to the championship when he brought Fermanagh back to Croke Park with a team who seemed to have discovered that Gaelic football is supposed to be fun.'

39

MILLER'S CROSSING: BOBBY MILLER

*Players can smell bullsh*t a mile off.*
Brian O'Driscoll

It was a shock of seismic proportions that reverberated around the rugby world. The fact that the Black Ferns enjoy such dominance in world rugby makes Ireland's victory over them in the 2014 Rugby World Cup all the more remarkable.

Indeed, Ireland set the Women's Rugby World Cup alight by defeating reigning champions New Zealand 17–14 in the sides' first ever meeting in Marcoussis.

One of the highlights of the victory came when Niamh Briggs countered brilliantly to set up Alison Miller for a wonderful try.

Alison has a great sporting pedigree. Her late father Bobby is a legend in both Laois and Carlow. To me Bobby Miller is inextricably linked in my memory with Jimmy Magee. I once went for lunch in the Montrose Hotel with Jimmy. The meal was spent enjoying one of Jimmy's biggest hobbies: selecting 'dream teams'. For the first course we picked our dream teams in football and hurling; for the main course we picked our greatest teams of footballers and hurlers never to win an All-Ireland; for the dessert course we picked our 'dirtiest teams', and then as we were having coffee Jimmy suggested we picked our dream teams of footballers and hurlers never to have won an All-Star. When I was struggling a bit, I asked him to get me going: 'Who is the greatest player never to have won an All-Star?' I expected him to equivocate but he answered immediately: 'Bobby Miller.'

I pushed him to explain why: 'I don't know any stories exactly like his. The great players like Christy Ring, Mick O'Connell and Seán Purcell were really loved in one county, but Bobby is loved and admired in two counties.

'He was a sensational midfielder, but the only time most GAA fans would see him play was on Saint Patrick's Day in Croke Park, playing for Leinster. That evening people would be saying what a marvellous player Bobby Miller was and how they'd have to wait for another year to see him perform again.

'At that time, Railway Cup football and hurling were prestigious events, and to be selected to play was the highest accolade of recognition for a player of exceptional talent. From the 1940s through to the 1970s, the rivalry between the provinces was as strong as it is between counties today. Once the Railway Cup finals were shown on television in the early 1960s they became huge national events and the interprovincial rivalries took a hold on the nation.

'In the 1970s, Bobby was in his prime. He was a joy to watch and had a very commanding presence. If he had played for either Kerry or Dublin, he would have won a hatful of medals and All-Stars, and he would have become a household name like Brian Mullins or Jack O'Shea. I was thrilled when Mick O'Dwyer led Laois to their first Leinster title because it is always sweeter the first time. I have to confess, though, that I thought of all the great Laois players who had never won a Leinster title and was sad for them. Bobby was the first player I thought of. If I was selecting my Hall of Fame of great Laois players I would have to nominate him first ahead of any of the great players from the 2003 side, such as Beano McDonald, who is a real hero in Laois today, or even "the Boy Wonder" Tommy Murphy, who was chosen on the GAA's official Team of the Millennium, and of course their hurling legends Pat Critchley and Cheddar Plunket, and the brilliant Sue Ramsbottom. Bobby was that good.

'Four times he was nominated for an All-Star and that is a great achievement for a player with a county that was well down the pecking hour at the time. I love the All-Stars but the odds are stacked against you if you are from a county that is not successful. That is not just my opinion. The stats bear that out. Today Micheal Murphy is rightly recognised as one of the greats of Gaelic football. He was lucky, though, to be around at one of only two times when Donegal won an All-Ireland. If he was playing intercounty football at the same time as Bobby Miller, he would not have the same profile because Donegal were not such a force then. If you wanted the archetypal Laois legend, it would be Bobby Miller. He had that understated manner which so many successful Laois sports people have.'

CARLOW'S KINGS

However, Bobby was destined to find fame in other fields, as Jimmy explained:

'Bobby managed both Laois and Carlow, but his managerial career will always be remembered because of his time in charge of Eire Og. When he took over the club, they did not have permanent dressing-rooms. They changed in prefabs. Yet he turned them into kings of club football. They won five Leinster provincial titles. They contested two All-Ireland finals. They were very unlucky to lose the 1993 All-Ireland final to Cork's O'Donovan Rossa in a replay and indeed there was a lot of controversy about the end of the game.

'We take it for granted now that the club championships are

central to the GAA calendar but that was not the case in the early 1990s. Eire Og played a part in changing that. The way they won the All-Ireland semi-final in 1993 against Mayo's Knockmore in Knockmore caught the public imagination. It electrified Carlow in particular and I think Bobby Miller deserves some of the credit for the enormous popularity of the club championships today.

'What Bobby did for Eire Og was remarkable. He took a club that was not a force outside Carlow and turned them into a super-power of Gaelic football. While Bobby was their manager, they were right up there with some of the most famous clubs in the history of the GAA like Saint Vincents, Austin Stacks and Nemo Rangers. That would have been an achievement in any county but it is astonishing that he could achieve so much in a county that was in the doldrums for so long.

'The reason they had such great success was that Bobby devised a method for them that played to their strengths. Under him they were really hard to beat. They played better than the sum of their parts and that is always a tribute to a manager who can do this consistently. He deserved all the plaudits he got, and he deserves to be a revered figure in Carlow for what he achieved in Eire Og.'

The GAA world was shocked in 2006 when Bobby Miller died suddenly. He was just 56. Jimmy Magee was very saddened by the news.

'A hallmark of Gaelic Games is "the GAA funeral" whereby fans from every county come to say goodbye to a fallen hero. I think immediately of huge funerals like that for a former Offlay hurling great Pat Carroll, who was taken from us much too soon. Bobby was also taken from us much too early. His funeral was unique because of the incredible affection he attracted both in Laois and in Carlow. It was a unique tribute to a unique story and an exceptional player and manager.'

40

DON'T BE AFRAID THE DREAM'S NOT REAL: LIAM GRIFFIN

I love me county.
John Mullane

In the faint clink of connection strange thoughts came tumbling out before falling away.

Many former players and managers have gone on to carve out a successful career in the media. Pat Spillane is one of the many in this category. Given his years on *The Sunday Game* Spillane takes a keen interest in other pundits. He is a big admirer of one occasional pundit.

'One of the reasons why *The Sunday Game* has prospered is that the production team are always on the lookout for new analytical talent. On the hurling side they brought in the greatest manager of the 1980s, Cyril Farrell. Some people in Galway were disappointed that he continued to work as an analyst with the programme during his second coming as Galway manager in the mid 1990s. Their point was that it is hard to hunt with the hare and hunt with the hounds. Cork's Donal O'Grady and Thomas Mulcahy are among a number of former great players who have made an invaluable contribution to the programme.

'The arrival of one of hurling's great evangelists, Liam Griffin, as Wexford manager would change his county's fortunes. Of course, hurling fans will never forget the way he steered Wexford to that All-Ireland in 1996.

'Teams reflect the personality of their team manager. Jimmy Barry-Murphy once said, "I want a quick, skilful, athletic team. I'd rather have greyhounds than elephants." His team did. So, too, did Liam Griffin's Wexford's team. He had a unique capacity to take the source material of a team not used to winning championships and to refine that ore into pure gold.

'When he stepped down as Wexford manager it was inevitable that his services as an analyst would be in great demand and RTÉ audiences have had the benefit of his passion for "the Riverdance of sport".

'With his knowledge of the game he quickly became the Alan Hansen of co-commentary. In a world where words are cheap the only pity is that Liam's sharp intelligence and clear elucidation could not be deployed by cross-channel stations for their soccer half-time discussions. Often the brightest things about their analysis is John Barnes's jacket.

'Liam is a great raconteur and has remarkable energy. I saw this at first hand in the Burlington Hotel the morning after RTÉ's Sports Personality of the Year awards in 2004. There was a virtual "who's who" of Irish sport walking around the hotel. Most people were still bleary-eyed from the night before. I was sitting down having my breakfast and Liam came over to me full of vim and vigour.

'He told me that at one of his first meetings with the Wexford panel he gave them a questionnaire to fill up. It had a number of questions such as "Where would you prefer to train?" At the bottom was an additional query, "What is your favourite position?" Most players answered in the obvious way, full-back, centre half-back, full-forward, etc. The exception was a former panellist on *The Sunday Game*, the joker from Faythe Harriers, Larry O'Gorman, who gave Griffin information he didn't really need. His reply was simply, "On Top!"'

WHO FEARS TO SPEAK OF '98?

Liam Griffin is a man with a very strong sense of Wexford's place in Irish history. He believes that Wexford people carry the DNA of the 1798 Rising in their genes because it was their 'rebel hands' that 'set the Heather blazing'. It was they alone who followed the call to 'Arm, arm.' They were martyrs to the cause, 'For Ireland's freedom we fight or die'. It was then that 'Father Murphy from County Wexford' swept o'er the land like a mighty wave'.

Amidst the hotbed of political intrigue and the reams of revolutionary rhetoric that rampaged the nation it was Wexford people, and Wexford people alone, who put their pikes where their mouths were o'er the bright May meadows of Shelmalier'. Griffin argues, 'We were the only ones who stood up when Ireland needed someone to take on the Empire.' In this perspective, winning the All-Ireland in 1996 was much more than winning a match it was another instalment in the county's unique tradition of defiance, determination and dignity.

Yet Griffin also embraced the modern. In 1996 he had a sports psychologist Niamh Fitzpatrick work with the team, but he kept it under wraps. A master of misdirection, on the press night he instructed her to 'run out there and rub Larry Murphy's leg' because he wanted the journalists to think she was a physiotherapist.

A CONCERN

Griffin is concerned about some recent developments in Gaelic Games:

'A lot of fellas have started to try and wind up opponents

during the match especially if they think he can be riled up. I think that has crept into the game in recent years. People see incidents which shouldn't happen, like in football Paul Galvin knocking the notebook out of the referee's hand against Clare in the 2008 Munster championship. Of course, he shouldn't have done it but people often don't realise the verbal provocation, not to mind the physical, that a player may endure. The other thing that I don't like is players diving. Think of the way Aidan O'Mahony went down after he got a little slap in the 2008 All-Ireland semi-final against Cork. That is not the Kerry way. These are two things we don't want in our games, and I would like to see them addressed. I think Gaelic Games are one of the few places left where the Corinthian spirit survives, where fellas are playing for the love of the game and "sledging" or trying to get a fellow player sent off are not part of our wonderful tradition; and we must ensure that they are not allowed to bring discredit to our games. Players are role models. What they do young kids imitate – the good and the bad. Coaches have a big role to play in this. I always believe it's no good just mentioning things to players. You have to repeat things to them. I believe in the power of twice.'

Former Armagh player Enda McNulty is less concerned.

'My most direct experience of sledging was in a Dublin championship match. I got a barrage of verbal abuse from my opponent. It was so bad I wouldn't even repeat it to my closest friend. Playing county football, I never really had sledging. I did get a bit of it in club football in Dublin. I was called "Nordy basta*d" or "Queen loving f***ker". Sledging is part of the game, but any coach who encourages sledging, their focus is in the wrong place. Their time should be spent developing the technical and tactical capacities of the players rather than focusing on something negative.'

PART VI

The Nearly Men

In conversation with me Micheál Ó'Muircheartaigh made an interesting observation.

'You know the difference straight away between the casual fan and the real thing. The casual fan will ask: Who will win on Sunday? The serious fan will ask: Who was the greatest player you ever saw? Or even more tellingly: Who is the greatest player never to win an All-Ireland?

'In hurling, generations of great Wexford players went without winning an All-Ireland. A lot of great Galway hurlers like Josie Gallagher and Seánie Duggan never won one, and if you like they laid the foundations for modern day hurling in Galway. They won a National League medal and a Railway Cup in 1947. Josie Gallagher was as good a hurler as I ever saw. Harry Gray of Laois was a great hurler. He did win an All-Ireland medal with Dublin in 1938. He went back to Laois and spent many fruitless years there.

'God, you could make a team of the footballers. There's Gerry O'Reilly, Jim Rogers and Andy Phillips of Wicklow, and if you moved north you would have Iggy Jones of Tyrone, PP Treacy of Fermanagh, and if you go west you have the great Gerry O'Malley of Roscommon and of course Dermot Earley, who played so well for Roscommon for so long.'

The annals of the GAA reserve special honours for the many great players who never won an All-Ireland medal. In this section we meet some representative samples.

41

CATCH OF THE DAY: JIM McKEEVER

Jim McKeever had magic hands.
Jimmy Magee

Some thoughts take precedence and others are relegated or become merely vestigial.

A rare few moments touch our deepest yearnings.

In 1958 the GAA world witnessed a shock of seismic proportions when Derry beat Kerry by 2-6 to 2-5 in the All-Ireland semi-final. The Foylesiders were led to the promised land by a prince of midfielders, Jim McKeever.

His ability to jump and catch the ball was the hallmark of his play. He could jump so tidily that he would be almost like a gymnast in the air, toes extended and fingers outstretched as he grabbed the ball, way above the heads of anybody else, and then he would hit the ground, turn and play. In Ted Walsh parlance he was 'a great leper' and one of his most famous feats of fielding was caught on camera and has been immortalised in all the great subsequent coaching manuals under the caption, 'the catch'.

The bonus of talking to him is the quiet, self-effacing warmth with which McKeever discusses matter-of-factly a career that must always, in the end, testify to talent so magical that it is too profound to be rationally explained. At the age of 17 McKeever made his senior debut for Derry.

'I remember listening to the famous All-Ireland final in the Polo Grounds in 1947. I didn't think then that a year later I'd be playing in a challenge game for the county against Antrim. It wasn't until the following year, though, that I made my championship debut. When I was in my teens Derry used to play in the junior championship. We didn't have a senior team then. At that stage there was a tremendous gap between Cavan and Antrim and the other seven counties in Ulster. We played in the Lagan Cup at the time, which featured the eight counties in Ulster apart from Cavan.'

A major impediment to Derry's advancement was the fact that its footballing base was so narrow, particularly without the foundation stone of a strong college scene.

'I believe that success in football or hurling is largely determined by population. In a county where the playing population is small you are always struggling to fill in the last three or four places.

'You need to be a big school to have a successful colleges side. St Columb's in Derry had a great team in the 1960s but as a boarding school they were mainly powered by players outside the city. I myself went to school in St Malachy's in Belfast. I went to train as a teacher in St Mary's in Belfast. After that I went for a year to do postgraduate studies in Physical Education in London. It was difficult to explain the intricacies of the game to some of my classmates! A few times in the year I flew home to play for Derry and Ulster.

'Derry was a soccer stronghold, which was a big disadvantage for us. By the law of averages, given the population of the city, it should be providing about 40 to 50 per cent of the team, but it has given us nowhere near that. The ban worked very badly against us in Derry.'

Seamus Heaney incisively exposed the way in which sport, religion, race and politics were inextricably twined together in the Derry of his youth: the way in which walking through a street on Ash Wednesday with a forehead badged with the mortal dust enforced a sense of caste created by the sectarian circumstances; the way in which Pioneers were referred to as 'the strawberry brigade' and the manner in which the green chestnut tree that flourished at the entrance to the GAA grounds was more abundantly green from being the eminence where the tricolour was flown illegally at Easter. For the GAA faithful in Heaney's eyes, though, football was central to their identity and an essential element of the fabric of their lives.

42

THE SLIGO SHARPSHOOTER: MICHEÁL KEARINS

Micheál Kearins was consistently brilliant.
Micheál Ó'Muirearchtaigh

Micheál Kearins is a momentary nostalgic portal to what we imagine things were like in a more innocent time.

In full flight, he was a sight to put a permanent tingle in the blood, leaving many a defender with a pane, where he never had a window. Gaelic football provided the ideal context in which to express his combination of cerebral gifts and extreme competitiveness.

As a boy, his hero was the great Sligo full-back Nace O'Dowd. It was only after he completed his education, at Ballinaleg National School and St Muirdeach's College in Ballina, that he really made his mark in the footballing world. He first played for Sligo minors in 1960, losing out in the Connacht championship to a Galway side powered by Noel Tierney and Johnny Geraghty that went all the way to win the All-Ireland. The following year he made his competitive debut, being marked by Gabriel Kelly, against Cavan in a league game in Ballymote, and he played for the county at all three levels that year. He played in 17 successive championship seasons with Sligo from 1962 to 1978. There were many disappointments, so what sustained him on the way?

'Losing the Connacht final of 1965 against Galway was one of many disappointments. My dedication and love of Gaelic football always kept me going.'

His introduction to championship football in 1962 was the story of his career in shorthand: so near yet so far. Sligo led by a point against the reigning champions, but Roscommon stole victory with a goal in the last kick of the game and went on to contest the All-Ireland final.

Football was in his genes, as his father played a lot of club football and lined out a few times for Sligo beginning something of Kearins dynasty. Not only did Micheál and his brother James play for the county, a generation later Micheál's son, Karl, lined out for the Magpies.

Micheál's place in the lore of Gaelic football is made additionally secure by his phenomenal scoring feats – a record that has no equivalent in the past and is never likely to find even an echo in the future in the Sligo colours. He was the country's leading marksman in competitive games in four different years (1966, 1968, 1972 and 1973). In the drawn 1971 Connacht final he scored a record 14 points: five from play and nine from placed balls, two 45s and one sideline kick. He won two Railway Cup medals in a 13-year career with Connacht, in 1967 and 1969. Two years later he scored 12 points for Connacht against the Combined Universities in the Railway Cup, all from placed balls. With the Combined Universities leading by 3-9 to 0-17, Connacht got a line ball 45 yards out in the dying seconds and Kearins calmly slotted it over the bar to earn Connacht a replay. Which score stood out the most for him?

'A side-line kick from 30 yards in the Connacht final of 1971 against Galway.'

Kearins was a natural rather than a manufactured talent. Although he ranks with stars like Johnathan Sexton as among the greatest place-kickers in the history of Irish sport, he did very little actual practice in that area.

'Especially in the early years I did a lot of physical training on my own. I would run a few miles early in the morning maybe four times a week. I never bothered much practising my free-taking, not even taking a practice one in the kick about before a match.'

Despite the longevity of his career, Kearins never shed the burden of having the weight of expectations of Sligo fans on his shoulders.

'I was always nervous before a game, knowing Sligo were depending on me. To slot the first free between the posts was always very important to help me to relax.'

He won an All-Star award in the inaugural year of 1971 at left-half forward, the first Sligo man to win the award – in 1975 Barnes Murphy became the second. In 1972, Kearins was also a replacement All-Star, though a major controversy ensued when he was omitted from the original selection. He won a magnificent seven football championships with his club St Patrick's Dromard – two junior and five senior. He also won two senior county medals with Ballisodare. He also played in three National-League-losing semi-finals with Sligo. He lined out in three Connacht Senior football finals, losing to Galway in 1965 and 1971 before finally winning the title in 1975.

With a Cinderella county like Sligo, it was inevitable that Kearins's career would be marked by pain: the anguish of seeing his team lose so often and the horrible inevitability of defeat. But his is also a story of hope and about dreams which sometimes, just sometimes, come true. Like the once-in-a-lifetime ecstasy of winning the Connacht final, when the joy is even greater because you've known the pain. It's about being willing to accept a lifetime of frustration in return for one day of utter wonderment. The fact that he scored 13 points in the Connacht final helped to make the occasion all the more memorable for him. Surprisingly, though, he does not see that game as the high point of his career?

'Winning the Connacht championship in 1975 was a great honour, but it was not the highlight of my career. Winning the senior county championship with St Patrick's Dromard in 1968 was the best moment of my career.'

AH REF

A cattle dealer, Kearins has been a familiar sight at many a cattle mart down the years. After his retirement from playing, he became a referee. His career with the whistle is probably best remembered for the time he sent off Colm O'Rourke.

'It was an incident after half-time and he got a heavy enough shoulder while in possession. It knocked the ball out of his hands, but he didn't try to retrieve it but came after me. The play moved down the field and he followed me the whole way down sharing "pleasantaries" with me! I had no option but to send him off.'

The two giants of the game had another heated exchange subsequently, in the 1988 All-Ireland semi-final when Kearins was a linesman.

'There was a line ball incident and he felt I gave it the wrong decision. I know myself now that I was wrong and he was right, having seen the replay on telly. I would have to say, though, he was a great player and actually made the Meath forward line while he was in his prime. He was their play-maker.'

Kearins did not have to think too deeply when asked about his most difficult game to referee.

'It was an All-Ireland semi-final between Cork and Dublin (in 1989). I had to send Keith Barr off that day. He got involved in an incident five minutes earlier and he ran 30 or 40 yards to get involved in that second incident. There was an awful lot of off-the-ball stuff that day and it's very hard to manage those games.'

In fact, the tension escalated to such an extent that Kearins publicly pulled the captains, Dinny Allen and Gerry Hargan, aside before the start of the second half and instructed them to warn their players about their behaviour. He didn't get exactly the response he hoped for from Allen who, when quizzed by the Cork lads about what the referee said, claimed Kearins had simply wished them well for the second half and hoped the awful weather would improve.

Sligo's most famous footballer rates Leitrim's Packy McGarty as the greatest player never to win an All-Ireland medal and selects a fellow Connacht man when asked about the greatest player he ever saw.

'It has to be Seán Purcell. He could play anywhere and had all the skills. Mick O'Connell's anticipation for fielding was great too. My most difficult opponent though was Donegal's Brian McEniff. He always made life very difficult.'

How did he react to be selected as the left half-forward on the Team of the Century for players who never won an All-Ireland senior medal?

'I felt greatly honoured to be chosen on the Centenary Team with such distinguished players.'

43

ANTRIM'S ACE: CIARÁN BARR

Antrim's All-Ireland semi-final win in 1989
points to the magic of the GAA.

Jimmy Magee

One of the biggest shocks in the history of the GAA came when Antrim defeated Offaly in the 1989 All-Ireland hurling semi-final.

Ciarán Barr went bravely where no one had gone before as Antrim's first All-Star hurler in 1988. Later in his career the former Irish international water-polo player would transfer to Dublin and give outstanding service in the blue jersey. The high point of his career came when he captained Antrim to a memorable All-Ireland semi-final win over Offaly. It was the first time that Antrim had qualified for the All-Ireland final since 1943.

It was Offaly who made the better start and their half-time lead was 1-10 to 1-6.

It was a different story in the second half, as Dessie Donnelly marshalled the Antrim defence superbly and Antrim ran out 4-15 to 1-15 winners. Ciarán Barr assumed the playmaker role, like a maestro playing the violin to provide ample scoring opportunities for Olcan 'Cloot' McFetridge (who with Dessie Donnelly won an

All-Star in 1989), Aidan 'Beaver' McCarry and Donal Armstrong.

Barr retains vivid memories of the game:

'It was a strange situation. We were confident we could beat Offaly as we had beaten them twice that year. Although it was an All-Ireland semi-final, we didn't think of it like that, we just thought we were playing Offaly. Although Offaly were the form team in Leinster in the 1980s we would have been a lot more scared if we had been playing Kilkenny. It was only after we had beaten them that we thought – gosh, we're in the All-Ireland final now.

'Although we started off slow enough it was a day everything went right for us. Things we had planned in training just came off for us unbelievably well. We were lucky in the sense that we had five or six players who could turn things around for us when the going got tough.'

That year also presented Donnelly with his sole opportunity to play on the highest stage within the game. Everyone was expecting the day of the All-Ireland hurling semi-finals to produce high drama – mainly because the second semi-final was between old rivals Galway and Tipperary. Eleven days previously, Galway had hammered the Glensmen in a challenge match, suggesting to neutrals that the Northerners would be like lambs to the slaughter against Offaly.

Barr believes the 1989 All-Ireland semi-final with Offaly is a parable for what GAA is.

'On the field both teams were trying their utmost to win but when the final whistle went the Offaly team gave us a guard of honour as we walked off the pitch. It showcased real sportsman-ship and all that is wonderful and positive in the GAA.'

44

THE MIGHTY MEATH MAN: KEN RENNICKS

*Frank made his championship debut in such a way
that he will never be asked to make it again!*
Meath club secretary's report

Meath football has always been a place where the weak do not survive.

Ken Rennicks was one player who consistently displayed the pride and passion that characterises the men who wear the green and gold of Meath. After playing for the county minor team, he made his senior inter-county debut in a game against Offaly in 1969. The following year he scored three points in one of the most exciting and dramatic provincial football finals of all time, which Meath, after trailing by 11 points, won by 2-22 to 5-12. The high of such a win was followed by a bitter disappointment when the Royal County lost the All-Ireland final to a Kerry team captained by Donie O'Sullivan. The match saw the coming of age of a young man who would go on to become one of the immortals of the game, 19-year-old John O'Keeffe, who gave a commanding performance at centre half-back on the great Matt Kerrigan. The game was the last hurrah for the great Meath team that Peter Darby had captained to All-Ireland glory in 1967. Younger players like Rennicks could not have foreseen that Meath would have to wait until 1986 to win another Leinster final.

In 1974, Rennicks won a Railway Cup medal with Leinster, the province's first title for 12 years, and the following season Meath won a National League title with a great victory over reigning All-Ireland champions Dublin. Rennicks ranks that match as his greatest game. The icing on the cake came in the shape of an All-Star award, 'the biggest honour I could receive in my career'.

In the mid 1970s, however, seismic shifts were taking place in the football landscape, and counties like Meath were struggling to maintain a foothold. Dublin and Kerry were pioneering a revolution, introducing a more professional and innovative approach into the game. How did Rennicks evaluate Heffo's army?

'They were one of the best teams I have seen, always very well prepared and very skilful. Sometimes it got very disappointing after they arrived, because we were out of the championship so early. If we were longer in it, we would have been better prepared to take on a side that good.'

Like many of the players featured in these pages, Rennicks has a great devotion to the club. An essential element of the appeal of Gaelic Games, that extra quality that distinguishes them from all other sports in Ireland, is the tribalism on which the structures are based. No other sports enjoy the intense rivalry that exists between clubs in the GAA. From time to time this creates problems, but in the main it generates a sense of community which has been all but lost in contemporary Irish society.

It acts as a unique bridge between rural and urban. Here, from time immemorial, pride in the honour of the parish is handsomely vindicated and vigorously defended.

The weekend matches provoke intense discussion. Great

sporting moments were dissected here with an insight and lyricism that a *Sunday Game* pundit would have been proud of. New influences were seeping into the lives of the locals in the guise of modernity.

As everyone proudly said in those parts, 'home is home'. This cryptic saying means that it is far better than all those places you could see on the television and that the blanket of green in which it wallows, sometimes uncomfortably, is to be preferred to the paved streets of the best cities of the world. Can anybody disagree with their logic? To dissent is to be disloyal to communal wisdom and to be disloyal to that wisdom so carefully and painstakingly distilled through the ages is arrogance. And arrogance is the eighth deadly sin.

Rennicks became involved in coaching young players with his native Bohermeen, which became St Ultan's. He looks back on his long association with a glow of satisfaction.

'Bohermeen won the junior championship in the mid 1960s and I started playing with the club when we were an intermediate team. For three or four years we were always in the shake-up of the championship but failed to get the breakthrough. Eventually our time came, and in 1974 we went back the whole way to the senior final. We were beaten by a point. The next year we joined up with another team in the parish called Martry and the name of the team became Bohermeen Martry Harps. That year we got to the semi-final of the senior championship, and again we lost by a point. Shortly after that the team broke up and some of the players went back to Bohermeen. I stood on with the existing team and we went intermediate. I coached them to a county championship victory in 1975.'

PART VII
Wired for Sound

Pat Shortt claimed in *Killnaskully*, 'There's only one crowd worse than the Black and Tans and that's that shower in RTÉ.' However, Gaelic Games have been at the heart of broadcasting in Ireland from its earliest days. On New Year's Day 1926, '2RN' Ireland's national radio station, began its transmission. On 29 August that year a Gaelic game was transmitted live for the first time. The All-Ireland hurling semi-final between Kilkenny and Galway was the first radio commentary outside America of a field game. When RTÉ television came on in air in 1961–62, the GAA initially adopted a cautious approach, restricting this coverage annually to the two All-Ireland finals, the two football semi-finals and the Railway Cup finals on St Patrick's Day. Over the years the GAA has spotted that television is not a threat but a useful ally in attracting people to our national games.

Seán Og O'Ceallacháin was the first presenter of *The Sunday Game* in 1979, a rare programme then devoted exclusively to Gaelic Games. Initially the chief football analyst on *The Sunday Game* was the late Enda Colleran, who was a key part of the Galway three-in-a-row All-Ireland-winning side 1964–66, captaining the side in the latter two years. He was selected as right full-back on both the Team of the Century and the Team of the Millennium. He used the knowledge he acquired to telling effect as an analyst and blazed the trail for the rest to follow.

In Seán Og's two years as a presenter many players, both active and retired, were called on to give their opinions. The hurling guest analysts included Limerick's Éamonn Cregan and Pat Hartigan; Kilkenny's Pat Henderson, Eddie Keher and Phil 'Fan' Larkin; Clare's Jackie O'Gorman and Johnny Callinan; Tipperary's John Doyle and Cork's Jimmy Brohan. The football guests were equally distinguished and included Kerry's Mick O'Connell and Mick O'Dwyer; Dublin's Kevin Heffernan; Antrim's Kevin Armstrong; Cork's Eamon Young; Mayo's Seán Flanagan; Cavan's Jim McDonnell; and Down's Seán O'Neill and Joe Lennon.

Down through the years, the programme has evolved and become indelibly imprinted in the national psyche. *The Sunday Game* does not happen in a vacuum, with the match and analysis. There is a complex and highly professional packaging operation designed to convey a more attractive and seductive context for the event. The packaging begins from the first minute with sophisticated graphics, evocative and carefully chosen music, with judiciously chosen and lively filmed images. These establish a mood of anticipation of an exciting programme to come. Powerful and dramatic opening sequences will almost certainly attract marginal viewers to certain sports.

The print media has always been pivotal to the GAA. When I was a boy the publication that captivated my attention to the greatest extent was *The Evening Press:* because of both Joe Sherwood's regular feature 'In the Soup' and the column written by the peerless Con Houlihan.

Local radio stations have become incredibly important and their GAA commentators, like Shannonside's Willie Hegarty, have become iconic figures in their local area. *Off the Ball* on Newstalk has brought a new dimension to Gaelic Games' coverage. The print media, national and local, continue to be hugely influential. Social media platforms have become increasingly important. This section pays homage to the media's role in the GAA.

45

DUNNE DEAL: MICK DUNNE

We need people to tell epic stories of our legends.
Dermot Earley

As a boy I thought his words were wondrous and full of heaven's delight, as if they were sanctified and blessed.

While Micheál Ó'Hehir and Mícheál Ó'Muircheartaigh have rightly been acclaimed for their magnificent contribution to Gaelic Games, Mick Dunne is one of the unsung heroes of the GAA, having served 21 years as the GAA anchor man with *The Irish Press* and an equal number of years as Gaelic Games correspondent with RTÉ. Yet but for a tiny jumper as he grew up at the foot of the Slieve Bloom Mountains in Clonaslee in County Laois he might never have got the opportunity.

'When I was four my parents were away for the day and I slipped the attentions of my minders. A river tumbling down from the mountain flowed by at the foot of our garden. It was the Brosna and it was in full flood and I fell in! Thankfully my little jumper got tangled in some overhanging branches at the turning of the river and this halted my progress all the way to the River Shannon. A neighbour heard my shouts and rescued me.'

Some years later sports journalism almost lost out again as Dunne, like so many of his contemporaries at the time, decided to enter the priesthood. After a year and a half in All Hallows, he decided that the clerical life was not for him. This was a time when there was a considerable stigma attached to being a 'spoiled priest' but his family, unlike many others in that situation, supported his decision fully.

Mick was born into a very political family – known as the Tailor Dunnes because of the number in the extended family who took up the tailoring profession, as well as distinguishing them from the many other Dunnes in the area. His father, Frank, went to America at an early age but during the War of Independence he was sent back by Liam Mellowes with an important message for the Big Fellah, Michael Collins. He stayed on to fight in the war and became second in command of the fourth Battalion. He spent time in a number of prisons and took part in a number of daring escapes. He was also very musical and enjoyed a great reputation as a Pipe Major. During the Civil War he spent 44 days on hunger strike in Mountjoy with Seán Lemass, who would go on to succeed Eamon De Valera as Taoiseach, and Seán Coughlan, who subsequently became the GAA columnist with *The Irish Press*, writing under the pen-name 'Green Flag'.

As a youngster Mick Dunne's journalistic hero was the 'Green Flag'. The fact that *The Irish Press* was the only paper allowed into their house might have influenced his decision. When he returned from matches with his father on Sundays, he would take out his copybooks and write reports of the game he had just watched, signing himself 'Green Flag'. In 1949 he got the opportunity to follow in his idol's footsteps when he joined *The Irish Press* as Junior Librarian before quickly graduating to the newsroom and rapidly becoming the GAA correspondent and later GAA editor. It was an experience he greatly enjoyed, though there were some painful moments on the way.

'I had a bit of trouble with my editor because, when I wrote my reports about Kilkenny matches, I always spoke of the "Diamond" Hayden. The editor hated me using pet names and read me the riot act. I replied, "I'll tell you what. You go down to Kilkenny today and talk to everybody you meet in the streets and ask them what the Diamond's Christian name is and I bet none of them will be able to tell you. He is known as the "Diamond" and by nothing else. He conceded the argument and I continued to write about the "Diamond".'

Had he been alive today, Westmeath's 'Jobber' McGrath, chosen at midfield on the Centenary team of players who had never won an All-Ireland hurling medal, would have been a must for this book. Mick Dunne has the inside story as to where the Jobber's nickname comes from.

'My wife's twin brother, Joe Fox, actually christened him "Jobber". He could really speak, I can tell you, but when he was small he couldn't say Johnny so Joe called him Jobba and that's where the name came from.'

In 1970 Dunne was head-hunted by no less a person than Micheál Ó'Hehir with a view to beefing up RTÉ's coverage of Gaelic Games. It was a daunting prospect, especially as there was no training. When his daughter, Eileen, began her career in RTÉ some years later that situation had been remedied somewhat. He made his debut as a commentator in handball, in the popular *Top Ace* series.

'Commentating is the nearest thing to playing because you get caught up in the game and you're living on adrenalin. Of course, sometimes things go wrong. One day I was commentating in Thurles and I was watching the game from my monitor when it tipped over and fell into the crowd. I had to carry on commentating and at the same time retrieve the monitor, which I can tell you isn't very good for the blood pressure!'

Of all the games he commentated on one gave him particular pleasure.

'It was when Laois won the National Football League in 1986. It was the first time in 60 years for Laois to win a national competition. Although I was euphoric, unlike the fans I could not show it. I met a friend from Cork the following day who said he enjoyed the commentary and in his best Cork accent he said, "And you know, boy. You'd never know you were a Laois man listening to your commentary," which I thought was a great compliment.'

One of the great privileges of his career was the fact that he came into contact with some great characters.

'The famous John Kerry O'Donnell of New York was a wonderful character. Back in the 1960s I was involved in selecting the team that would travel to New York to play in the Cardinal Cushing Games to raise money for the Cardinal's mission in Peru. It was almost the precursor of the All-Stars. We tried, especially, to pick some good players from the weaker counties. In fact, the former GAA president John Dowling always maintained that one of the reasons why Offaly eventually made the breakthrough in hurling was because of the boost it got when players like Paddy Molloy got one of these trips.

'John Kerry dined out for years in America on the story of what happened when this gang of Irish journalists got together. The importance of picking players from the weaker countries led us to speak about the terms of reference in selection decisions. One of our number blurted out immediately, "Let's pick the team first and we'll sort out the terms of reference later"!'

For many years Dunne was secretary to the journalists who selected the All-Stars. The fruit of their deliberations often generated controversy – for their perceived sins of omission as much as their actual selection. Selecting the best 15 often provoked passionate disagreements among the journalists in question.

'When he was president of the GAA Pat Fanning said, after seeing us picking the teams, "The amazing thing is that they are such good friends after a night fighting like this!"

'The President and Director General of the GAA sat in as observers. The only time they ever intervened was if there was a tie over a particular position when somebody abstained. They then, having listened to all the arguments, went out of the room and decided who got the nod.'

Controversy erupted in 1985 when Paul Earley was chosen at full-forward on the All-Star football team ahead of Monaghan's Eamonn Murphy. An article was written by a prominent GAA personality in Monaghan which claimed that Earley was awarded the honour because he was an employee of the sponsoring bank. Was there an informal canvassing will disqualify policy in operation?

'The accusation that the bank interfered in Paul's selection was totally wrong and very unfair to his abilities as a player. If they had tried to persuade us to pick Paul it would have ensured that he wouldn't get the All-Star!

'The only time I ever got "approached" was when I got a phone call from a manager of a team the day before the team was picked. After a bit of casual conversation he blatantly started talking up some of his players with a view to influencing my selection. I simply said, "It would be much better for their chances, Brian, if you didn't interfere in this way".'

46

THE DOYEN: RAYMOND SMITH

He was as confused-looking as a Kerry man in Paris.
Con Houlinhan

The legendary Tipperary hurler John Doyle enjoyed the humour of hurling, like the story of the former hurler who is in an accident and is rushed into hospital. Two men are in the ward with him. One dies almost immediately. Then the second. The player in panic screams when the consultant appears: 'Doctor, doctor. Get me out of here quick and stick me in the backs. Things aren't going well in the forwards.'

Another example was the headline in the *Tipperary Star*: 'Death of hurling immortal'.

Doyle was good friends with the 'doyen of the print media in the GAA' Raymond Smith. Once I asked Raymond who it was that first described him in those terms; he replied with a twinkle in his eye, 'I did!'

When I was in my early 20s I got involved in writing about sport and one of the first people I spoke with was Raymond Smith – who at the time was to the print media what Micheál Ó'Muircheartaigh is to broadcasting. He told me the story of how Hill 16 got its

288

name – how it was built with the rubble from the 1916 Rising and he told me about the time he had a drink with a man who got five shillings for wheeling the rubble into Croke Park. This story and this belief were, I thought, universal – the only problem was that I discovered that the hill was actually built in 1915. I would have bet my house that story was true, and it was such a shock when I found out that it was not – that I almost had to go into therapy.

HARRY'S GAME

Raymond loved a 'good one'. Shortly after Luis Suarez's bite on Branislav Ivanovic in 2013, Cooles under-tens played the Burren. A very quick-witted Harry Minogue, after spotting a hole in his jersey, remarked, 'Look lads, Suarez must be in town.' Raymond would have given Harry the thumbs up.

Then he might have claimed the quote as his own!

When he was good, though, Raymond Smith was very good. Witness: 'Christy Ring, the undisputed genius of three decades of competitive hurling, yesterday drew the crowds for the last time. But never did they return out in such spontaneous tribute as they did for the final, sad procession as the nation's superb hurler went back to the soil of his native Cloyne.'

47

A SPEECH FOR ALL SEASONS: IGGY CLARKE

People of Galway we love you.

Joe Connolly

It is the greatest speech in the history of the GAA.

Iggy Clarke was part of it but not the way he would have wished.

The four-time All-Star player was part of the new era in Galway hurling when he captained the county to their first All-Ireland under-21 title against Dublin in 1972. Three years later, a National League medal came to Clarke. Unfortunately, injury prevented him from lining out in Galway's historic All-Ireland triumph over Limerick in 1980. However, his presence was publicly acknowledged following Joe Connolly's tour de force in his acceptance speech. Iggy looks back on the time with undisguised affection:

'I have many incredible memories and heart-warming thoughts from my hurling days. The most memorable day of my hurling experience that will forever remain etched in my heart is 7 September 1980. As a Galway man, I remember sitting beside the then President, the late Paddy Hillery.

'I was overcome with raw emotion as Joe Connolly made the

most powerful, profound speech that will remain in the annals of hurling history. I could feel my heart pumping rapidly as I heard the crowd calling for "Iggy" in the middle of Joe's speech.

'This moment is one I greatly treasure and one that has touched the very essence of my soul and that will last me a lifetime. The unforgettable rendition of 'The West's Awake' by Joe McDonagh will forever endure the passage of time.

'Joe paused and passed the McCarthy Cup to me. I was both honoured and thrilled to be able to hold it aloft with one hand. My hurling ambition was to be able to hold it with both hands.'

The day before there was one unforgettable moment for Iggy:

'I will never forget passing Mike Keary's pub in Loughrea on the team bus as we went through the town on the way to Croke Park. There was a big banner with a mnemonic that said:

I.	G.	G.	Y.
It's	Galway's	Golden	Year.

It was so thoughtful and uplifting to see.'

It was a time which captured like no other the Saw Doctors idea of the maroon and white of Galway 'forever and for a day'.

48

THANK YOU FOR THE MUSIC:
JIMMY SMYTH AND THE GAA BALLADS

The Wind is wild to-night, there's battle in the air
The Wind is from the West and it seems to blow from Clare ...
In suntide, moontide, startide, we thirst, we starve for Clare.

Jimmy Smyth

The trials have faded from Jimmy Smyth's consciousness like pain from a wound as it heals.

Appropriately, his words are immortalised on stone on the sculpture in Ennis dedicated to the hurling heroes of 1995.

'Hurling is special – the body and soul of a people – surviving to speak of a past that is noble, distinctive and proud with a game that is surely unique.'

The Clare legend of the 1950s proved his commitment to his native county on the playing fields. Off the field he also wrote a book on the ballads of Clare.

'The GAA achieved three very different purposes. It encouraged local patriotism. It inculcated among its members an uncompromising hostility to foreign games, and it revived local and national pride. Its philosophy is that love of country draws its strength and vitality from love of neighbours, fellow-parishioners and fellow countrymen and women from love of the scenes, traditions, culture and way of life associated with one's home and place of origin: that a club or county provides a sense of importance, belonging and identity, shared goals, a pride and a purpose. All the texts are equally charged with such values and aspirations.

'The ballad makers write about hurling and the ash, the glory of Munster final day as a symbol and inspiration to the Irish nation: about hurling and football and their association with the land, the sea, the plough and the spade, and the atmosphere of All-Ireland day. They write with feeling about the role of the priest, the transience of life, the belief in a God and the power of prayer. All these assumptions are woven into the complex web of understanding. They are content in the knowledge that they have great games, great heroes, great people and great places. They tell us who we are, where we come from, and where we stand.'

When I asked Jimmy to sum up the core message of the hurling ballads, he told me:

'Hurling is old, as old as the hills
And tough as the rocks that lie under.
Hard as the metals that smoulder within
A simmer of passion and wonder.
Hurling is part of the soil and the land
A mixture more polished than gold
And comes to the surface expressive and free
As a skill that is daring and bold.'

49

SHE WAS LOVELY AND FAIR LIKE THE ROSE OF THE SUMMER: AOIFE KELLY

We need to see more women playing our games.
Eugene McGee

According to William Thackery, the world gives back to each of us a reflection of ourselves. The GAA gives us a window into our inner selves but like us it mutates with events.

A major boost for the GAA is its increasing appeal for women. Ireland's fastest growing sport is ladies' football. One of ladies' football's biggest champions is the 2008 Rose of Tralee, Tipperary's Aoife Kelly. Aoife has made her own mark in the game.

'I went to San Francisco for a summer. I discovered there was a clique of Irish people there and I decided that sport was a good way of meeting some of them. I wasn't sure which sport to choose but I met a girl who persuaded me to play Gaelic football. I had never taken a football in my hand in life. I decided I would try it for the craic and joined the Clann Na Gael club there. I had the best time. We lost the All-American final in Boston in 2004. When I went back to university in Scotland, I decided to get involved playing Gaelic football there and we won the five-a-side championships.

In the five-a-sides I played midfield but otherwise I played wing-forward. My problem is that I have weak ankles – which become a serious problem when the opposition get to know you have weak ankles!

'I have a good friend Fiona May who played for Sligo and she was kind of my idol because she was so fanatical and so dedicated. When I came back to Ireland to work in Dublin in the National Rehab Hospital as an occupational therapist, I had planned to get involved in a club but then the Rose of Tralee intervened.

'During the Rose of Tralee contest, we were brought up to see the ladies' football final in Croke Park. We had the best time. My then fiancée, Leon, who is from South Africa, had seen many hurling games but had never seen a Gaelic football match before and he thought it was wonderful.

'The great thing about playing I found is that it is great for character building – because you have to learn to win and lose. It's not just about the winning. It's about the experience. I am obviously Tipperary-biased and I think Eoin Kelly was unbelievably skilful but I don't like singling out individuals because Gaelic Games are team-based and it is teams who win and lose matches, and being part of a team appeals to me. There's also a great community involvement behind it. I think the GAA is so important when you are away from home. I lived in San Francisco and the one time the community gather, whether its three or five in the morning because of the time difference, is to watch a match. It is then you really see how important the GAA is for our identity of being Irish. It brings people together.

'In my travels, I have never met anybody who doesn't love the Irish and the one thing I would like to see happening is for the GAA to reach out more to other nationalities. In terms of ladies' football, the one thing I would like to see is a greater emphasis on it in the schools. In the school I went to the emphasis was on basketball and we had zero exposure to ladies' football in either primary or secondary school. I don't think women get the same recognition as the men. I think people think men are tougher, but I think women withstand a belt from an opponent much better whereas men would fall down and look for a free! Women have a higher pain threshold, which is reflected on the field. So, I would like to see more media exposure for ladies' football and camogie.'

50

THE MONAGHAN MYSTIC: PATRICK KAVANAGH

All our sporting hearts beat as one.
> Donal Ryan

Why is it so easy to build our lives on treacherous hopes?

Monaghan produced perhaps the most famous man to play Gaelic Games, one of Ireland's greatest poets Patrick Kavanagh.

An American film crew went to make a documentary about Kavanagh in Iniskeen. When they visited the local pub, they expected a great reception after they announced their mission and went out of their way to state publicly, 'Patrick Kavanagh was a great poet'. The wind was taken out of their sails when one of the locals replied: 'Ah sure there's a man down the road, Peter Bunting, who could poetry the sh*te out of Kavanagh.'

It is noteworthy that Kavanagh's star is rising internationally. In 2010 Russell Crowe quoted his poem 'Sanctity' in which he describes the intense heartbreak of being a lover who has the singular talent of repelling all women, and to be a poet without knowing the trade in his BAFTA acceptance speech. In 2015 Barack Obama quoted 'let grief be a fallen leaf' from one of Kavanagh's most famous poems, 'Raglan Road', when he delivered the eulogy at the funeral of Joe Biden's son, Beau.

Kavanagh was an abrasive character. He argued that all sporting subjects are 'superficial', as 'the emotion is a momentary puff of gas, not an experience'. The fact that Kavanagh's own sporting career was an unmitigated disaster may have fuelled his cynicism. Like Albert Camus, Pope John Paul II and Julio Iglesias he was a goalkeeper. In the early thirties he played for his local team, Inniskeen Grattans – succeeding Tom 'The Collier' Callan, who in the words of his brother Peter was 'so stiff from farm work that he could only stop a ball that hit him'.

Kavanagh's most famous contribution was to wander off to buy either an ice cream or a drink, depending on whose version of events you listen to, while the opposition scored a goal between the deserted posts. The final ignominy came when he conceded the match, losing a goal in the county final by letting the ball roll between his legs. His own supporters shouted, 'Go home and put an apron on you!'

His career as a sporting administrator fuelled even more venom. As club treasurer he kept club funds under his bed, which prompted some nasty rumours. Like Father Ted who famously did not steal money but merely had it 'resting in his account', Kavanagh's own response to the innuendo was, 'It is possible that every so often I visited it for the price of a packet of cigarettes, but nothing serious.'

Kavanagh once took time off work on the 'stony, grey soil of Monaghan' to attend the county final. He was asked to predict the outcome of the match. After a dramatic pause, he responded, 'The first half will be even. The second half will be even worse.'

Kavanagh once let in two soft goals: one of the fans shouted at him, 'Use your hands to stop the ball.'

The poet replied, 'That's what the f**king net is for.'

PART VIII
A Holy Show

I was an altar boy for a few years. I soon discovered the three Bs, which are prerequisites of a successful altar boy: 'Be on time, be neat and be alert.' The big perk was that you got a bit of money for serving Mass for weddings and funerals, which was like winning the Lotto back then.

As a child people still spoke fondly about the Eucharistic Congress in 1932. There were special Masses, rosaries and novenas to prepare the country for this solemn occasion. It was a big event just to travel up to Dublin. The capital was like a rainbow with all kinds of bunting and flags on the street to mark the arrival of the Cardinal Legate on 20 June. It was noted that the most elaborate decorations were hung in the poorest regions, a sort of supernatural toy shop. There was a lovely piece of graffiti on a wall which stated, 'Long live St Patrick'. Someone obviously thought that reports of his death 1,500 years earlier were greatly exaggerated. The event attracted a huge audience and was just a small indication not just of the importance of the Catholic faith in Ireland at the time, but of the type of religion.

Holiness at the time was virtually compulsory. Catholicism cast a long shadow over all aspects of Irish society in the 1950s. There was a heavy wooden crucifix nailed up on a wall in most homes, flanked by pictures of sickly yellow and gloomy apostles. More saints and wounded martyrs watched over other rooms. Reading material consisted largely of religious magazines like *The Sacred Heart, The Far East* and *The Messenger*, though amongst the farming community *The Farmer's Journal* was their bible.

Sunday, though, was the GAA day. Hence the description of the former Roscommon star Jimmy Murray as 'a GAA Catholic' – he went to one Mass and two matches every Sunday.

Jimmy was there to see me play my first club game when I was picked to play for St Brigid's under-12s in Knockcroghery. When we got there the dressing-room was locked, so we had to tog out in the field next door – which was a graveyard. It was to be a real metaphor for my football career!

It was so cold that I thought I discovered God's frozen people. My opponent was not the quickest. The milk in our kitchen turns faster.

Things did not go well for the team but I was really happy with my performance because I was playing corner-back and any time the ball came in my direction I was first out and cleared it and my man never got a touch of the ball. At half-time we gathered for what I hoped would be an inspirational speech from our manager, who was the local parish priest. As he was God's ambassador on earth I was more than a little surprised when he came in to the circle and grabbed me by the jersey, with his face red, the eyes almost popping out of his head, the veins of his neck bulging like crazy and the flecks from his spit as he spoke were all over my face.

All he said was 'They're bleeping killing ye.' Then he let me go and told me he was taking me off. The first half was not great, but the second half was even – it was even worse! We lost narrowly. The final score was 7 goals and 21 points to 2 points. The guy I had been marking was on fire in the second half and destroyed us. To this day I still can't understand why I was taken off. I really think it is the kind of injustice that Amnesty International should consider taking on. I started at the bottom and sunk still further.

This short section looks at the role of religion in the GAA.

51

A NUN'S STORY: PAULINE GIBBONS

They should hope the fixture is played in Lourdes.
Christy Ring on an injury-ravaged Cork side

It was a summer where there seemed to be more rain than sunshine.

The Catholic Church have always played a central role in the GAA. I still remember the late Bishop Eamon Casey throwing in the ball before the 1978 Connacht final. Before doing so he said to the midfielders, 'Well, lads, are ye nervous?'

The long relationship between the GAA and the Catholic Church is complex. Although culturally and, in many respects, spiritually close with the Catholic Church at the forefront of promoting the GAA, the Church banned its priests and seminarians from actually playing intercounty football for years. Seminarians and priests had to assume a name to allow their footballing careers to continue at the highest level despite the curious irony of men who so often preached the truth practising deception. Everybody knew who they were, including the bishop, and a blind eye was turned. It was a Jesuitical solution to a uniquely clerical problem.

In 1955 the late Fr Michael Cleary was in line for a place on the

Dublin team to play Kerry in the All-Ireland football final. The problem was that he was also attending the diocesan seminary in Clonliffe at the time. Under College regulations, there was no way he would be freed to play the match. It was a straightforward choice: which was the more important to him, to play in the final or to become a priest? He chose to become a priest but as the final was being played, he could practically see the ball down the road in the college. After his ordination, he played for Dublin under the name of Mick Casey.

As a result of his playing career with Saint Jarlaths of Tuam, Seán Freyne was often described as one of the greatest colleges' footballers of all time. In 1952 he captained the Mayo minors. The night before he was due to lead out the team to play in the All-Ireland final, he entered the national seminary in Maynooth. Not only was he not allowed go to the match, he was not allowed to listen to the result on the radio either. The night of the final, he went out to the college gates and his winning team stopped outside the gates on their way home to tell him the result and show him their cup.

The Association banned government ministers from the VIP section in Croke Park in the 1980s in a row about VAT on hurleys. In their absence, the seats were given to Catholic bishops.

With this in mind, Pauline Gibbons blazed a unique trail.

She was the first nun to line-out in an All-Ireland football final. After leaving the Roscommon football team mid-season to join the Augustinian Order in England, 18-year-old midfielder Pauline was given a special dispensation to travel home to play in the 1977 All-Ireland Senior Ladies' Football Championship final against Cavan.

Sister Pauline was denied permission to play in Roscommon's semi-final clash against Kerry. However, when the team reached the football final, the Roscommon County Board pleaded with

Mother Superior Sister Leonie to allow Pauline to travel home from her Sussex convent to play against Cavan. Their prayers were answered.

To the surprise of her fellow nuns, Sister Pauline trained for the football final within the convent grounds. Roscommon's unique player received great interested from the media and, as a consequence, 3,000 spectators turned up to watch the final held in Dr Hyde Park. Sadly, there was to be no divine intervention for the women in the primrose and blue as Cavan took the title.

The final score was Cavan 4-3 Roscommon 2-3.

52

WORSHIPPING AT THE ALTAR: FR COLM McGLYNN

We're all in the same family.
Donal Ryan

The last smear of light was draining from the sky. Swallows dived and looped across the window as I spoke to Fr Colm McGlynn, a member of the Servite Order based in Dublin, to see how important the GAA was in his life. Colm is keenly aware of the power of the club:

'St Peregrine GAA club in Blakestown was founded by another Servite priest, Fr Joe Madden, in the late 1970s. Peregrine is patron saint of cancer sufferers, and his body is in our church in Forli in Italy in the Tuscany region. During my time as school chaplain in Blakestown community school and curate and as a parish priest, I was in and out of St Peregrine's a lot for fundraising nights, birthday parties, etc. When I was based in Rathfarnham, I was also involved with St John's Ballinteer with an annual Mass for deceased members in each club. I discovered at first hand the power of the club in the community.'

However, his abiding memories are of a more personal nature:

'The last memory of a visit to Croker was with the man who introduced me to Hill 16, my father James Victor McGlynn. I'm holding the stub of the ticket. It reads Saturday, 11th August 2007, section 711 Row W Seat 30; Senior football quarter finals, after the Nicky Rackard Cup final and ESB minor quarter final. Earlier we had taken the 14 bus from Rathmines, thinking it would stop on O'Connell Street but instead it ended up at Merchants Quay. Very soon Dad got tired of walking and for the first time ever I had to flag a taxi to get us to Summerhill.

'We then made our way through the gauntlet of match day sounds: "Get your teams colours... official programmes... programmes of the game ... apples, pears or chocolate, four cents each the bananas" and a whole lot more, finally arriving into our seats high up into to the newly built Cusack Stand, in which my father, a plasterer by trade, was enthralled by its engineering work. Dublin comfortably beat Derry that day to reach the semi-final and Dad and I were very happy with another victory for the boys in blue. Then suddenly from a place deep within, walking out the gates of Croke Park, I began to cry tears that flowed, doing my best to hide them from Dad. It was the dawning realisation that this would be my last visit with Dad to this Dublin theatre of sporting dreams of heroism, skill, enjoyment, fun and song as well as darker, sadder memories of thrilling games ending in defeats that Dad had initiated me into since my teenage years. I just knew in my bones it was his final goodbye and sure enough three months later on Remembrance Sunday, 7 November 2007, he died and went to his maker, whom he loved so much. 'Molly Malone' was sung as we lowered him down into his Bohernabreena cemetery grave after the religious formal prayers.

'That day, we said goodbye to the da who had regaled us with the stories of the heroes of Dublin teams of his generation in both football and hurling – Lar and Des Foley, John Timmons and the great Kevin Heffernan, all of whom got battered by the county teams the length and breadth of the country. That's where the magic of the Dubs began to happen in our generation, with the emergence of Heffo's army on that famous All-Ireland day in 1974 when we beat the great Galway team of Liam Sammon and to finally win the Sam Maguire Cup after long years of footballing famine.

'I guess the games that I remember most are the 1975 hammering by the emerging young Kerry side of probably the greatest GAA manager of all time, Mick O'Dwyer, and then probably the most exciting game I'd seen to that point of my life, Dublin beating Kerry in the magnificent 1977 All-Ireland semi-final when Anton O'Toole, the Synge Street stallion, ran riot, and years of epic rivalry and the great friendships made between both those teams in Listowel races after their footballing escapades. The names flood back: Paddy Cullen who was famously outfoxed by Mikey Sheehy's goal in the 1978 final, Seán Doherty, Brian Mullins, Jimmy Keaveney, Tony Hanahoe, Bobby Doyle, Gay O'Driscoll, Kevin Moran and Kerry's Ogie Moran and Páidí "Mucker" O'Sé, a target for the Hill with their chant "All coppers are ba*t*rds."

'Fortunately the Dubs rose again with other great memories like on a wild wet 1983 day when only 12 Dublin players were left on the pitch beating Galway that day thanks to Brian Mullins midfield efforts and a boxing match of legendary fame at the half-time tunnel dressing-room walk. Heffo's armies brought so much joy and a lot of heartache too, but I look back with immense appreciation of such fantastic memories to savour.'

THE FINAL WHISTLE

It is the simple things in life that make us rich.

As John B. Keane's wonderfully evocative play *The Field* demonstrated, land is crucial to Irish people, not just in economic terms but in terms of identity. Irish people waited for centuries to own their land. The Land Acts of 1870 and 1881 began the process by which Ireland was transformed from a nation of peasants to a nation of landowners. In rural Ireland nothing caused such bitter feuds between neighbours as disputes about land. This was particularly the case when a neighbour was negligent about mending their fences, which meant that their cattle or sheep broke into their neighbour's fields doing untold damage to the farmer's reserves of grass. In the 1950s two farmers in Clare had an acrimonious falling out over a dispute about fences. As was often the case in such disagreements, things were said which never should have been said and could never been unsaid.

For 43 years they never spoke to each other.

Then on 3 September 1995 Clare won the All-Ireland hurling final for the first time in 81 years. That night the two neighbours found themselves in the same pub. There was magic and grace in the air. The two men squared up to each other like two cowboys in a gunfight not really responding apart from a really cursory, almost imperceptible movement of their heads.

Then they did the unthinkable.

They hugged each other without embarrassment.

Forty-three years of hostilities were dissolved because of a hurling match.

A little parable which captures the power and the glory of the People's Games, where our thoughts and feelings intersect and where our lives reverberate to the pulse of the heart.

The secret of having it all is knowing that we already do.

GAA fans know that feeling.

THE LAST WORD

The GAA is the greatest family in the world.
That's why I love it so much.

Michael Duignan

AFTERWORD:

A TRIBUTE TO WEESHIE

As I began working on this book, the sad news broke about the death of the legendary broadcaster Weeshie Fogarty. I wanted to pay a tribute to the man who added so much to the lore of Gaelic Games and whose award-winning programme on Radio Kerry *Terrace Talk* was a national institution. Having had the great good fortune to know him in the end, I decided the most fitting way to pay homage to him was to publish the final letter I received from Weeshie in September 2014. It also serves as a tribute to Dermot Earley to mark the tenth anniversary of his death.

Dear John

Thank you for the privilege of attending the launch in Croke Park of your beautiful new book on the life and times of the former Roscommon mid field star the late Dermot Earley before a huge crowd of GAA and army personalities by An Taoiseach Enda Kenny. I had befriended Dermot during my time as an inter county referee and later in my life with Radio

Kerry. When you very kindly contacted me of course refusal to travel was never an option. My good Killarney friend and stalwart Roscommon man Tommy Regan was my companion on the night and in many ways I felt I was representing Kerry football as Dermot had often spoken to me when we met about all things Kerry.

It can and has been argued that Dermot was the greatest Gaelic footballer never to win a senior All-Ireland medal. He was a member of the Roscommon senior team from 1965 until 1985 and during that time he played against and matched the most supreme mid-fielders the game has known. His status as one of the all-time greats is self-evident and in a magnificent career over all those years he won five Connacht titles, one National League, two All-Star awards but sadly the ultimate honour of winning that All-Ireland medal eluded him. When his senior inter-county career was over, Dermot managed both the Roscommon and Kildare senior teams with little success and your book details vividly his feelings as managerial success eluded him.

Your book is a beautiful, intimate and touching account of the life of a very special person, because Dermot Earley was one of those people who literally touch the lives of so many in such a positive way. I first had the honour of meeting him back in the early eighties as I called the captains together for the toss of the coin before an All-Ireland seven-a-side final in Dublin; Roscommon and Offaly were the contestants that day. It was his strong firm warm handshake and warm smile which I remember most of all and his words to me, 'nice to meet you Weeshie, my name is Dermot Earley'. Those moments remained etched in my memory and later before National League games we would meet again. He had about him that special aura very few encompass.

Then in 2007 when he was appointed as the Irish Defence Forces Chief of Staff, the highest honour available in our army, I contacted his secretary in relation to having him as a guest on Radio Kerry. He accepted without a moment's hesitation and a few weeks later I sat opposite him for a full hour as we discussed his life and times in the Irish army and his playing career. Needless to say it was an amazing and uplifting experience. And of course one of the topics we discussed was Roscommon's defeat by Kerry in that dramatic 1980 All-Ireland final and you cover this in great detail in the book.

I was very sad when Dermot died. Dermot Junior told me in an interview that he had first noticed something was wrong with his dad in September 2009. 'They were simple little things but unfortunately the little things started to get bigger and January brought the diagnosis. The one thing he kept was his smile. I knew there were times he was aware he was unwell and it was tough for him, but the man he was always had the smile.' How right he is, Dermot's smile and handshake were two things that I will always treasure myself.

My final meeting with Dermot occurred following Roscommon's magnificent minor win over Kerry in Ennis in that re-played final back in 2006. We met on the field, and as always the gentleman he agreed without hesitation to an interview and unashamedly shed tears of joy as he spoke about his beloved Roscommon and what that meant to the county. His friend Fergal O'Donnell, a Garda, was the manager of that brilliant minor side.

Enda Kenny visibly emotional, as his father and Dermot's dad had been personal friends, spoke to me following the launch. 'Dermot Earley epitomised all that was good in his professional career as Chief of Staff of our Defense Forces and was truly an iconic figure, the Taoiseach added. 'He illustrated in his professional career and sporting career as well as his family life the finest qualities of what Irishness is all about.'

Your book is one of the finest GAA books I have ever read. It was an honour and privilege to have known Dermot if only in a very small way.

Give me a shout if you are coming down to the Kingdom.

Yours in friendship,

Weeshie

ACKNOWLEDGEMENTS

My particular thanks to Michael Darragh Macauley for his assistance with the foreword.

My profound gratitude to Eddie Keher and Kieran Donaghy for their help.

Special thanks to Mary Earley, John O'Mahony, Sarah MacDonald, John MacKenna, Michael Duignan, Nicole Owens, Kevin McStay, Iggy Clarke, Colm McGlynn, Bernard Flynn, Charlie Redmond, Zak Moradi, Peter McVerry, Karol Mannion, John Tiernan, Christy Grogan, Julia White, Anthony Daly, David Burke and Peter Canavan for their support.

My deep thanks to the great Michael Foley for a masterclass on Bloody Sunday.

My profound thanks to the many players, past and present, who generously shared their stories and thoughts with me and who made this book possible.

Special thanks to my former star student Rosanna McAleese for her insights.

Thanks to Simon Hess, Campbell Brown, and all at Black & White for their help.

Leitrim lost a much-loved son in February with the passing of Michael Sammon. He will be much missed by his loving family, including his daughter Mary and son-in-law Leitrim football royalty, Mickey Quinn.

This year we said a final goodbye to Ashling Reynolds. She will always be an inspiration for all seasons.

In December Michael McGrath left us peacefully after 99 years of life. Although he had left Cork for many years he retained until the very end a deep passion for Cork hurling.

One of the many sad things about the COVID-19 crisis was that many people were deprived of the collegiality of 'the GAA funeral'. A case in point was Peadar Duignan, father of Offaly legend Michael, a great husband, a great father and a proud father.

Former Roscommon footballer Conor Connelly was also lost to us as the crisis took a grip on the country.

Former Meath manager and selector Eamon O'Brien has made his own mark on the playing fields but this year he made his mark in other fields too. I salute his achievements.

As this book was being written, Dublin hurling gained a full-back of the future with the birth of Séamus O'Brien to the delight of his proud parents, Breda and Cormac, and grandparents.

After a life of dedication and service to teaching the pride of Clones Fintan MacKenna stepped off the playing fields this year. May he always know joy and happiness.

For over 20 years, Carol Hennessy showed extraordinary care, commitment and creativity to help thousands of needy children. I wish her every good wish for the next exciting chapter in her life.

My thanks to Maureen Condon for her efforts on my behalf.

Liam Lee has climbed dizzy new heights this year. The best is yet to come.